NATIONAL CATHOLIC REPORTER
AT FIFTY

NATIONAL CATHOLIC REPORTER
AT FIFTY

The Story of the Pioneering Paper and Its Editors

Arthur Jones

ROWMAN & LITTLEFIELD
Lanham • Boulder • New York • London

Published by Rowman & Littlefield
A wholly owned subsidiary of The Rowman & Littlefield Publishing Group, Inc.
4501 Forbes Boulevard, Suite 200, Lanham, Maryland 20706
www.rowman.com

16 Carlisle Street, London W1D 3BT, United Kingdom

British Library Cataloguing in Publication Information Available

Library of Congress Cataloging-in-Publication Data
Jones, Arthur, 1936–
National Catholic reporter at fifty : the story of the pioneering paper and its editors / Arthur Jones.
pages cm
"A Sheed & Ward book."
ISBN 978-1-4422-3611-0 (cloth : alk. paper) — ISBN 978-1-4422-3612-7 (electronic)
1. National Catholic reporter—History. 2. Catholic Church—United States—Periodicals—History. I. Title.
BX801.J66 2014
282'.7305—dc23
2014008857

♾ ™ The paper used in this publication meets the minimum requirements of American National Standard for Information Sciences Permanence of Paper for Printed Library Materials, ANSI/NISO Z39.48-1992.

Printed in the United States of America

For Joe Feuerherd

"NCR's Man for All Seasons"
NCR intern, staff writer,
Washington correspondent,
Washington bureau chief,
editor-in-chief and CEO/publisher

in tandem with

Tom Fox

"NCR's mystic, maestro and mentor"
The newspaper's Vietnam War correspondent,
twice its editor, three times its publisher,
its institutional memory—
and always its guiding spirit

CONTENTS

PREFACE

*I have always felt that NCR was located poorly, but that a combina-
tion of extraordinary events helped it to overcome that disability.*
S. J. Adamo, "The Press," *America* magazine, July 24, 1971

This is a book for reading in the lounge chair, or at the beach or in bed
for ten minutes before lights out.

It is about the people who have led a small, national Catholic newspaper into the thickets of church and secular, national and international
news for a half-century. It is an account, more a summary, of the news
flow across these past fifty years of our lives—wherever the reader
might fit into that era.

The *National Catholic Reporter* was founded at the halfway mark of
the Second Vatican Council (1962–1965). *NCR*, as it is known, became
not merely the council's chronicler, but its flag-bearer, then its defender. Its defender until, finally, it was one of the few publications that—
like monks working in the Dark Ages—still carried the great message of
the great church council into the future.

The great message of the Second Vatican Council was that the
church had thrown its arms wide open to greet the world in a new way.
Vatican II also told the Catholic laity it was its job to pick up the load
from that point on. *NCR* held fast even as the institutional church
began to backtrack and renege on the council's ideals.

For five decades, *NCR*'s coverage has chronicled social changes and
the church's response, has taken its readers into worlds of the hope-

filled and valiant as well as into the saddest corners of human life and the darkest corners of a secretive church.

In its fifty years, *NCR* has been hailed and damned.

Twice, local bishops called for it to remove the word "Catholic" from its masthead. Twice, the editors, publishers and board declined. Fellow journalists have a different view. To the *New York Times*, we are "a brave little paper"; to *TIME* magazine, "a global powerhouse." The *Kansas City Star* dubbed us the church's "Loyal Gadfly"; Religion News Service spoke of the *National Catholic Reporter*'s "fierce independence and liberal tilt," while the *Washington Post* sees *NCR* as "the go-to source for all things Catholic."

What the reader will not see is much by the way of current critique of *NCR*. Just as it needs a full-scale history, it requires a detached observer. Not since the University of Notre Dame's Scott Appleby's fifteen-page paper in 1997 has anyone thoughtfully taken the *National Catholic Reporter* to task in a scholarly way. Even then, Appleby's critique was simply an element within "Taking Hold of the Dirty Stuff of History: Robert G. Hoyt and the Founding of the *National Catholic Reporter*."

What Appleby in part contended was that

> the paper was nonetheless vulnerable to criticism that it was narrowly theological, biased, and contentious for its own sake, thereby undermining Catholic unity. Obsessed with ending the hierarchical church's governance by secrecy, it was too frank at times, transgressing the bounds of good taste and decency—not a happy legacy for our own frayed "culture of complaint." Hoyt's "thirst for the fray," [as first board chairman John] Fallon put it, inclined the *NCR* to strongly partisan stands in its editorials, influenced it toward the selection of controversial news, and contributed toward an atmosphere in which sloppy reporting might slip by if it represented a certain side on an issue.

In September 1966, Bishop James Shannon, auxiliary bishop of Minneapolis–St. Paul, gave a talk at Saint Thomas College. He cited *NCR* "as an example of journals which slip into bad taste, discourtesy and sloppy reporting" in their eagerness to promote free discussion. Hoyt invited Shannon to submit an article to *NCR*. Shannon agreed and wrote that *NCR* was too much into "good guys, bad guys" and was "often foolishly simplistic" in its view of the world and the church.

Hoyt's extended reply explained *NCR* was not a teaching agency of the church. Nor was it a public relations agency for the bishops. Hoyt said the newspaper's inadequacies "bother us but not enough to weigh us down. We are doing an essential job and that is being done well enough to justify continuing."

Certainly the newspaper has been the dependable source of behind-the-scenes stories on the church for a half-century.

It revealed the secret findings of the Papal Birth Control Commission. (In 1968, Pope Paul VI overrode the commission members' recommendations to approve contraception for married couples.)

It spearheaded the earliest debates on the role and rights of women and women religious in the church.

Its open forum on celibacy brought to the fore a topic the institution contended was a non-issue.

In 1985, seventeen years before the national outcry created by the *Boston Globe*'s investigation into Cardinal Bernard Law's behavior, the *National Catholic Reporter* front page revealed the widespread nature of clerical pedophilia abuse nationwide.

And when, in the 1990s, nuns were being raped in Africa by priests who wanted AIDS-free sex, it was *NCR* that carried yet another story no one wanted to hear, and none could ignore.

Those, however, are the highlight exposés. This book's overview of the news flow under each editor is more impressionistic than detailed. There are occasional samples of the news flow, but the focus is more on the trends and major issues of the moment.

The newspaper has always had two underlying themes: revealing the social Gospel at work through the lives of the church's current prophetic witnesses, and doing so through some of the best American Catholic writers of the times. The writers—lay men and women, priests, nuns and brothers—have explored in depth the scriptural, spiritual, moral and theological imperatives in the light the ever-changing times demanded.

Editorially, the paper has been, foremost, a defender of prophetic witnesses, those living according to the Gospel mandates.

Whether the topic is women's ordination, or gay Catholics and their rights and needs, or of theologians being battered by an inquisitorial

Vatican, or Vatican-orchestrated punitive measures sought against any who dare dissent, the newspaper has been there, arguing for justice.

From the start and down to the present, NCR's enduring five elements have been race and poverty; peace and U.S. foreign policy; nuns and women; sexuality; church and papacy. In the 1990s, then-editor Tom Fox added ecology and cosmology. As a later editor remarked, "Any headline that has 'transcendence' and 'ecology' in the same headline is a winner with our readers." Issue by issue, the topics switch around as to which make the front pages, and admittedly, a multitude of stories can appear under headings as broad as those. And have.

Through Gospel and spiritual exploration, through a Lenten series and an Advent series, our spiritual depths and needs as Catholics have been examined, our joys encouraged, our sorrows understood, our lives placed in perspective.

This book is not the newspaper's history; it is the *National Catholic Reporter*'s personal story—the inside story told by an insider who cares. Think of it as NCR's biography (with a dash of autobiography) as the editors are introduced.

The book's structure introduces the editors as individuals. What drove these editors—most of whom could have had or did have prominent or promising careers in mainline secular journalism—to follow the journalistic path less-traveled? Who are they or who were they? And why? Through these editors' family backgrounds and religious formation, their hopes and driving forces, the reader gains a sense—from the news highlights—of how the paper prioritizes, ebbs and flows under a particular editor's leadership. What they all have in common is the constant tension between remaining loyal to their faith while fostering a deep—and occasionally withering—critique of the church institution and its leaders.

This is a very human story; not everything turns out all right all the time.

Yet what becomes obvious is that despite the individuality of the editors in charge, beginning with founding editor Robert G. Hoyt and his initial team, the *National Catholic Reporter* has stayed the course.

By the twenty-first century it had adopted and adapted to the online age with www.ncronline.org. But, miracle of miracles, it still has a circulation of thirty-five thousand (print and e-edition).

I had twelve months from a standing start to write this book, to rapidly page through forty-nine volumes of the newspaper as the 50th was coming into being. In comparison to a history, this is journalism— as in the remark of *Washington Post* publisher Donald Graham that journalism is the "first rough draft of history." This is that rough draft, firsthand and personal. Even though it has been more than forty years since Adamo spoke of *NCR*'s "combination of extraordinary events," only now is "how extraordinary" set down for the first time.

To borrow from Bob Hoyt, I am well aware of the book's inadequacies, and they do bother me, but not enough to weigh me down. I can only hope it is "being done well enough to justify continuing it" through to the end.

INTRODUCTION

The fifty-year home of the *National Catholic Reporter*, for all but its first fifteen or so months, has always been in the light-red-brick-and-dressed-stone mansion that is 115 E. Armour Blvd., in the Hyde Park area of Kansas City, Missouri. The "Armour" was Simeon Armour, owner of the Armour Packing Company in Chicago, a firm famous for its hams. Armour was a man who preferred Kansas City to the Windy City for his home; it made him a very big name in a very small town.

Armour is a true boulevard: spacious, tree-lined and pleasant (and now faded). *NCR*'s elderly mansion is unassuming. It is set back sufficiently that its four-story mass doesn't intimidate. Nor, despite episcopal condemnations by the local prelate of the day at each end of its fifty years, is *NCR* intimidated. Some two blocks away, the chancery office of the diocese of Kansas City–St. Joseph at the time of *NCR*'s October 1964 founding was also in the Hyde Park area, at 300 E. 36th Street. After the bishop of that era, Bishop Charles Helmsing, began to express his displeasure over *NCR*'s content, the chancery office was always referred to in the newsroom as the place "a stone's throw away."

Not only was *NCR*'s birth extraordinary, but so were the times in which it was conceived.

NCR was founded during the 1960s. Those were turbulent years, an explosive interlude in the rapidly changing post–World War II environment, and Catholics expected their church to change too.

The American Catholic church was something neither the universal church nor the Vatican, i.e., the church-in-Rome (popes, cardinals, curia, senior hierarchs) had ever witnessed: a highly educated laity, enthusiastic about its faith and church, determined to take its place in its church and civil society. To Europeans, the American church was "arriviste," a post–World War II church, neither adolescent nor fully matured. After all, thirty-five years earlier it was still mission territory. Of course, many Europeans felt that way about the United States in general.

Once in the spotlight, however, the American church practically stole the global show. Wealthy by any existing world standards, the American church was not only well educated but also well organized. In the decades ahead, the church in Rome, understandably, would come to fear American Catholicism's strength as a strength capable of rivaling its own on a world scale.

In all of this, a low-circulation newspaper (just under ninety-thousand-plus at its peak in a church of tens of millions of U.S. Catholic families) has played an outsized role.

The paper has made history as well as reported it. Its stance rests in its determined coverage. Its influence in its editorials. Its authority is drawn in part from its supportive readership, just as its strength rests in the quality of its reporters and commentators. A 2003 Northwestern University study argued that *NCR* is progressive Catholicism's local paper, but that didn't quite capture its role. Melissa Jones, in a 2013 paper before the American Academy of Religion Western Region, described *NCR* as a "community newspaper that looks out for [the readers'] interests," a veritable "sandbox" of unique content—offering coverage and editorials that churn up difficult questions in digestible form—*and* a publication that has successfully continued into the digital age.

That's a close reading of the present and the augury for the future.

Generally speaking, if *NCR*'s is a readership largely drawn from the like-minded, they are like-minded as to what the Second Vatican Council (1962–1965) intended.

This newspaper's original readership was the generation of Catholics maturing in the late 1930s to mid-1960s and into and beyond Vatican II.

By the 1960s, the American Catholic—layperson, woman religious, priest, brother and bishop—was part of large group held together (beyond their mutual faith and love for the church) by a rapidly expanding U.S. Catholic literati of sorts. These were fresh generations of Catholic writers, journalists and doers in a country led by a Catholic president, in a church headed by a lovable pope. However, while Washington, DC, and Rome are exciting, the adventure story that is *NCR* could only have been born in the quieter, rooted, independent-minded Catholicism of the Midwest. In Scott Appleby's 1997 remarks at a Hoyt tribute, *NCR* "could only happen in the progressive Catholic Midwest, not on the [Cardinal Francis] Spellman–[Cardinal Richard] Cushing conservative-minded East Coast, not in [Cardinal James] McIntyre's Los Angeles."

In 1912, in England, the Rev. Francis Henry Wood, in the introduction to his twelve-volume *The Hebrew Scriptures in English*, described the prophets as the editorial writers of their day. To that extent, *NCR* is about prophetic witness in a changing church. Most often that is seen in interviews with and intensive news coverage of contemporary Christianity's prophetic witnesses: laypersons—women and men—and nuns, priests and bishops living, suffering and sometimes dying for their witness.

Wood used the English term "leader writers" for editorial writers because those are seen as a newspaper's "leading columns." Under its founding editor Robert E. Hoyt (1964–1971), *NCR*'s prophetic witness was most clearly stated in his profound editorials, his "leading columns"—the columns on which the newspaper actually rested. It was Hoyt's gift as an editorial writer that led to the newspaper's birth. Its first publisher, Michael Greene, said it was not his marketing but Hoyt's editorials that sold subscriptions. Hoyt handled words as precious commodities. As Fr. John Reedy wrote, "Other men had *control* over Church institutions; Hoyt had *influence*."

NCR's fourth editorial staffer, Art Winter, whose position was assistant news editor, these days has above his desk in his home a text sent to him by a religious brother. It dates to the time when Kansas City Bishop Helmsing condemned *NCR*.

> Prophets are not particularly pleasant people. It is their function to unsettle, to disturb, to criticize and to convert. The reaction of established authorities to prophetic voices is usually not pleasant either. They rebuke. Some they suppress—and some they crucify.

While prophetic witness marks the paper's consistency throughout its first half-century, the *NCR*'s taproot is in the New Testament, which the newspaper holds close as its implied mission statement: Jesus' good news in Luke 4:16–19, and the Sermon on the Mount in Matthew 5:1–12.

The New Testament came easily to the paper's lay editors: Three had been seminarians, one had been ordained, one was and remains a woman religious; the others were cradle Catholics. Founding editor Robert Guy Hoyt was a Norbertine ("Frater Guido"). Donald J. Thorman (1971–1975) was in two seminaries, the Servites and the Viatorians. Thorman was never a shirtsleeve editor and was rarely down from his fourth-floor office to visit the third-floor editorial offices. Thorman, however, was *NCR*'s shepherd, and a manager who saved the company financially. (In 1973, he persuaded the board that the company should buy the 115 E. Armour mansion. The board agreed.)

Thorman always wanted to maintain a balance between *NCR* and the bishops, especially wanting to defuse those topics where animosity or mutual recrimination seemed most likely.

Then, from 1975 to 1980, came Jones (that's me, a lifelong journalist untouched by a higher calling), followed by Tom Fox (1980–1997). Though their contributions differ, Fox ranks with Hoyt in significance as the newspaper's editor. With such longevity in the chair—he served as publisher, then retired, then returned as editor in 2010 for two years—Fox has served as *NCR*'s guide ever since 1980. As an editorial writer, he was Hoyt's equal, and he exceeded all other editors as an extemporaneous speaker and public presence. Fox is also one of those who carry *NCR*'s institutional memory—he began his journalism career as a war correspondent in Vietnam writing for Hoyt. (The longest-serving member of the company is Vickie Breashears, display advertising manager, who started as a clerk in 1966.)

Fox is a man to trust with *NCR*'s soul.

After Fox, came Michael Farrell (1997–2000), previously a priest, *NCR*'s best-educated editor and, though mainly unrecognized as such, its Jonathan Swift. Most saw Farrell through his columns as an entertainer, without quite recognizing his wit (in the eighteenth-century sense) or the razor-sharp acuteness of his range. He was an editor with a knowing view of the world, and warily so.

Tom Roberts (2000–2007), musician and journalist, followed—an editor so open and warm he could be trusted with *NCR*'s heart. He was another newsroom rebuilder. St. Anne Sr. Rita Larivee was publisher (2005–2008), and she spent her final year doubling as editor in chief.

Then, all too briefly (2008–2012), came Joe Feuerherd, another essential layman, *NCR*'s man for all seasons. He was snatched away by cancer. His term—in this book—is characterized as a Joe Feuerherd/Tom Fox duo, with Feuerherd as publisher/editor in chief and Fox, editor, as a strong second-in-command.

Today's editor, Dennis Coday, was a Society of the Precious Blood seminarian. He is the extremely industrious, low-key, twenty-first-century anchorman of the paper's print and online editions. He came with digital-era skills previous editors lacked, skills that accelerated *NCR* (the newspaper) in its fledgling moves into the digital era. Coday has expanded the news team with the youngest newsroom since the 1970s. A man to trust with *NCR*'s future. The editorials have regained a Hoytian quality—though these days it generally takes a team effort to achieve it.

But all that is for later in the book.

NCR has been led by men and one woman. On three other occasions, it appeared the next *NCR* editor might indeed be a news-oriented woman. ("Editor," as used here—and as the paper requires its editors to be—means someone coming from a news-and-reporting background. That has not always happened, and the results have never been satisfactory or long-term when it has not.) In 2007, Pamela Schaeffer was executive editor. There was a proposal under publisher Larivee to change *NCR* into a magazine with Schaeffer as editor.

The proposal was dropped. Schaeffer left.

In 2010, another woman candidate, a prominent national newspaper journalist and editor, after extensive talks with *NCR* and trips to Kansas City, finally decided against moving there and becoming editor in chief (and publisher).

Kansas City, for all its charms, remains—for editors and journalists who've worked elsewhere—somewhat off the beaten track.

The people behind the scenes who keep the company functioning are not totally neglected. The appendix carries a corporate report that introduces board members, sister-publication *Celebration* magazine editors, and folks in the back office who keep the corporate side functioning.

NCR was indeed born out of a combination of extraordinary events. The fertile soil was turned in the mid-1940s by a new American lay

Catholic "rising class." It was a post–World War II Catholic religious-and-sociopolitical awakening. Awakened to do what?

If there was hope and optimism, it wasn't evident everywhere. There was unbelievably crushing rural and urban poverty.

Poverty was intermingled with—in many states inseparable from—a brutal, visible, unconscionable racism against African Americans in the East and South, against Hispanics (primarily Puerto Ricans) in the East, against Latino Americans in the West and against Native Americans in every state into which they'd been hounded from wherever they'd been uprooted.

By 1947, the House Un-American Activities Committee had begun blacklisting Hollywood writers. Within three years, under Wisconsin Senator Joseph McCarthy, HUAC would spread the cancer far wider than Hollywood. The ever-lurking fascism of the far right was exemplified too by remnants of the German American Bund, formed in the 1930s to promote a favorable impression of Adolf Hitler and Nazism in the United States. It had its congressional sympathizers. Demagoguery was back.

There was anti-Catholicism and anti-Semitism, anti–East Coast establishmentarianism and a North-South divide precious to those who did not want to relinquish it. The aftermath of World War II saw a reinvigorated anti-communism, which the Cold War heightened into a nuclear terror—a genuine terror, a pressing reality, never then and not now a figment of excitable imaginations.

Wartime had altered the American psyche. Americans had not known America, or other Americans, except through the distorted fantasies of Hollywood. To the East Coast American of the 1930s and 1940s, California was as exotic as the South Pacific. The Army shipped out many Easterners through the West Coast to the Pacific, shipped Westerners and Heartlanders out from East Coast ports to Europe. War introduced Americans to themselves: to Americans from other states of the union, Americans from a multiplicity of ethnic backgrounds.

Previously separated and segregated by distance, or sequestered, hidden away, in ethnic and religious ghettos and neighborhoods, American servicemen—Catholics, Protestants and Jews—lived together under the same reeking, inadequate canvas shelter. Many were imprisoned together, or wounded together, or died together on the same foreign ground.

New Year's Day 1946 promised unprecedented prosperity and peace but also a new world peril: The year was the dawn of an atomic age that would worsen into the nuclear age—if a quantum leap from total atomic annihilation to total nuclear annihilation could count as a worsening. Millions of young Americans were now swapping their uniforms for a worker's overalls, perhaps a suit, or slacks and a jacket, or on dozens of college campuses, for sweaters and slacks. Many, for the sake of their psychological health, suppressed their view of other war-torn worlds, their fright-filled days and death-threatened hours-minutes-seconds as friends around them perished. Yet the experience had brought the deepest form of reflection. Many had seen the worst of what man can do to man, and woman and child. In war, that is not a trite phrase.

Scarcely anyone in America had escaped the images of the Holocaust. The photographs in newspapers and magazines and on the Movietone News and Pathe News in the cinemas, and the survivors' testimony in film and (for a few wealthier Americans) on television indelibly stamped the Jewish plight on a generation. The Holocaust—the genocide that slaughtered six million Jews and countless others the Nazis hated or thought superfluous to humanity—had an evil twin: the U.S.-inflicted holocausts on Hiroshima and Nagasaki.

Harry Truman was president and not expected to be reelected. (He famously was.) New York's party bosses, among others, were arraigned against him.

On Broadway, audiences could seek relief and laughter at *Born Yesterday*, or agonize with Eugene O'Neill's somber *The Iceman Cometh*. Top radio shows included *Fibber McGee and Molly* and *The Shadow*, but switch the station and there'd be Rosemary Clooney, Bing Crosby, Frank Sinatra and dozens more singers and crooners.

In 1946, in war's aftermath, Pope Pius XII was far too occupied with war-torn Italy to pay much attention to the United States. He was fearful Italy would fall to the communists. Few Catholics were yet aware that war had also cast a pall over the church's reputation. The pope's impartiality was clouded by his silence in the face of Shoah, the Holocaust—charges that will never satisfactorily be laid to rest. Further, some in the Vatican, plus bishops and some religious orders, were implicated in "rat lines": escape routes for Nazi war criminals fleeing the Allied victors' wrath and headed primarily but not exclusively to South America.

What Pius XII did realize, as war ebbed, was that the church was short of cardinals—it was down to thirty-eight. There was only one cardinal in the United States, Philadelphia's archbishop, doughty eighty-one-year-old Cardinal Dennis Joseph Dougherty. In the hastily called February 1946 "Great Consistory," Pius created thirty-two new cardinals to meet the maximum seventy. The number included the archbishop of New York, Francis Spellman, whereupon another page was turned in U.S. Catholic history. This time in the pages of *Life* magazine.

In 1946, *Life* magazine was everything that television became: the major source of pictorial news entertainment, national in circulation, international in scope, often a feast for the eyes and a dominating force in deciding which trends were newsworthy. (Television, beamed from New York, had spread as far south and west as Tennessee, but very few Americans could afford a television set.)

Time-Life's founder, Henry Luce, undoubtedly prompted by Clare Booth Luce, his Catholic convert second wife, decided Catholics per se were newsworthy (and an audience worth cultivating). That meant, when Archbishop Spellman was raised to the purple, *Life* magazine decided Spellman was worth a two-part series. *Life*'s reporting included the fact that war-induced shortages meant the new cardinal couldn't obtain fresh silks to match his new status; he had to settle for the cut-down, hand-me-downs of his predecessors.

For Catholics in particular, the return from war produced self-confidence, a brio, an energetic forward thrust not unallied to an increasingly rapid improvement in Catholic personal income as a group. Their education in Catholic schools and colleges had a great deal to do with that. The awakening American Catholics were 24 percent of the U.S. population. (When questioned in a 1949 twelve-page article in *Life* magazine, Evelyn Waugh "finds his Church here is maturing as its zealous educators seek to raise its proletariat to a bourgeoisie." Michael Greene, *NCR*'s first publisher, encapsulated this emergence when he described John Fallon, *NCR*'s first president, as a "'New Wave' Catholic.")

These were the years when the Catholic bishops met as the National Catholic Welfare Conference (NCWC). In the East Coast church, the

initials were said to stand for "Nothing Counts West of Chicago." Hoyt
& Co. were out to change that as Catholics everywhere began to pour
out of the ethnic parish ghettoes to take a new place in society nationwide. Some remained where they were. In the west, a young man called
Cesar Chavez worked with his family picking tomatoes, grapes and
lettuce.

In the East, two men dominated all: Archbishop Edward Francis
Hoban of Cleveland, and Cardinal Francis J. Spellman of New York.
Between them—in competition—they created the nation's bishops.

Popes and the Vatican had long distrusted American democracy.
"American Catholics" and American bishops were "too American" and
too independent by half. Papal infallibility was only one of the bones of
contention. Though American bishops had finally fallen into line, they
had, in the main, been opposed to the pope making himself infallible.
(Arguably, Pius IX had the bishops do it for him, but he wanted it, and
the result was the same.) Popes issued encyclicals to score their points:
against democracy—whether "Americanism" (Leo XIII; *Testem benev-
olentiae*, 1899) or "modernism" (Pius X; *Pascendi dominici gregis*,
1907).

The old church's idea of a modern nation—if a Catholic theocracy or
a Catholic absolute monarchy was too much to hope for—was Francisco Franco's Fascist Spain. Fascism has been described as "capitalism at
its most nude and crude." In Spain, the church was one of the players,
along with the government and the military, in alliance with those who
controlled the private economy. Spain also gave birth to Opus Dei, the
secretive, fundamentalist, clerical and lay Catholic organization that
sees itself as the papacy's antidote to the Jesuits.

Yes, that was then. But it's also now.

In 1946, one of the Americans doffing his uniform after three years
in the Army Air Forces was twenty-four-year-old Robert Guy Hoyt.
While mothers, wives and sweethearts were humming "When Johnny
Comes Marching Home" to welcome back their solders, Hoyt was a
young man with no home to go to.

Four years later, he was on page 90 of the October 16, 1950, edition
of *Newsweek* magazine. The photograph is of an angelic-looking Hoyt.
It is the only column of "religion" news on the page. The two other
columns are dominated by advertisements.

"Connolly of Minnesota, 'soft leather' shoes, $11.95 to $18.95."
"Your car starts instantly with a Stewart-Warner 'Electric' Fuel Pump."
"When You Have a Headache, Take Alka-Seltzer."

Nonetheless, in close competition with the ads are the large, heaven-fixed eyes of Hoyt above a Mona Lisa smile. (Obviously, the *Newsweek* photographer had told him to gaze heavenward.) On the wall behind Hoyt's editor's chair, the photographer had caught part of an illustrated poster. There are fishes, loaves and wine, and Jesus is seated at a table. The photographed legend reads, "Multiplied loaves and fishes and converted water to wine. Do thou come to our [table; the word is obscured by Hoyt's head] as giver and guest to dine."

The cutline reads, "Hoyt: Poverty is a condition."

The four-paragraph story announces to the world, or at least to *Newsweek*'s 1950 million-plus circulation readership, the birth of a Catholic-inspired Christian daily newspaper, the *Sun Herald*, located in Kansas City, Missouri. Hoyt had been elected the *Sun Herald* editor by its twenty-person start-up team. The team's journalism was there, in *Newsweek*, for all to see: Jesus, U.S. lay Catholics and poverty. The courageous, five-day-a-week, eight-page sheet squeaked by for seven months.

The *Newsweek* article was a brief pen-portrait of an editor. The term "editor" here implies a shirtsleeve journalist who determines the newspaper's editorial policy in his leading columns. He confers with staff members with more breaking-news experience than he possesses, and he reads everything before the newspaper goes to press. He takes the blame for everything misstated, misunderstood or inaccurate.

Twenty-three years later Hoyt, after the *Sun-Herald*'s brief appearance, was founding editor of the *National Catholic Reporter*.

Fifty years beyond that, the half-century-old *NCR* requires its story be told. Fifty years of *NCR*: 60,000 pages; circa 3 million words. Each decade is boiled down from 400,000-plus words into a 5,000–7,000-word chapter.

Alas, there are many writers and topics and people deserving greater coverage than this book provides; for example, the writers behind the Lenten and Advent reflection series and the writers tackling anti-Semitism, housing, education and health care. Tragically, yet with no slight intended, many writers who appear in *NCR* across a half-century, some extremely well known, scarcely make an appearance in this book, or get no mention at all.

That is why, in time, a three-volume, footnoted history is needed.

I

1966: BOB HOYT

It was toward the end of the 1920s, perhaps 1927. There is a photograph of two young brothers, "slim, dark and somber": James Hoyt is aged about seven, his younger brother, Robert Guy, perhaps five. They are in a goat cart. Was it taken at Aunt Rene's house near Torch Lake, Wisconsin? They look solemn. Were they afraid of the goat? Or had they been taken there because their father, Guy, a grain mill manager in Ironwood, Michigan, had died of pneumonia? Ironwood was their mother's birthplace. The family had moved around. The boys were born in Clinton, Iowa, but now the widowed Ella Wynn Hoyt moved to Detroit. In order to have an income, she trained as a beautician and later opened her own shop. Bob Hoyt said that at this time his mother sent both boys to a boarding school. Or had she temporarily placed her sons in an orphanage? He was certainly in one at some point, as others referred to it later as fact.

The actual record is somewhat clouded. The certain facts are that in 1933, in the depths of the Great Depression, Bob Hoyt graduated from Detroit's Gesu Catholic School, part of the Jesuit-run Gesu Parish, and, obviously a bright student, he was sent to St. Norbert's High School, a boarding school in DePere, Wisconsin. Jim Hoyt remained in Detroit, presumably in high school. In March 1935, when Bob Hoyt was a high school sophomore, his mother died. She was forty-six. Already orphaned, the boys would soon be abandoned. Though Jim, who probably graduated from high school that year, could fend for himself, he and Bob needed a guardian until they reached "legal age"—twenty-one.

The task of finding official guardians for the two lads fell to the Gesu pastor. Two families stepped forward. One couple was not well-off. This was possibly "Aunt Rene" and her husband, for it is known this couple "loved the boys." The other possibility was Arthur and Irene Cronin. They were wealthy. Arthur D. Cronin was president of the Pine Ridge Coal Company and the Cronin Coal Company. He was a member of the Detroit Country Club, the Grosse Pointe Yacht Club, the Detroit Gold Club and the Detroit Riding & Hunt Club. The Cronins, with five children of their own, lived in Detroit's prestigious Woodston section just north of Seven Mile Way, at 19160 Woodston Drive.

The pastor decided on the Cronins, though apparently it was only Mrs. Cronin, active in the League of Catholic Women, who was prepared to act as guardian.

Mrs. Cronin obviously met her legal responsibilities. Bob Hoyt's fees were paid regularly, but according to his son Mike Hoyt, neither boy was ever inside the Woodston Drive house after the one visit, nor had either any further direct contact with the Cronins. Bob said he was too young to understand much of what was going on but that Jim was "deeply angry and never really got over it."

The quick-witted and intelligent young Bob must have done well enough at school and been sufficiently inclined to religion and piety to be accepted, in 1939, into the Norbertine order. He had completed his freshman college year. The Norbertines—more formally the Premonstratensians, for their founding in Prémontré, France—led austere lives. The austerity did not rule out activity; at some point during these years, Hoyt learned to box. Nor did it rule out fun: Hoyt apparently had a taste for practical jokes. At heart, however, he was a serious young Catholic at a time when these college-educated Catholic young men and women were beginning to see greater possibilities for service within the church than had been possible for their parents' generation.

He entered the Norbertines as "Frater Guido." Norbertine Fr. Albert McBride recalled that in 1942, Frater Guido was teaching in Philadelphia at the Norbertine-staffed South Central Catholic High School. By the 1940s, few Catholics of college age were unaware of the work of Dorothy Day and the Catholic Worker movement she'd cofounded in the early 1930s with Peter Maurin. If, by the early 1940s, Hoyt was an editor in embryo, the *Catholic Worker* at a penny a copy must have been a considerable inspiration.

Hoyt was enamored, too, of the teachings of an activist priest in Flanders, Fr. (later Cardinal) Joseph Cardijn. This was a region close to Prémontré, home of the Norbertines, and the order may have admired Cardijn as a model. In 1912 as a young priest, Cardijn had founded the Young Christian Workers (YCW) movement in Laeken (Dutch; Laken, in French), Belgium, then on the outskirts of Brussels. Cardijn developed a manner of approaching problems—"see, judge, act"—and expected this of his Young Christian Workers protégés in their workplace. Each was "challenged to Christianize" his or her workplace or area of responsibility.

Cardijn's "Christianizing" would be a strand never severed in underpinnings to Hoyt's writings. As Hoyt matured into his early twenties, YCW was in more than three dozen countries worldwide, including the United States. The U.S.-founded Catholic Worker and the European YCW shared common impulses: to put Christianity forward as an alternative to communism. The *Catholic Worker* was a direct stand against the Marxist *Daily Worker*.

The Catholic Worker–Cardijn approach to the lay Christian life, fully lived, required giving of oneself to aid others. To Hoyt, who had experienced the austere life of the Norbertines, that came as a matter of course. Nonetheless, whatever was whirling around in Hoyt's head in 1942 in Philadelphia, it was not about a future as a priest: there was an ongoing war. He left the Norbertines and, in 1943, enlisted in the U.S. Army Air Forces. Once there, with the cooperation of a couple of recruit friends, he played a practical joke on their peers. A brooding Hoyt pretended to be a transfer in from the French Foreign Legion who never spoke because he'd lost the love of his life to a Nazi bomb. Their hut mates were not amused when Hoyt and his friends admitted to the ruse.

He was accepted into flight training but never made it as a pilot. The tide of war in Europe was turning in favor of the Allies. Demand for pilots was down. Mike Hoyt said his father "washed out" as a trainee pilot—along with many others: "I think he liked the service, but remember, he had lived in institutions all his life." He'd scarcely known any other. The elder Hoyt recalled fondly, Mike said, a boxing bout in the military, not because he was knocked out but because when he came to, there was a beautiful blonde standing there looking down and smiling at him. (But when Bob Hoyt wed, it was to a brunette, both times.)

Discharged in Denver, Colorado, in 1946, he started job hunting: he wanted to be an editor. There was fresh post–World War II leavening now: the New York–based *Integrity* magazine was founded that same year, 1946, by Wellesley College graduate Carol Jackson, a convert, and Ed Willock, an artist from the Catholic Worker movement. Jackson founded the magazine with $400 and succeeded by opening the pages of her publication—"published by lay Catholics and dedicated to the task of discovering the new synthesis of RELIGION and LIFE in our times"—to names now icons of that period, names that included Dorothy Day; Pax Christi cofounder Eileen Egan; founder of Madonna House, Catherine de Hueck Doherty; publisher Maisie Ward; a *Commonweal* editor, Anne Freemantle; and Maria von Trapp (whose family became famous because of the musical *The Sound of Music*). Six women no less.

Intellectual thought, however, was gathered by *Integrity* from many fields: from seers of technological development to philosophers such as Cardinal Emmanuel Suhard, archbishop of Paris, who in July 1942, despite his support for the Vichy government, had written a public protest against the deportation of Parisian Jews and condemned Vichy collaboration with the Nazis' anti-Jewish policy. Edith Stein's first writings on women appeared in *Integrity*, along with sharp, sometimes biting assessments of current U.S. social issues from Paul Hanley Furfey, plus poetry from Thomas Merton and the Modernist poet Franciscan Sr. M. Bernetta Quinn, whose small collection, *Dancing in Stillness*, was published in 1983.

Integrity was a radical, feisty, highly intellectual and witty Catholic publication. The hierarchy regarded it as subversive. But it galvanized young, thinking, activist Catholics such as Hoyt and his friends. He later described it as "lively, sometimes very funny, a sort of radical, lay-apostolic, remake [of] the world. There were implicit in it some tendencies toward extremism on the right, although I didn't recognize it at the time."

On the social side, fastened in faith, the Catholic riptide was reaction against the Industrial Revolution, augmented by Leo XIII's 1891 encyclical *Rerum Novarum*, which placed the church solidly on the side of the laboring classes, industrial and rural. There were stirrings among the educated German and French Catholics. Le Sillon is the best known of the French movements, but it was not the only one. By the early twentieth century, English Catholics of the "ChesterBelloc" (G. K. Chesterton and Hilaire Belloc) movement joined in the general reaction. In the United States, Catholic Worker cofounder Peter Maurin had come out of the French Le Sillon tradition.

On both sides of the Atlantic, the Catholics in these movements were taking a stand against atheistic socialism. They mirrored their opponents in their concerns for the poor and the workers, but pitted a Christian communitarian approach against communism, and Christ against godlessness. Radical Catholicism of the Hoyt era found encouragement from individual priests, and subtly—in the liturgical area, for example—in magazines such as *Orare Fratres*. For these Americans, a secondary networking factor was the existence of a Chicago Catholic–Notre Dame axis, where more young Catholics were also likely readers of *Integrity*.

In 1947, Hoyt found a job with the Denver-based *Register System* of Catholic newspapers group of Denver, Colorado, where the overall editor in chief was Monsignor Matthew Smith, who had "a self-awarded LL.D degree," said Hoyt. The *Register* published thirty-five or so Catholic diocesan newspapers from West Virginia to California. The reasons were economic. Many dioceses found it relatively inexpensive to have the *Register Systems* "edited, composed, typeset, laid out, printed, and in most cases, mailed from the central Register plant in Denver," Hoyt said. He was on the copy desk as an associate editor.

From there, he could scout for editor opportunities as they arose with the chain. Also on the copy desk was Bernadette Lyon. They courted and were wed in 1948. Hoyt was in love—"I ended up getting married to another young proofreader, Bernardette Lyon"—but not with the *Register* chain, nor it with him.

That was obvious when Hoyt was directed to a job offer in Santa Fe, New Mexico, by Maryknoll Father Don Hessler, who traveled around Colorado converting priests to the lay apostolate and self-sacrifice. The job was to make the *Santa Fe Register* more *au courant*. Hoyt resigned from the Register, and he and Bernardette were about to sell his house in Denver when the Santa Fe Catholic chancery—the diocese's headquarters—telegrammed to say the job no longer existed. The reason, Hoyt later learned, was that the *Register* group's overall boss, a Monsignor John Cavanaugh, had told Santa Fe they could hire anyone but Hoyt. Hoyt blamed the long arm of the Catholic powers-that-be in Chicago, and his *Integrity* connections.

He probably hadn't helped matters by daring to mention sex. Hoyt was also writing the advice column under the *nom de plume* "Roberta Guido." Most of the letters were invented, but a real one from a young Catholic college woman raised a moral question. Should she quit her secular college because her classmates were sleeping with men, an occasion of sin? Roberta Guido assured her that while she had to be aware of peer pressure, "you can't run aware from all temptations—and if you stay you can set an example of how to be happy though pure."

Cavanaugh was handed the galleys by someone. The editor in chief exploded, but while Roberta Guido was dispatched, Hoyt remained—until he applied to Santa Fe.

So it was off to Chicago for the Hoyts (with one-year-old son Mike), for it was there, not Denver, where Bob and Bernadette and their Catholic Worker–oriented Chicago-based Catholic colleagues—prompted by *Integrity*'s Carol Jackson—decided to start their own Catholic daily newspaper.

He and Bernadette circulated a newsletter, *The Precursor*, drumming up the idea of a Catholic daily and soliciting ideas and interested participants. Home was a Chicago apartment that had rats. Dale Francis was one of those on the Chicago–Notre Dame axis. He was the Notre Dame University's head of communications. In June 1949, Francis hosted in his home a two-day "convention" of Catholic daily-newspaper idealists. From this definitive meeting emerged the idea for a Catholic daily, the *Morning Star*. Under a corporate structure called the Apostolic Press, Hoyt was elected publisher and editor. The *Morning Star*'s promotional material was unique for a U.S. daily newspaper, though it offered nothing strange to progressive Catholics. It introduced itself to would-be backers and subscribers as "a new daily paper of truth, clarity, and service, looking to Mary, Morning Star, and under the patronage of Saint Paul the Apostle."

The editors wrote (the exclusive language of the era is maintained),

> Christ is King. Charity rules. Today man decides his stand in time and eternity. *The Morning Star* will report these truths daily as they live in the news. It will repeat the good news of the Gospel. It will cover the human scene, where a man is either for or against God.

> This new daily will look at the global situation, see it through the
> eyes of faith, and attempt to present it in the context of the whole
> truth.

The brochure continued in that vein and declared it intended to "inform the conscience of individuals" and "help build a world society which will provide the proper environment for a free choice of right." The paper was in the process of setting up a "corps of correspondents" that "will eventually include more than 100 writers strategically located."

Hoyt got down to the nub of why he wanted to be the editor when he wrote, three pages into the promotional material, "Editorials and features will in many ways be the most important parts of the paper. Their function will be to give the principles of Christian living and to show them lived." Unfortunately, "many people" were prescient when Hoyt also wrote, "According to many people, *The Morning Star* is an economic impossibility if [it] is not backed up with two or three millions in ready cash. At present it is sustained by work, prayer and trust in God. Unto these, it is hoped—rather, expected—the financial means will be added in due time."

Behind the campaigning for readers, the admirable optimism was coupled to some genuinely groundbreaking proposed content. The material closed with a prayer from the Roman Ritual "used by the group. You are invited to pray with them."

At this juncture, prayer proved insufficient. Publicity material was prepared, then the Chicago archdiocese was heard from. The chancery told Hoyt that any attempt to launch his paper in the archdiocese would be condemned from the pulpit. The *Morning Star* as such was not to be. Not only was it banned from Chicago, but also as a result, perhaps, of reverberations from Chicago Cardinal Samuel Stritch's advance condemnation, the expected surge of interest in a purely Catholic daily newspaper was not forthcoming either.

The versatile group shifted gears. Barred from Chicago, where a huge Catholic population offered the paper at least a *chance* of economic survival once the newspaper began to hit the streets, Hoyt had to go "bishop-shopping." This was an era when the need for episcopal approval for Catholic publications was not questioned but was simply understood as the way things were.

Immediate possibilities included St. Paul, Minnesota, and Kansas City, Missouri. One of the would-be newspaper's key people, Geraldine Carrigan, was close to Kansas City Archbishop Edwin O'Hara, and Hoyt approached him. What Chicago's Stritch—or his officials—had apparently found offensive, O'Hara took in stride. However, the archbishop did not reply for months, and the project still seemed doomed. Candidly, and—as it proved—accurately, O'Hara wrote that they were stupid to come to Kansas City with its small Catholic population. He continued, however, that he had no authority to tell them where to start a daily newspaper promoted as a project of Catholic laypeople. O'Hara understood, again accurately, that the proposed newspaper was not focusing on church issues but gathering news and delivering commentary from a Catholic Christian viewpoint. But the daily *Kansas City Star* was not about to permit another newspaper called "Star" into its circulation area, so "Morning" became "Sun," and "Star" became "Herald."

O'Hara would become a major supporter, freely giving the new effort both his blessing and some of his money. He provided a chaplain, and O'Hara entertained the staff in his home.

But what was it that Stritch in Chicago objected to and O'Hara ignored? Not the intended content. It was straightforward and respectful. Not the initial *Morning Star* team line-up: Robert Hoyt, editor; Geraldine Carrigan, associate editor; William Martin, circulation director; Dennis Howard, staff writer; Isabel de la Vega, foreign editor; Norma Ann Krause, feature editor; Adolph Schalk, staff writer; and Bernadette Hoyt, treasurer. But there was one name on the new the *Sun Herald* letterhead, essentially the paper's advisory board, that when listed on the earlier *Morning Star* masthead had alarmed Stritch: "Carol Jackson, co-editor, *Integrity*, New York." Either O'Hara didn't know who Carol Jackson was, or he didn't mind—and the latter seems more likely.

And so the trek to Kansas City began. The initial five were soon joined by recent Princeton graduate Bill Martin and pre-med student drop-out Dennis Howard. They'd be joined by Jeb Byrne, who ran the city desk. Otherwise, staff members and scores of volunteers came and went.

There was a benefit to setting up shop in a Baptist-dominated city where Catholics were a distinct minority: the Catholics soon got to know one another. As such, the communalists of the *Sun Herald* did not arrive without introductions. Notre Dame connections to local alumni helped. A rundown and empty storefront at 702 12th Street was offered to the fledgling newspaper, rent-free.

But it wasn't just the newspaper that needed a home. So did the *Sun Herald* commune-community. Hoyt sold his decrepit Buick. The money was the down payment on a huge, semi-ruined, three-story, old stone house on a hill and eight acres he bought for $12,000. It was far out from downtown but within the city limits. When Mike Hoyt was a boy, an elderly man told him that before the grand house was abandoned, its spacious third floor had been the venue for country dances with fiddlers. By 1950, there were holes in the roof and missing glass in the windows, the second floor was barely habitable, and, though winter was already moving across Missouri, there was no furnace.

Outside, weeds, overgrown bushes and towering trees flourished everywhere and pushed against the building. Next to the extensive woods were an overgrown orchard and the bed of a former boat pond. The *Sun Herald* crew set to. They repaired the holes in the roof. Windows were fixed, and, in time, the second level was re-floored to accommodate bedrooms. This is where Bernadette and Bob continued to have and raise their six children: Michael, Timothy, Mary Theresa, James, Mary Jo and Anne.

The house became known as "Withering Hoyts."

But the Hoyts were not alone. "Withering Hoyts" accommodated an entire group of people, "a kind of commune," said Mike Hoyt. Bob Hoyt wielded a scythe on the unkempt wilderness, and the "commune" created a large garden. Bernadette bought three goats. Like Mary's little lamb, they followed Mike Hoyt to school one day. Bernadette was an early believer in natural foods and natural living—influenced by Adele Davis, a biochemist and a popular healthy foods nutritionist and dietician. The Hoyt family bought unpasteurized milk from a dairy in Independence, Missouri.

Back in Kansas City, the *Sun Herald* was shaping up by day in an area that once had lived by night. This area was all that remained of Kansas City's wide-open jazz scene of "Twelfth Street Rag" fame. It had been a hotbed of hooch, hookers and high-class, jazz-laden entertainment (with the mob barely behind the scenes).

The production department of the five-day-a-week *Sun Herald* was in a storefront basement. A photograph from the early days shows five staff members, one woman and four men, hard at work typing on Vari-Typers, the technology that immediately preceded offset photographic printing. The copy was printed out and pasted up on layout boards. At the printers in Independence, the boards were photographed, and in time, the presses began to roll.

In the basement photograph, notes and notices were taped to the rough and dusty whitewashed fieldstone wall behind the staff. The machines were on old desks or tables made of planks, with well-used desks, chairs and cabinets for part of the circulation department. The basement was crowded.

The street-level storefront housed editorial, advertising and the rest of circulation. Once the paper came out, the first issue was dated Tuesday, October 10, 1950, with volunteers by the dozen pasting on the mailing labels. Initially they pasted around 2,000 a day. By Christmas they were working at a furious pace, pasting almost 7,000 daily, five times a week. The labeled and bundled newspapers were carted to the *Sun Herald* truck, an old hearse, and delivered to the main post office.

But what was it that the *Sun Herald* was trying to deliver? Across two columns of the front page, the newspaper asked the same question: "What is a Christian newspaper?" Hoyt continued (unsigned),

> A difficult question, granted. The members of the *Sun Herald*'s staff have been thinking about it for a year and still have no very complete answer. In fact, we began to realize about six months ago that there just isn't any neat, easy answer. Tomorrow today will be dead, and today's "Christian daily paper" will be dead, too. No formula or words can be invented to tell you on Tuesday what Friday's issue will be like. So definitions are out. But though the world changes, it remains the same world. Next Friday, as today, it will be God's world still, and you have to take that into account if you are going to report the world's news rightly.

Hoyt's word selection was always superb. The word "rightly," even in 1950, sounded old-fashioned. But there is no suitable synonym in this case. "Rightly" conveys the unspoken element of the phrase "right and just," and by itself carries a religious connotation into the secular arena. A beautiful opener, and one much longer, of course, than excerpted here.

The *Sun Herald* was pacifist, well almost, in a time of war. The Korean War began in June 1950. The "almost" is present because while condemning the use of napalm bombs and indiscriminate bombing, the editorials supported "the U.S.–UN action to roll back North Korean aggression." Hoyt and his colleagues would move steadily down an anti-war path in the years ahead. Even in the first issue, *NCR* editorially approved of a U.S. and allies–supported scheme to develop a United Nations peacekeeping force.

Viewed pragmatically, the *Sun Herald* enterprise was foolhardy. Another view is of the charming naiveté of launching a national Catholic daily in a Baptist backwater six hours hard driving from the nearest megalopolis, Chicago. It was launched, not so euphemistically, on a wing and, literally, on a prayer. (And there's a reason the newspaper receives so much space here. It is an example of the sheer energy bubbling up in the pre–Vatican II lay community—and the laity's issues—and the open-mindedness of some bishops, and the close-mindedness of others.)

The October 10 paper had a women's question-and-answer column by Mary Reade. Its first headline: "Will woman's ability to earn living jeopardize marriage?" From Rome there was a news story that reported, "More modern dress for nuns will be proposed at an important series of Conferences to Open Here Nov. 26."

Among the *Sun Herald*'s first news columns: "Latin Americans can't eat Cadillacs; malnutrition ahead." A report from Saigon in French Indo-China was prescient of *NCR* reporting ahead: "Powerful Viet Minh rebel forces are pushing . . . ." There were "Tough times in tomato fields" in California. Stooped over in those fields somewhere, twenty-three-year-old Cesar Chavez was yet to be heard from.

On a lighter note there was "herself at home," a column by Peggy Wink. The initial temptation is to assume the writer was Bernadette Hoyt under a nom de plume—given the number of small children bounding around the writer's home. In fact, Peggy Wink lived and wrote in Long Island, New York.

Wry asides and reporting weren't absent from the *Sun Herald*. A one-paragraph item told of a World War I veteran who had written to his local American Legion commander in Kansas City to apologize in advance for missing the next meeting. It was signed "Harry S. Truman."

Where these young Catholic Worker–influenced *Sun Herald* journalists shone brightest, as they personally sacrificed a chance at a livable income and career opportunities, was on the one issue Americans did not want to touch: racism.

Racism, segregation and the concomitant poverty was the United States' deliberate blind eye. The evil many Americans did not want to change.

Under the headline "Fight against segregation," the *Sun Herald* first announced, "The United Press reports that the US Supreme Court, in its first business session of its 1950–51 term, today reaffirmed its ruling that state universities must admit Negroes if equal educational facilities are not otherwise provided for them."

Earlier, in his *Morning Star* promotional material, Hoyt had said the editorials and features were to be the paper's most important writing.

Nothing was more important than the regular column, "Color: Ebony," by an African American writer and student nurse, Helen Caldwell Day. No other white daily newspaper in the nation was deliberately trumpeting that it would have a black columnist. Day was twenty-three, born in Marshall, Texas, and training at a Brooklyn hospital, but at that moment she was confined to a sanitarium, probably with tuberculosis, ever-present in New York.

She began,

> "How is it down South?"
>
> "I guess you people have it pretty hard down there, don't you?"
>
> Such questions as these are not too infrequent in a mixed sanitarium such as I was in, and even when they are not put into words, I have seen them in the eyes and trembling on the lips of a white patient too "well bred" to ask, "What's it like being a Negro?
>
> How strange it is that such a question should have significance in a Christian country. How strange that it should have so much significance that a great many friendly white people dare not ask it at all for fear of causing pain or giving offense. How often have you wanted to ask your colored neighbor, coworker or friend about the problems, the hurts of the needs peculiar to him as a Negro, and dared not, but remained in a shamed silence, feeling the chasm between you as a pain and not knowing how to cross it?

This is going to be a story about a Man who did cross it, more than it is going to be my story. He has shown us the way, but we have come a long way from Him, farther than we think.

Helen Caldwell Day went on to an interesting life of dedicated service. She continued to write for the *Sun Herald* but was known later for her Catholic Worker commitment and the house of hospitality she opened in Memphis.

As these words are written, there is a black president in the White House whose policies, with very few exceptions, are one with those of Helen Caldwell Day. But the racist hate—barely more shrouded than before—is still out there. In everyday life, in its many forms, the chasm Day wrote of remains.

Keeping to its agreement with Archbishop O'Hara, the *Sun Herald* was a Christian paper covering the secular world and applying a Catholic understanding and critique on what was reported.

The constant drumbeat that is news ranged from the French government ordering its civilians out of Indo-China's Tonkin province and the war in Korea to Canada's government going on the record against using the atomic bomb in Korea. There was analysis, Hoyt style, noting "that even news stories are pervaded by the spirit of propaganda. A UN advance is a 'surge forward by powerful American-British forces;' a Chinese attack is 'a fanatical attack by enemy *hordes*,' a Russian or Chinese argument in the UN 'drones on interminably.'"

The drumbeat reported that a young mother in Buffalo, New York, fearing Korea was the tinderbox for a world war, touched off an area-wide appeal for peace under the auspices of the local Council of Churches. "Many miracles have come through prayer," she said.

The *Sun Herald* needed a miracle itself—in the circulation department. Attempting to produce and deliver a national newspaper from a minor hub city was a daunting challenge. "Dear (and maybe disgruntled) subscriber," wrote circulation manager William Martin, "with a prayer that you have not yet given up on us, we tend this report/appeal. By way of apology—we feel incompetent and ineffectual when told that our paper is arriving days late in some places . . . circulation is a terrific problem . . . we had to make many adjustments . . . before we could meet particular train and plane schedules. But before long (if not right now) you will be able to go to your mailbox . . ."

Circulation rose to eleven thousand , but even with help, the newspaper as an enterprise was steadily losing ground.

Pope Pius XII had declared 1950 a Holy Year, and made the Assumption of Mary a dogma. To television personality Bishop Fulton J. Sheen, that one act, "the definition of the Assumption, will cure the despair and pessimism of the modern world." But the *Sun Herald* editorially analyzed the news and suggested that it was not the Assumption dogma or Christians who were rising to meet the world's needs:

> The communists have been ruthless, shrewd, double-dealing and double-talking, but ironically enough, their greatest triumphs have been built on the failures of Christians. In a world where Christians have been numerous and well-organized, communism not Christianity has voiced the indignation of millions. In a world full of inequality and injustices, communism not Christianity has been the revolutionary, radical thing. Neither the rich nor the powerful, the exploiters nor the comfortably indifferent have feared Christianity . . . The big danger is not that Christians will be persecuted—that is no more than they have been warned to expect. The big danger is that Christians will be persecuted for the wrong reasons—not because justice was loved but because injustice was condoned.

For the next eight and a half months, until the *Sun Herald* ceased publication on Saturday, May 26, 1951, the forty-seven staffers who passed through its doors, its editors and editorials, stuck to the mission statement and its top three concerns: peace, poverty and racism.

When the *Sun Herald* announced its end in Kansas City, that was not the lead headline on the final front page. Instead, the lead headline read, "Score one for racial justice." It was a report on Kansas City's city council voting to insert a non-segregation clause into all its contracts regarding the leasing of public spaces, such as the city-owned Starlight Theatre and the airport restaurant.

The announcement the newspaper was shutting up shop in Kansas City and moving to New York was the second lead. Hoyt, as the funds dried up, had taken to selling brushes door-to-door to help support his family. Many members of the staff had already left. Others were moving east with "bag and baggage, subscription files and equipment, morgue and miscellany" to Manhattan. The idea was to raise enough funds to start the *New York Banner* as a monthly until there was sufficient cash in hand to convert it into a daily. The monthly appeared several times but by November 1951, it was facing its own fiscal cliff. In January 1952, with $38,000 in liabilities and without even sufficient funds to liquidate the Apostolic Press Association, the dream of a Catholic daily newspaper was dead.

Back in Kansas City, Robert Hoyt, a future cab-driver by night, tried to be a Fuller Brush door-to-door salesman by day. Instead, as he admitted to Bernadette, he sat in a diner drinking coffee while trying to pluck up the courage to knock on people's doors to give them his canned sales pitch.

He failed.

2

NCR'S LABORED BIRTH

As the 1950s moved forward, Hoyt, slightly less desperate than one imagines, was teaching at Jesuit-run Rockhurst High School in Kansas City. He could face students with a confidence he'd never felt on Fuller Brush sales-calls. Before Rockhurst, there'd been a stint as managing editor of an Independence, Missouri, daily newspaper. It had folded. Then he drove a cab.

In this chapter, the reader is in danger of being confused by the fact that Hoyt is involved in three newspapers in the diocese, one after the other. Here is the playlist: The diocesan newspaper was a product of the *Register* chain of Denver. The diocesan *Register* was replaced in 1959 by the *Catholic Reporter*.

In 1964, the *Catholic Reporter* and the *National Catholic Reporter* were produced weekly by the same people in the same offices: the *Catholic Reporter* on a Tuesday or Wednesday; *NCR* on a Friday. When *NCR* became independent, one of its topics was birth control. It was an *NCR*-generated birth-control controversy that caused then Kansas City–St. Joseph Bishop Charles Helmsing to change the diocesan newspaper's name to *Key to the News*.

Back to the narrative.

In 1956, the Kansas City and St. Joseph dioceses merged. In 1954, the ambitious Bishop John Patrick Cody was appointed coadjutor in St. Joseph. With the merger, he was coadjutor to Kansas City, Missouri's, O'Hara (whose "archbishop" rank was an honorary title). Cody succeeded him in 1956.

Cody wanted the *Register* improved. He sought an editor to improve it, asked around the chancery, and two priests, both friends of Hoyt, recommended him. "Both knew I'd rather be editing than teaching; Fr. Vince Lovett was one of them," Hoyt said in a later *NCR* interview. Lovett, a firm friend and ally of everything that led to the eventual creation of *NCR*, was a late vocation. His bearing and reliability were respected by Cody and later Helmsing—who would make Lovett publisher of his diocesan newspaper.

"Vince was appointed liaison between the *Register* paper and the bishop [Cody]. I wouldn't have taken the job without the [editor title] because I know how it works." Hoyt and Lovett "worked out an elaborate rationale for the paper and reached an agreement with Bishop Cody." Hoyt said Cody wanted "a good and lively paper" because it was a way for the bishop to get his name known. "He was on the way up and everybody took it for granted he was headed for Chicago. He got there by way of New Orleans."

The fact the *Register* had been "a lousy paper didn't mean it didn't make money," said Hoyt. "Certain advertisers had to use it: funeral directors, religious-goods stores and so forth. Cody had Vince Lovett, who was diocesan assistant treasurer or comptroller, figure out how much money the paper had made over the years, and credited the paper with that amount in the archdiocesan accounts. So we had a lot of money to spend."

Hoyt began writing his signature editorials, and he and Lovett hired Jack Hare from the *Register* chain's central office in Denver as managing editor. "He and I knew what we were doing style-wise. And we were able to introduce an interesting mix of columnists, and to professionalize the publication within the unspoken or tacit code of diocesan papers."

The diocesan *Register* in essence was the product of two copy-desk editors, one of whom was a superb editorial writer. Hoyt at that time was almost blind to important news, and he admitted it. For example, as editor, he learned from a layman professor at Rockhurst College that there had long been an agreement that the lay teachers' sons would receive a free college education. At the college, said Hoyt (he'd taught at the then adjacent high school), "the lay teachers were the mainstay of the faculty. As some of their sons were about to be eligible, the Jesuits changed the policy. They simply took it away unilaterally. A friend of mine told me about it. It should have been a news story. It simply didn't cross my mind at the time." Hoyt admitted, "We didn't really have reportorial instincts. I'd not come up as a reporter—I did feature writing in Denver—but we gradually got better at it. Outside the diocese we covered stories NCWC [National Catholic News Service] missed, or gave a propagandistic twist."

As he began to achieve a better grasp of the task at hand, Hoyt wrote about and gave speeches on the mission of the Catholic press. As the paper became somewhat known, Cody was invited to address the Catholic Press Association. Hoyt was asked to draft the talk. According to his standard practice of handing in his copy just after deadline, he gave Cody the speech as the bishop headed for his plane. Cody gave it verbatim, and thereafter Hoyt could defend almost anything in the newspaper by stating, "My bishop said . . . " The key understanding was that Cody said that the "only thing that expresses the policy of this diocese" was anything that appeared over his signature and under the heading "Official." The rest, said Cody, was up to the staff.

Hare left and Michael J. Greene came in as managing editor. Greene was a Notre Dame graduate, a university he described as "all winds and football, to all intents and purposes an extension of the all-boys Catholic high schools and a long ways from being a credible university."

He was a philosophy major in literature—"neither philosophy nor literature." He enrolled in a graduate summer program on French Catholic writers and received a scholarship to Notre Dame's first graduate liturgy program. He and a colleague were hired to rewrite the "very wooden English" translation of a French book. They did. Praxis Press in South Bend published the English translation. Greene had never held a job. In 1953 he was drafted into the Korean War, and Army paperwork required he list a civilian occupation. He wrote, "Rewrite specialist Praxis Press." The Army made him a *Stars and Stripes* (the U.S. military newspaper) battalion reporter and sent him to Korea.

"Set loose with a typewriter, no designated place to sleep or eat, I picked up journalism along the way," writing articles about the men on the frontline, he said.

When Greene was back in America, out of uniform, a friend who headed the Catholic Press Association suggested Greene try diocesan journalism. He did, at the Baltimore diocesan newspaper, the *Catholic*

Review, edited by an Englishman, Gerard Sherry. "And after six months of Sherry, who gathered the entire staff around the table while he dictated his editorials to a secretary, I'd had enough. I came [to Kansas City] because Hoyt was a good editorial writer," said Greene, who was named managing editor. "That Hoyt had a point of view plus an ability to write it well constituted the paper's strength. I saw his editorials as an opportunity to kick off a newspaper that focused on reporting. It took me a while to get a first impression of him."

To Greene, Hoyt was idiosyncratic. Greene also referred to Hoyt in the orphanage, at a young age.

> He was the little boy raised in an orphanage who came by a Clark's bar, took it down the basement, had one taste of it, knowing he could put it away for a week until he took another taste of it. That was the only way I could explain to myself his secretive behavior. He was unwilling to communicate, really. It took me a while to get used to someone who would say yes to everything and not deliver on it.
>
> He didn't really want to get involved in anything, except what he was doing, writing the editorials . . . [and here] we had a newspaper on the threshold of the Vatican Council, the local diocesan *Catholic Reporter*.

The sixteen-page *Catholic Reporter* was first published on December 4, 1959, launched in the same year that Pope John XXIII announced, in January, he was convoking a Vatican council. Fr. Vincent Lovett was executive editor and business manager, Hoyt its editor, Greene the publisher, Betty Fitzgerald assistant to the editor, and John Rotterman the photographer.

There were innovative Protestant-Catholic dialogues, and the complete text of John XXIII's *Mater et Magistra* [Mother and Teacher]. In January 1962, with Bishop Cody transferred to New Orleans, Bishop Charles H. Helmsing of Springfield–Cape Girardeau, Missouri, was named Kansas City–St. Joseph's bishop. The *Catholic Reporter* continued under Helmsing, and once the Second Vatican Council began on October 11, 1964, *CR* became a major U.S. Catholic source for council news independent of the regular religious news services. James M. Johnson, former *Kansas City Star* religious news editor, filed regular reports to *CR*. Desmond O'Grady, a Rome freelancer, and Desmond Fisher, editor of the *Catholic Herald* in London, were regular contributors, as was Larry Guillot, a Kansas City priest studying for his doctorate in ecumenism.

In addition to its straightforward yet incisive Vatican coverage, *CR* offered superb editorials. As a handful of diocesan newspapers exchanged their best coverage, Greene set up a syndication service, Catholic Cooperative Features, which gave the Kansas City publication an impressive national edge and following.

Given the nationwide Catholic attention *CR* attracted, Hoyt and Greene were soon discussing greater things for the "lively newspaper." Hoyt said the newspaper was attracting extra-diocesan circulation without promotion: "Mike [Greene] was a terrific feature writer." Greene said it was Hoyt's editorials that were the main attraction, and would remain so. Hoyt said he and Greene toyed with the notion of putting out a supplement on the lines of *Parade*, which accompanied Sunday newspapers,

> to be sold as a package to newspapers everywhere. That had two drawbacks. One was editorial control. All these editors around the country would be frightened to publish some of the stuff we were running—or contemplated running. And the other was that to pay for the thing you'd have to have a million circulation before you could afford to put it out. Without national advertising, you just couldn't do it.
>
> So then we began to think of a . . . I don't really know who had the idea—I suspect it was Mike—the idea of, instead of going for a supplement, putting out a separate and independent newspaper. Entrepreneurial and apostolic—a term that is less used now than it was then, a good paper that was a good service.

Mike Greene would later say that Hoyt took credit for the idea that became the *National Catholic Reporter*. The credit was certainly bestowed on Hoyt by most because he was the founding editor. Perhaps on occasion Hoyt did not refute it. But there is no public evidence in hand to suggest he made that claim.

Greene was a go-getter, Hoyt was not. Hoyt admitted,

> The independent newspaper idea just lay fallow. There'd been a meeting in the chancery basement, the rudimentary idea fleshed out, a board was formed. Chairman was John J. Fallon, a lawyer in Kansas City. Fallon was someone Greene had known at Notre Dame. Fallon

was in the same year as Greene's older brother. Fallon and the elder Greene had been drafted for World War II and were then back on campus.

The "independent paper" president was Frank Brennan, a successful local businessman. Also aboard were Dan Herr, chairman of the Thomas More Association, a prestigious Catholic publishing house; Joe Cunneen, who, with his wife Sally, founded the inter-religious magazine *Cross Currents*; plus Greene and Hoyt.

"Fallon was important," Hoyt said,

> but I think Dan Herr was the most important, not only for having an inventive reputation and knowing about publishing, but he'd dealt with boards of directors and laid down the law of editorial control. The editor served at the pleasure of the board.
>
> Nothing happened to the proposal [to start an independent paper] because I just didn't do it. Some complications in my own life. So Mike became extremely exercised [and] without saying anything to me, wrote a letter to the other members of the board laying out his complaints with great vigor. So that was our first personnel crisis, I suppose.

Greene's complaints galvanized everyone into action, not least Hoyt, who immediately began churning out pre-publication subscription solicitations, and a mission statement. "I got endorsements from Gene McCarthy and Bill [William F.] Buckley and other eminences of the time. I'd defended Buckley's right to speak as a Catholic about encyclicals—one of two diocesan editors in the country to do so. I didn't agree with Buckley, but he wasn't a heretic for disagreeing with the moderates."

The burst of activity brought help from an unexpected quarter: Bishop Helmsing. He made the separate and independent newspaper possible. He proposed the team continue to put out his newspaper in the first half of the week, remain on his payroll, and then use the same facilities to publish their *National Catholic Reporter*, as it came to be called, with Hoyt as editor and Greene as publisher. Hoyt said, "Two men contributed $1,000 to make the idea known and solicit further support." There was promise of a $15,000 loan from the Benedictine Sisters at St. John's University, in Collegeville, Minnesota. As part of its plans, *NCR* intended to include a regular special section, Sisters Forum, which Lovett would oversee.

Fallon and Brennan held a dinner to raise money. Greene was the keynote speaker. About $2,000 (some $15,000 in today's dollars) was pledged. That, plus the loan, made the launch possible. "It gave us a little cash to get started," Greene said. And there was advance marketing in *Commonweal* and *America*, which endorsed the idea editorially and encouraged Catholic readership to take a look. Among those attracted to the dinner were Catholic publishing luminaries, including Philip Scharper, editor in chief of Sheed & Ward (and later cofounder of Orbis Books).

Board member Dan Herr was unhappy with the idea of a Hoyt-Greene "two-headed horse" running the proposed paper. But rather than resolve it by firing one of us," said Hoyt, "he healed it. Mike and I [after the 'crisis' when Greene had written directly to the board] were never on as good terms from then on as we had been, but we worked fine together. He worked extremely hard [at being publisher], but he lacked the experience. This is not just my judgment."

The first issue of the *National Catholic Reporter* appeared in 1964, on October 28, the feast day of Saint Jude, patron of hopeless causes.

Greene later wrote a fourteen-page, single-spaced letter of his difficulties managing the paper in the light of Hoyt's work habits, late nights, last-minute writing and inability to make a decision. After a year, Greene resigned as publisher. Donald J. Thorman succeeded him. Hoyt resigned as *CR*'s editor in 1966, and three months later *NCR* moved to 115 E. Armour Blvd. Nonetheless, the two papers coexisted for a further twelve months. Ultimately, *CR* changed its name due to an uproar over *NCR* and the Papal Birth Control Commission.

In 1967, Hoyt wrote that by the time *NCR* was launched it had eleven thousand advance subscriptions. "In October, 1964," he wrote, "the memory of Pope John XXIII was still very much present to the world, a memory of human warmth, wit, peasant realism and great openness. The mid-1960s offered the best opportunity in history to bring the traditions and professional techniques of secular journalism fully into the service of the church."

Greene generously said the many advance subscriptions were "not due to my promotional pieces in the mail, more due to the Second Vatican Council—the best promotional activity possible for this particu-

lar paper at this particular time." The advance mailings usefully included kind words—though not testimonials—from such well-known
reform-minded people as Jesuit Frs. John Courtney Murray and Karl
Rahner and Benedictine Fr. Godfrey Diekmann.

By December, less than three months after the launch, subscriptions
had reached the 22,253 mark. A year later, the circulation was close to
60,000 and would peak in 1968 at 88,578, four years after the launch.

For the first twelve months, at $6 a year for a subscription, the paper
priced itself too cheaply. "We were gaining 5,000 readers a week for
that first year," said Greene, but the back-office organization was primarily volunteers. Subscribers were complaining about the fulfillment
department and not receiving their newspaper. NCR was losing money
on its "short-term" subscriptions—three issues at an attractive price to
get people to look at the newspaper. Most decided to change their
subscription to a longer term one, Greene said. However, he said, "Our
staff was not competent enough, not trained enough to handle the
changeover. We only had one experienced circulation department person" on board after several months, and "the rest were clerks and volunteers."

As the end of the first year approached, Hoyt said, "we were losing
money the more subscriptions we sold. So we came close to financial
failure. We added only one staff member, Bob Olmstead. He'd been
night editor of the AP, and previously had worked with Young Christian
Workers. He wanted to get back into religious or church-related work.
He tested us out."

Olmstead was told the *Oklahoma Courier* or NCR were the places to
go. Oklahoma City was early into Vatican II advancements. It had
opened the first non-territorial "parish," the John XXIII Community.
The *Oklahoma Courier*, deep in the Baptist South, where the Catholic
population barely registered on any religious Richter scale, was a fine
example of Catholic diocesan newspapering.

Said Hoyt,

> Olmstead asked if we'd be interested in an Allis-Chalmers strike in
> Milwaukee—because Marquette University had given Allis-Chalm-
> ers [a machinery manufacturer] the freedom to recruit students on
> campus to work as strike breakers. He would call me every couple of
> days to tell me how the story was going, teaching me, really. He was
> beginning my education as an editor. A down-the-middle reporter,

>he got quotes from everybody involved in the story. He applied, so
>we accepted him. He was important from the word go.
>He taught me; I absorbed from him. But the same is true for the
>next two people I hired—Tom Blackburn and Art Winter.

Of Olmstead, Hoyt said he made every story in the paper read like a news story. Art Winter said, "I'd second that."

However, there was trouble brewing at the top about the problems in the back office.

As had the *Sun Herald* before it, *NCR* depended heavily on volunteers. There were plenty of them, incredibly loyal volunteers, people such as Mike Greene's wife, "Biz" (Mary Elizabeth), who turned up like clockwork to help lay out the issue, paste on mailing labels and do the dozen and one other tasks a start-up always needs done on the spur of the moment.

Such reliance on a volunteer back office was no way to run a fledgling national newspaper. Greene needed more experienced help. It worried him, and he "shared that concern with [board chairman] Fallon." Fallon accused Greene of incompetence. "He made me quite angry, so pissed given the stress factor, that it led to a blow-up and my departure. I felt secure enough to not feel I depended on *NCR* to survive."

He was not as secure as he sounded to Fallon, he said later, because he and Biz had "two or three children by that time. I was physically, psychologically and spiritually stretched further than I could go."

Spouses of Catholic newspaper people have to be long-suffering. The pay is rarely good, so the enterprise is, to a greater or lesser extent, a burden on the family's economic well-being. As future editor Tom Fox told an applicant for a job in Washington, DC, *NCR* couldn't afford to pay what a family needed to live in Washington. (Future Washington correspondents knew the story all too well; their families subsidized the position, rather than vice versa.)

With Greene's departure, the other—in some ways more serious—casualty was Mike Greene's wife, Biz. Barbara Thorman, wife of the new publisher, later said that Greene's break with *NCR* "practically destroyed Biz. She'd worked really hard for it, a tremendous mover. They had literally put the *NCR* together on the dining room table. It was very difficult for Mike to come home, and it caused Biz to have a great breakdown. And that's the environment into which we came."

In 1966, Hoyt and Olmstead were joined by Blackburn and Winter. Tom Blackburn grew up in Evanston, Illinois, and attended Marquette University for both his undergraduate and graduate journalism degrees. He wed in 1956, all the while knowing the draft board was eyeing him. The military sent him to Germany. Out of uniform, he worked for the *Evansville Press*, then edited *Marquette Magazine*, a journal "with intellectual pretensions," said Blackburn. While he was there, said Blackburn, a "*Milwaukee Journal* friend, Jerry Peters, wanted to leave daily journalism and was looking for something else. He was active in the Christian Family Movement (CFM)."

There was an ad in *NCR* looking for an editor. "'Jerry,' I told him, 'this is something you'll love.' This was right after great John Howard Griffin . . . wound up speaking and of course Jerry was there—great night." (Griffin had published *Black Like Me*. He had dyed his skin and traveled as a black man in white America. The modest volume, aimed at sociologists, achieved classic status and sold 10 million copies.)

Peters said, "I can't go to KC why don't you write to them?" Blackburn contacted Hoyt and was invited to fly down to Kansas City to talk about it. It was the fall of 1965. At the airport, waiting for his flight, Blackburn met a law professor he knew. He told him about the *NCR* job interview. The law professor encouraged Blackburn and said the newspaper had "a smell of history about it."

Hoyt told Blackburn the main job was layout, but the job wasn't defined; the editors did what came along. Blackburn accepted it.

Blackburn said he and his wife were in CFM

at a time when we thought something like the Vatican Council would come along and change the church to the way we knew it could be. I knew guys in YCS [Young Christian Students] and YCW [Young Christian Workers]. Hoyt struck me as a grown-up example of the Jocist [a follower of Cardijn] movement, the Cardijn kid. My second and third impression—I'd been reading his editorials—was I thought, "Here's a guy who just sits down and it flows." After I saw how he wrote editorials—it was blood.

He would put a cigarette on the side of his metal typewriting table. He would put his hands on his head, he would pound his feet, his cigarette would roll into his wastebasket, start a fire, Betty Fitz [Fitzpatrick, the editorial secretary] would run in and put out the fire. Hoyt would go through the whole thing again, and afterwards he would have one line of type, 28 lines crossed out. That's the way he wrote those smoothly flowing editorials. He *really* worked on them. They were a two-day operation.

On Thursdays he'd disappear. We did the rest of the stuff. On Fridays Hoyt would work until midnight and turn in his copy just past deadline.

Blackburn said, "Olmstead was there already and they hired Art [Winter] six months after I got there."

Perhaps because Hoyt admired experienced newsmen, Blackburn found Hoyt

very, very easy to work for, but there were a few hot spots. I was in Cursillo [an informal retreat movement]. I remember one day I said something totally unexceptional and he accused me of pietism— which I'd never even heard of.

Whatever, I'd made it all sound too easy . . . written too much on the Holy Spirit, and he bristled at that. I found that kind of funny because he didn't usually bristle. He didn't get along as well with everybody as he did with Olmstead. Olmstead was the one who was really reserved, you didn't know how he felt about anything. He was a really professional reporter. If he had a quote that would hang somebody, he'd call back the next day and make sure [the] quote was solid.

Blackburn's own approach to journalism and interviews was that "if someone who has hung himself [during an interview] decides he doesn't want to be quoted that way, he can call me; I'm not going to call him and give him the idea to change his mind. Olmstead came out of the [Chicago] City News Bureau and had those standards."

(The Chicago City News Bureau was a cooperative that covered city hall, county hall and much else for ten Chicago daily newspapers. Charles MacArthur, who with Ben Hecht wrote "The Front Page," was a City News Bureau reporter. It operated around the clock. The requirements were always check quotes twice and give two sides on every issue. Because its clients ranged the ideological and political spectrum, the stories themselves were neutral, but the reporting was superb and the writing tight. Its graduates included Pulitzer Prize–winner Seymour Hersh, novelist Kurt Vonnegut and David Brooks of the *New York Times*.)

When Blackburn met Bernadette Hoyt, "the first thing she said to me was 'Thank God you're coming because maybe I'll see my husband once in a while.' But it wasn't true [that she would see Hoyt more]. He was a workaholic. If he'd had a staff of 900 down there he still would have worked those hours." The worst-kept secret—only Bernadette was unaware of it—was that Hoyt was having an affair with volunteer Mig Boyle. Blackburn simply said, "I never did understand [the] Bob and Mig thing. Don't know how he got away with doing it. But Hoyt didn't tell you what was on his mind."

He did tell Blackburn he'd been in an orphanage. "I heard Bob say several times that he had been in an orphanage, but I don't recall any details."

Art Winter was raised on a farm in northeast Iowa. Once he had graduated in journalism from the University of Iowa, he was soon drafted. Out of uniform he wrote for daily newspapers in Iowa and Nebraska for the next five or six years until,

> unfortunately, I got religion. I'd had a perfectly normal life up to that time. It coincided pretty much with the 1960s. Betty and I were married, we didn't know anything about Catholicism particularly, except you had to go to Mass every Sunday, which I did . . . for the most part. Then suddenly there was all this Catholic stuff. At the daily in Iowa, and since I was known to be Catholic and there weren't many around it seemed, it was, "Did you have to vote the way the pope tells you?" and so on. I started to read about Catholicism in self-defense. My family were old-fashioned German Catholics; they not only marched to the drummer of their German heritage, but also their Catholic faith.

"I kept on reading," Winter said.

> I became pious and was daily a communicant. What I found was that the more interested I became in Catholicism the farther I was drifting from what I was doing in my personal life and my work life. I was split between church and society and had the feeling that the only real Christians were priests and nuns. No one was really living a Christian life, but . . . [it was as] if we are reasonably good we find place in heaven after all.

If not bewildered, at least perplexed, Winter quit secular news-papering for a small Catholic magazine in Atchison, Kansas, and a $40-a-week pay cut. He was married with three children. That pay cut didn't sit too well. The job was providing quotes for priests' homilies, and that didn't sit too well either.

It was the mid-1960s. Winter shifted gears and enrolled at the Institute of Lay Theology at the University of San Francisco—one in the first wave of lay pastoral associates. His wife, Betty, a nurse, kept the family afloat. Graduated, he was placed in two parishes in Peoria, Illinois—"It was like being first-wave Marines to hit the shore." The contract was for three years. Twelve months later, both pastors felt they'd had enough of Winter. "One told me I was too aggressive, the other I was not aggressive enough." He was summarily dismissed. "Needless to say my wife and I were pissed."

Winter had subscribed to *NCR* from the start. Out of impulse and necessity, he applied for a job.

"By grace of God, I got it," he said. "I should have been somewhat cautious about it because the call from Bob Hoyt to come for an interview came on a Sunday morning. We were just going to Mass and were late, and Betty said, 'Shouldn't those people be in church?'"

In May 1966, Art and Betty Winter and family moved to Kansas City.

Hoyt became Art Winter's idol. "He was very private, wasn't a stand-around-the-water-cooler type. All work, worked unbelievable hours." Winter said that if Hoyt's workaholic style affected all the staff, especially on press day, Fridays, which began at 9 a.m. and ended after midnight, "I don't remember much complaining. We were a small staff trying to do a big job. Hoyt led the way. I admired him. I wanted to be like him. I didn't think of it so much as a job, but as a cause." (Publisher Thorman thought such a work routine was unnecessary and a waste.)

Winter continued,

> Tom Blackburn was bright, a hard worker, and wrote columns, even the fourth editorial. He did everything. Wrote a lot of stories, re-wrote a lot, handled the letters and the travel budget. I thought he was one of the smartest guys who ever worked there. Whenever you saw him outside, he was reading. On the sidewalk, waiting for a bus. They never had a car. He'd been in the Army in Germany and when-ever some bishop did something crazy, Tom would go into his Ger-

man army officer routine and we were all treated to his monologue goose-stepping around. He was a fast writer. I think he would have made a good editor.

I went around and did a series on floating parishes, small faith communities in Atlanta, New Jersey, Oklahoma. I thought they'd turn into alternative parishes. None of them made it. It was post–Vatican II euphoria.

Seymour Hersh was sort-of the Washington correspondent. His reports in *NCR* usually came by way of smaller news services, but there were Hersh "specials to *NCR*." One concerned the United States spending $350 million a year on gas, germ, chemical and biological warfare. Early details of the My Lai massacre first appeared in *NCR* and some other smaller journals after the *New York Times* and *Life* magazine had turned the story down. Later, in 1970, Hersh received the Pulitzer Prize for international reporting for his highly detailed and far-reaching account of the massacre for Dispatch News Service.

Hoyt had his team.

Now to look at those early news pages.

3

NCR: "RELIGIOUS YET WORLDLY"

Hoyt's first *NCR* editorial, volume 1, number 1, October 28, 1964, was a quite lengthy one, and why not? This was 1964; he used exclusive language:

> One significant element in our program . . . results directly from the paper's lay character. One of the few positive ways of describing the layman is to say that he is a man who takes the temporal order seriously. The Catholic layman as such may have no more certainty about temporal issues than a Methodist or an agnostic, but as a layman he is under obligation to carry his grappling with those issues past the realm of principle to the point of decision and action . . . Our orientation then is toward reporting the news, toward enterprise and relevance, toward dialogue with practically everybody. We are a religious paper with worldly interests. We are committed to the Church and secure enough in our commitment to keep wondering what the Church is and will become.

In his phrase "enterprise and relevance," Hoyt was in fact referring to a type of reporting.

It was not necessarily investigative reporting as we know it today. It was more identifying a topic on which there was a conventional opinion, but no one had actually thoroughly examined the situation to see if the conventional opinion was, in fact, correct.

Olmstead launched straight into an enterprise story with the first issue: what, in the confessionals, were confessors telling Catholics about birth control, specifically the newly marketed G.D. Searle contraceptive pill?

The previous year, gynecology professor Dr. John Rock had published *The Time Has Come: A Catholic Doctor's Proposals to End the Battle over Birth Control.* Boston Cardinal Richard Cushing, speaking personally and not officially, wrote the foreword in which he expressed hope for a "refinement" of the church's current teaching. In the subsequent twelve months, *NCR* carried three dozen stories and editorials on birth control. All this was four years before the great 1968 crisis of *Humanae Vitae*, the encyclical with which Pope Paul VI continued the church's ban on contraceptive use by married couples.

Racism was a major theme. The top-left lead story was "Report: Negroes leaving Church."

The inside pages carried a Selma, Alabama, photograph of religious sisters linking arms with "Negro leaders" as they sang freedom songs and protested the denial of voting rights. The March on Selma call had gone out earlier: "Send more nuns!"

Scores of sisters had responded. But after Mobile-Birmingham Archbishop Thomas Toolen cabled congregations stating their nuns would be "most unwelcome" at Selma, many more stayed away.

Toolen forced out of town Emundite Fr. Maurice Ouellet, pastor of a parish prominent in the Selma voting-rights drive. (Twenty-five years later, *NCR* was in Selma for an evening filled with sacred song and emotion as Selma's many churches joined en masse to honor an invited Ouellet. It was the faith community's way of thanking him in person for his courageous work.)

Mobile-Birmingham's Toolen was not an exception when it came to driving out priests fighting for racial justice. That same issue of *NCR* reported that in Philadelphia, Dominican Fr. Clement Burns was removed from La Salle College and ordered out of the diocese—on the Philadelphia chancery's instructions—after Burns was arrested in the city during protests against racial segregation in public accommodation.

In Los Angeles, it was Fr. John V. Coffield, fifty-year-old pastor of Ascension Parish, who was driven away. Cardinal James Francis McIntyre reprimanded him for his advocacy of racial and civil rights. Coffield went into "self-imposed exile," serving in a South Side Chicago parish with a large black membership. The bishops' "old boys' network" quickly clicked into action, and newly installed Chicago Archbishop John

Patrick Cody ensured that Coffield's Chicago speech-giving was also curtailed.

In Los Angeles, Fr. Phillip Berryman, two years a priest, gave his first sermon on racial justice and was transferred two days later to an all-white girls' academy where his only duties would be to hear confessions and say Mass.

NCR also reported on enlightened dioceses. The Detroit and St. Louis archdioceses announced programs to direct business only to firms that practiced the "fair hiring of Negroes," and in New Orleans the first U.S. black bishop in modern times was named. Fr. Harold Perry, son of a Louisiana rice-mill worker, became an auxiliary bishop.

In that first NCR issue, the human sexuality headline was Olmstead's "Confessors 'pinned to the wall' by pill question, says Jesuit expert." On papacy and the church, a Vatican council story: "Schema's tough issues rule sixth week of session." The poverty story also was a Vatican II report: "Ask dramatic council action for world attack on poverty." Nuns/women and peace/U.S. foreign policy were inside as, respectively, the Sisters Forum and "Pope: 'No more war, war never again.'"

The reaction to the first issue was a flood of accolades, and one canceled subscription. (In the second issue, a reader offered to pay for the canceled subscription.) Many in officialdom and some in the Catholic press were nervous because NCR obviously wasn't nervous as it dove straight into the toughest current church and secular topics. The founding news team and NCR board knew they had a winner as the newspaper, in publisher Mike Greene's words, "added 5,000 new subscribers a week."

It seems important in this narrative, at this point, to focus on the high-impact stories of the first couple years rather than provide a potpourri of the news flow. It was the high-impact stories that established NCR's reputation.

Nothing, not even birth control, created the attention, uproar and flood of mail to match a story that simply dropped into the editor's lap. Publisher Greene had suggested putting the occasional feature article on the front page. Hoyt agreed and placed on page one on June 9, 1965, a "Special to the NCR" opinion piece on celibacy from *Sacerdos Occidentalis* [Western Priest] (he wrote under a nom de plume). The unidentified Latin rite priest, living in the western United States, wrote that celibacy was "a problem in the church that must be faced honestly"; that the number of priestly defections was enormous; and that a defecting priest was treated as excommunicated, his action a crime. This was a strange outcome, he wrote, because the practice in the Western Roman Church was first seen as "a counsel of perfection" and not obligatory; that history suggests "there is no inherent connection between the priesthood and celibacy"—instead, it ought to be completely voluntary, he wrote, a joyful choice, not a permanent state, an end in itself; and that the church regularly dispensed religious from a vow of chastity but did not regularly grant dispensations from celibacy to clergy, who had not taken a vow of chastity.

The reaction lasted for months. In some issues, *NCR* ran two pages of "celibacy" letters. There were letters from "a happily married couple" who observed there was a "fairly unrealistic, overly romanticized thread running through all of [the responses]." Dominican Sr. Albertus Magnus confessed herself a heretic in her letter to *NCR* because she had been teaching that an ordained priest is not the only *alter Christus* [another Christ]—so is every male and female.

In one letter, a seminary faculty member asked the council to study the celibacy issue—probably so the faculty member could time how fast the Vatican could backpedal. (He didn't have to wait long.) *NCR* columnist Garry Wills and theologian writers Redemptorist Fr. Bernard Haring and Fr. Tom LeClerc joined in. Another writer, *Pater Pussilanimis* [Father Cowardly], said that if it was known he questioned celibacy, he would be exiled.

Rosemary Radford Ruether wrote that the real issues were Christian freedom and humanization. If celibacy ceases to be authentic, she said, take down the wall. She also said that *NCR*, when publishing articles and letters, should start using the writers' real names—and stop this "*mickius mousensis*." (Allowing correspondents to write anonymously was still fairly common in newspapers at the time. Even in the early 1970s, *NCR* had a columnist who wrote as "Calliope." In 1975 this muse was not amused when told she must use her real name. She refused. Calliope mused no more in *NCR*.)

Hoyt editorialized in August 1965 that "celibacy is an unavoidable issue for the Church" and described the issue as "delicate," "complicated" and one that "should be studied." Msgr. George Higgins, an expert on social and labor issues, said at that point that in his many decades as a priest he'd never heard a priest question celibacy. A year later, when confronted with the evidence, Higgins publicly ate his words.

The seemingly never-ending *NCR* open forum on celibacy caused a reaction in Rome. As the final council session of Vatican II reconvened in September 1965, *NCR* carried an extensive story based on correspondent and news service reports. Pope Paul VI intervened by letter and took celibacy off the council agenda.

Hoyt wrote, "It is possible to remain wholly loyal and to acquiesce as gracefully as possible in such a decision and yet to register a degree of disagreement with [the letter's] content."

Stalemate—four pontiffs later.

The following year, in June 1966, when the newspaper moved to 115 E. Armour Blvd., its circulation had moved well beyond the fifty-thousand mark.

Shortly after Art Winter's arrival, Kansas City–St. Joseph Bishop Charles Helmsing, at publisher Donald Thorman's invitation, visited in 1966 to bless the new offices. That day the fabled *NCR* elevator went on strike. Winter and Hoyt each offer a version of what happened. In Winter's tale, the elevator stopped between floors. Finally, the ancient, hydraulically driven system was persuaded to restart. Hoyt's version was that Helmsing, after the elevator failed, in full episcopal regalia, had to walk up the flights of stairs. Either way, the staff was embarrassed and the bishop was not amused.

In the 1960s, the Vietnam War also competed for front-page headlines. Jesuit Fr. Daniel Berrigan and two fellow Jesuits were ordered to quit an interfaith planning committee that was preparing a seminar on U.S. policy in Vietnam. Baltimore's Cardinal Lawrence Shehan became the first principal U.S. prelate to tackle the Vietnam issue. In a statement that drew heavily on Vatican II documents, he cautioned the United States to "keep the law within moral limits." *NCR*—in agreement with *Christian Century* and *Commonweal* that they'd all say something in the first editorial of 1968—encouraged draft resistance.

In September 1966, news editor Olmstead, according to an editor's note inside the paper, "wandered into a session in a Shawnee, Oklahoma," summer theology institution he was covering. The speaker was not part of his assigned coverage. However, "when his other assignments were completed, he hunted up tapes of the talks, interviewed the priest by telephone, and wrote a personality piece about a little-known lecturer that ended, "As one of the bright young men coming in on the winds of change, Father [Charles] Curran seems assured of a place near the storm front." How right Olmstead was.

The following month *NCR* headlined an article: "What are you doing talking to that nigger?" It was an account by Franciscan Sr. Matthias (Carole Rinderer) of time spent volunteering in a black Chicago ghetto.

She and other sisters were in a rat-infested building that was home to twenty-one families, there to teach them

> how to live in the best possible way in their surroundings. But it took us close to 13 minutes in the place to realize that these surroundings were not the sole responsibility of the 50 people who lived there. Somebody owned this place and not only that, somebody was collecting $95 a month from each of these families for the dubious privilege of existing there.
>
> So we assumed our dumb nun look and marched into the office of the biggest cigar-smoking slum landlord in Chicago. . . . Only we were even dumber than we thought. We were so dumb we didn't know this was the man Martin Luther King had confronted in personal battle over the tidy fact that he controlled about two-thirds of the real estate in Lawndale. We were so dumb we didn't realize that he needed a reputation saver and we were it . . . and that what our services in the building were doing were giving him an excuse to perpetuate a horror that should have been burned in a new Chicago fire.

Rinderer went on to say that when picketing a real estate office with Don, a black-history student and poet, they talked about "Camus and LeRoi Jones and the whole gamut of literature and history. And all the time people kept shouting, 'Hey, nun, what are you doing talking to that stupid nigger?' He could have outthought them all."

She also wrote,

> It took the SCLC [the Southern Christian Leadership Conference] to teach me what Christianity is all about . . . One afternoon Rev. Jesse Jackson called us out of line and said, "I'd like you sisters to lead the march today." I believe I mumbled something about massacre.
>
> "Do you believe in Easter Sunday?" he snapped back.
>
> "Yes."

"Well, do you believe Good Friday came first?"

Jackson must have believed that too, Riderer wrote, for he and another minister walked ahead to take the first barrage of rocks.

Shortly after the article was published, Riderer left her order and returned to the Chicago ghettos to work.

In December 1966, Bishop Helmsing, who attended *NCR* board meetings as a self-described "spiritual adviser," told chairman John Fallon, "I have lost confidence in the editor." Hoyt and the bishop continued to talk, intermittently, usually when Helmsing again felt offended by the facts or tone of an article, such as birth control.

The following timeline may help keep track of the emergence of birth control as a focus of discussion and *NCR*'s role in that discussion during 1967–1968.

In January 1967, Helmsing wrote a pastoral letter, "Some reflection on growth in faith in the post-conciliar era." He concluded by criticizing *NCR* for causing confusion on birth control and celibacy, for speculation on conflicts both between bishops and the clergy, and between clergy and the laity. Hoyt replied editorially, "We think the resolution of the birth control issue is the single most important problem of the church, and readers have a legitimate interest in developments relating to this question, and that the interests of the church as a society require full discussion."

On April 19, 1967, *NCR* broke its biggest story to date. These were the documents prepared by Pope Paul's special advisory commission on birth control. The papal birth control commission, called to study whether contraception was morally acceptable within marriage, had sent its findings and decision, in secret, to Paul VI. To his dismay, the pope learned the commission favored ending the ban. That report was leaked to two Catholic newspapers, *Le Monde* in France, and *NCR*. A 1988 interview with Hoyt and a 2012 interview with Larry Guillot fleshed out what happened next.

A group of Dutch journalists had founded the International Documentation on the Contemporary Church (IDOC), and in the fall of 1966 someone on the commission, possibly one of the cardinals—but certainly a "clerical person," Hoyt contended—approached IDOC with the commission's documents. The Dutch asked Irish journalist Gary

MacEoin, long connected with *NCR*, about releasing the documents to *Le Monde*.

According to Hoyt, MacEoin said, "'Fine, they certainly should be published. But you should also get it into the English language press, either the *New York Times* or the *NCR*.' Of the two, he suggested the *NCR* because 'it would be their big story, they would handle it competently, and the *Times* would carry it anyway.' So we just got that shipped to us." The packet "had no return address or anything." The contents were primarily in Latin, with some in French. "Translation was a big job," Hoyt said. "The arrangement was we would publish it simultaneously with *Le Monde*."

By that time Guillot was back in Kansas City from Rome, following doctoral research on the Anglican Roman Catholic International Commission. During the council, he was an accredited journalist reporting for the diocesan *Catholic Reporter*. In Kansas City, he took on the translation of Hoyt's birth control documents; Fr. Philip Tompkins handled the French documents for *NCR*. Once they'd finished, Tompkins and Guillot checked each other's work.

A publication date was agreed to, but *Le Monde* held the story for twenty-four hours longer, so "we had a world beat on our hands," Hoyt said.

> The signal to go ahead came a bit too soon. We weren't quite ready. So I was 36 hours I think, sometimes I say 48, but at least 36 hours at my desk—I left it only to go the bathroom. I knew there was a storm coming. I asked Olmstead, Tom and Art whether we should go ahead. They said, "For sure." The question almost answered itself. It was a storm. Secularly and religiously.
>
> The secular papers were onto us, and the networks, even from Australia, Germany, France. Then, of course, the reaction began in the Church press. I think Helmsing called me into his office, but tensions had risen long before that.

The Catholic press reaction was generally negative—strong exceptions were the *Catholic Star-Herald* of Camden, New Jersey, and the *Western Catholic Reporter*, of Edmonton, Canada. Later Hoyt wrote the standard editor's lament—one every editor since can look back on and repeat with confidence: "Now of course it is old news, in fact moldering. So with other news beats . . ."

In the May 3 edition, *NCR* recapped their mainly critical response. The Boston archdiocese's *Pilot* called it a "massive blunder" (a critique so irking Hoyt that he reprinted and rebutted it in the next issue); the Brooklyn, New York, diocese's *Tablet* labeled it "untimely and sensational"; both *Our Sunday Visitor* and the Chicago *New World* saw it as a betrayal both by *NCR* and the document leakers, with the *Visitor* deeming the latter "Judas" and asking "if he has collected his 30 pieces of silver—or was it more?—for betraying the vicar of Christ."

Some support came from Camden's *Catholic Star-Herald*: "One good effect of *N.C.R.*'s publishing the 'secret' documents is that they reveal the terrible dilemma that besets the Pope," leading them to conclude that "the best course the Pope could follow is to make birth control an open question, leaving the faithful to adopt whatever theological view convinces their consciences most sincerely." From outside the United States, Canada's *Western Catholic Reporter* headlined an editorial with "Secrecy must go."

Celibacy was back as a major theme when, in June 1967, *NCR* reported, "Pope reaffirms celibacy for Latin rite priests." Paul followed with *Sacerdotalis Caelibatus*, affirming the celibate clergy tradition. *NCR* replied with the editorial "The pope decides."

In March 1968, *NCR* ratcheted up the tension with the Vatican and the hierarchy when the newspaper printed an extensive excerpt from a forthcoming book by Mary Daly in which she argued for women's ordination and gender equality in the church hierarchy. In June the pope issued a new three-thousand-word creed ("Credo of the People of God") that *NCR* described in July as "flat and unrewarding." Rosemary Ruether then tackled the issue of the virgin birth in September.

Finally, Helmsing felt he had to act. His letter exudes a personal anguish and feeling of betrayal. "Now, as a last resort," he wrote, in a three-page statement, printed in the October 16, 1968, edition, "I am forced as bishop to issue a condemnation of the *National Catholic Reporter* for its disregard and denial of the most sacred values of our Catholic faith . . . [for] belittling the basic truths expressed in the Creed of Pope Paul VI; it has made itself a platform for the airing of heretical views on the church and its divinely constituted structure"—noting specifically an attack on the perpetual virginity of the Blessed Virgin Mary and the virgin birth of Christ, by one of its contributors. . . . It has given lengthy space to a blasphemous and heretical attack on the Vicar of Christ. It is difficult to see how well-instructed writers who deliberately deny and ridicule dogmas of our Catholic faith can possibly escape the guilt of the crime defined in Canon 1325 on heresy, and how they can escape the penalties of automatic excommunication entailed thereby.

He urged the board to have the newspaper "change its misguided and evil policy."

Helmsing's condemnation severed a relationship that had gone beyond simple benevolence. Hoyt was thrown by it. His editorial reply was one of those rare occasions when Olmstead or Blackburn or Winter should have told Hoyt to cut to the chase. Hoyt more than adequately answered Helmsing in the November 6 issue, but it took him almost 2,300 words to get there. It was discursive, defensive and dissembling before it came into focus.

[Helmsing] expected the editors to accept his "guidance" . . . It became clear that what the bishop meant by it was reducible to ultimate control of policy.

. . . In our reading the condemnation contains hardly a word of *criticism*. It is an exercise in labeling. It employs language that is intemperate and abusive. It attempts to make the paper an outlaw publication, but without anything faintly resembling due process of law.

Hoyt continued,

One element of Bishop Helmsing's statement reaches through our defenses: the section in which he speaks of the need in the church for continuous *metanoia*, conversion of heart. . . .

. . . Again, this is a newspaper, not a pious journal. It does not pretend to meet all the spiritual needs of its readers; its preoccupations are with issues in the church that can be treated in political terms, and it quite deliberately adopts a language that cannot be confused with the saccharine and submissive vocabulary once considered the mark of Catholic loyalty.

Concluding the editorial, he wrote,

> To make an end of it: We intend to go on being a Catholic paper, concerned with Catholic activities, values and ideas, trying also to be present to the world. We do not consider ourselves to have been severed from the community, though communications with part of it have become extraordinarily difficult. We plan to go on reporting as competently as we can, and we don't plan to consciously move either to the left or the right. As long as people are interested, and the U.S. post office stays in business, we'll be around.

Helmsing had not specifically mentioned one headline that may have deserved censure, for if ever a headline could be misinterpreted it was the previous week's "How to get the papal monkey off the Catholic back." The topic was infallibility.

When *NCR*'s five editors in 1969 pulled together a compendium of their favorite stories and articles as *Special to the N.C.R.*, the "papal monkey" article made the cut. The editors wrote, "If you must know which article the editors consider to be the most important work to appear in this book, this is it." In the issue before the condemnation, the editors had reprinted an article by Catholic philosopher Daniel Callahan (at one point executive editor of *Commonweal* magazine) titled "Getting the papal monkey off the Catholic back." In it, Callahan wrote,

> Along with many others, my first reaction to *Humanae Vitae* was to prophesy the imminent demise of the papacy. How could papal authority possibly survive the criticism and rebellion the encyclical was bound to unleash? The answer, I felt, was obvious. It couldn't. The encyclical, an autocratic blunder, would signal the need—evident to all—for a total overhaul of Catholic authority. The moment had come.

He continued,

> [This was] naïve. Wishful thinking. Just plain silly. The papacy has survived and its authority remains intact.
>   . . . In a church of some 500 million people [today 1.2 billion], the public complaints of a few thousand scattered priests and laymen are of little consequence. They create a flap, much excitement and plenty of news. But they do not necessarily and have not yet, in fact, brought down the papacy or shattered its hold on the church. . . . The main power which has kept the papacy alive through the centu-

ries, a power even stronger than episcopal support, has been the papacy's own self-image. It has been an institution within an institution, displaying all the marks of a self-justified, self-contained and self-perpetuated body.

Callahan continued, writing that papal infallibility "was the finest gift which the bishops ever gave the pope—perfect for the man who has everything . . . [yet] it is a doctrine which the popes themselves have apparently found useless, for they have not once openly invoked it by name, even in the instance of the proclamation of the Assumption.

In his conclusion, he said,

> It is utopian in the first place to be a Christian. Once that decision is made one might as well be utopian about the papacy. A passionate interest in the future possibilities of the papacy, combined with a cool detachment from its present clutches, would seem to me the best way to bring the utopia about. We won't reap the benefits of this utopia, but our descendants might. That's not much perhaps to get enthused about, but it is all we probably have. It is no offense for a drowning man to grasp at straws.

NCR's headlines frequently punned, and under many editors, that lighter touch—considered insulting by some—brightened pages packed solidly with hard news and frequently tough commentary. When Boston's Cardinal Cushing announced he would build no more Catholic schools, Tom Blackburn quipped, "Cushing throws in the trowel."

Olmstead, however, never liked the puns. He was also far more middle-of-the-road on church issues than the newsroom's tenor suggested. He left in 1968 for the *Chicago Sun-Times*, where he spent the remainder of a distinguished career. He also wrote for the *National Catholic Register*, an indication of his differences with some aspects of Hoyt's *NCR*. Before he left, however, he pressed Guillot into further service. When Guillot agreed to translate a purloined Latin document on mixed marriage, Olmstead said, "I didn't know if we could get you to do another in the light of the last one."

Original board members began departing, too. In order to quell any thoughts of cause and effect, chairman Fallon left after Helmsing's blast at the "evil" newspaper. Blackburn left in 1969. His career took him to daily newspapers in Detroit (the *News*), Trenton (the *Times*) and finally, the *Palm Beach Post*.

What marks the caliber of Hoyt's news team was that each departing senior reporter was able to move back into mainstream American newspapering.

Hoyt's *Sun Herald* editorship had stepped straight into the Korean War. His *NCR* covered the Vietnam War, and it remained a searing national and Catholic issue. In Saigon, a recently hired correspondent, Tom Fox, reported that Cleveland priest Fr. Harold J. Bury, one of a group of protesters who'd chained themselves to the gates of the U.S. Embassy, intended to travel to Hanoi to celebrate Christmas Mass. The cathedral there was still undamaged, but most of the city's Catholic churches had been bombed into rubble.

Furthermore, in the early days of the decade's second half, black Catholics were trying to help themselves. A delegation of African Americans to Rome included the Black Clergy Caucus, the Black Sisters Conference, the Black Catholic Lay Caucus and the National Office for Black Catholics. Among other issues, they were pressing for black bishops for Washington, DC.

These American Catholics did meet with several curial cardinals, then returned home to learn the U.S. bishops had not even included the National Office for Black Catholics in its budget.

4

1971: DONALD J. THORMAN

It was the early 1950s in Chicago. Donald Thorman and Barbara Jean Lisowski were courting. This particular morning, however, after he dropped Barbara at church—probably St. Giles in Oak Park, Illinois, where they wed in 1952, Donald headed to his mother, Adolphine's, house.

He had to hurry, for his stepfather, Mr. Dittmar, was threatening her with violence. The stepfather apparently "was not a pleasant person." Thorman grew up under that experience. These days he was quite capable of keeping his stepfather in line, for Don Thorman was a big man, broad-shouldered with a ready, if slightly shy, smile. He was an ex-Marine. He would not tolerate violence and was quite capable of ensuring his mother didn't have to either.

Thorman was the youngest of three children. There was a sister, Iris, and a brother who died in an industrial accident. Thorman was baptized in St. Angela's Parish, Oak Park (as was the late Catholic scholar and author Fr. Andrew Greeley). His father was first a Chicago policeman and then a funeral director. His father died in his fifties when Don was two. It was hard times. His mother, a homemaker of Franco-German descent, had quickly remarried, to Dittmar, a much older man and a friend of her father's.

Barbara, born in Kenosha, Wisconsin, was an energetic brunette. Her mother had died in childbirth delivering Barbara's sister, Joyce, so Barbara was raised primarily by her Polish grandmother, who had already raised ten children of her own. Barbara's father remarried and the result—her daughter, Betsy, recalled—was Barbara telling her children she had "a wicked stepmother." After her father's death, Barbara quickly returned to her grandmother's home.

Thorman attended public schools but completed his senior high school year at St. Philip High School, run by the Servite Fathers. After graduation, he entered the Servite monastery but left in 1942 to serve in the U.S. Marines. After military service, in 1946 Thorman again entered the seminary, this time with the Viatorians. Once again he left after a year, then graduated from DePaul University and was studying for his master's degree at Loyola University Chicago when he and Barbara met. She worked in the Loyola registrar's office and contended she noticed the handsome young ex-Marine before he noticed her. After Loyola, which included a semester at the University of Fribourg in Switzerland, Don went to Fordham University in New York for his doctorate. When his sister's husband was stricken with a brain tumor, Thorman left Fordham for Chicago to help out his family. He eventually took a teaching position at Loyola.

Thorman was a loyal son of the church and a daily Mass-goer when opportunity permitted. Barbara was an activist—outside the home. Thorman had come up through seminaries; she'd come up through Cardinal Joseph Cardijn's Young Christian Students and the Young Christian Workers. He was cautious, she was prepared to get involved. She participated in the 1963 March on Washington and the 1968 Poor People's Campaign. Domestically, however, by her own admission, she was a typical "demure" young Catholic woman of her era.

Barbara Thorman told of being at a natatorium, "pregnant with my sixth or seventh child." She was there with a Jewish friend from the South Bend Council of Catholic-Jewish Women. When the friend asked, "'Well, how many children are you going to have?'" Barbara Thorman recalled, "I honestly said—she must be laughing to this day— 'Well, it's not up to me.' I mean I believed that crap, believed it with my whole heart—more Catholic than the pope."

The newlywed Thormans moved to South Bend, Indiana, when Donald Thorman became managing editor of the *Voice of St. Jude* (later *U.S. Catholic*). From 1956 to 1962 he served as managing editor of *Ave Maria* magazine. The couple was deeply involved in the Christian Family Movement. For years, the two of them edited and pasted up the movement's *ACT* magazine for its founders Pat and Patty Crowley. Some thirty years later, Barbara, in an interview for *NCR*'s archives, said she saw her role "back in the 1950s as a Martha-Mary role. Hell, I'd had to paste up *ACT* when I was in labor. But that's the kind of brainwashing that I was very much a part of." There were now seven children: Peggy, Judith, James, Elizabeth, David, Daniel and Damien.

Though the growing Thorman family continued to live in South Bend, by 1962 Donald Thorman had decided to branch out on his own. He formed Catholic Communications Consultants and, as a resident five days a week of Chicago, was industriously building up a small but flourishing business as well as working as a National Catholic News Service columnist and a public speaker.

His mother had gone to live with her widowed daughter, Iris, in Wheaton, Illinois, to help with her four children while Iris worked in a doctor's office. Thorman lived with his mother and Iris during the week while he worked the Chicago Catholic scene weekdays and returned to South Bend on weekends. Barbara Thorman said that with the 1960s council and changing lay-Catholic attitudes, each issue of the Kansas City diocesan *Catholic Reporter* was enthusiastically anticipated in South Bend. "There was a feeling you could be a part of change, real change for a viable church," she said. Then *NCR* was born.

In 1962 Thorman wrote his well-received *The Emerging Layman*. With keen insight he had taken the pulse of the Catholic awakening and reported on its condition and ambitions. Peggy Thorman Hartig, Don and Barbara's oldest child, later recalled that as a result of that book— the first of four he wrote—her father was gone for most of the year giving talks. He was only home "for a three-day weekend for Mother's Day."

As a communications consultant, Thorman also ensured everyone in his Rolodex had a signed copy. That caused sharp-tongued *NCR* board member Dan Herr, chairman of the Thomas More Association, to quip he had the only unsigned copy of the book. Peggy Hartig said her father was scrupulous about keeping his contacts fresh. "Making and keeping connections was important to him from a professional perspective," she said. When he traveled, as to the 1971 synod in Rome, she was briefly an *NCR* clerk. She had to type out Avery labels so he could send postcards to his contacts and his personal friends. The children all learned at an early age what the word "itinerary" meant because, Peggy said, "Dad's was always posted on the refrigerator."

So it was that in late 1965, the struggling *NCR* company was looking for a publisher. The board—essentially Dan Herr, the quintessential businessman—looked around for possible candidates. From his years on *Ave Maria* magazine, Thorman was a known quantity in the Notre Dame–South Bend-Catholic publishing milieu. He had taken management courses, taught himself business practice, and was a cautious man on church issues. Nonetheless—as his book showed—he was open to the changes underway in the church. Herr approached Thorman to gauge his interest. Thorman (possibly unaware of Herr's quip about his book) was looking at his options. His little company was growing; he was thinking of taking on a partner. The stark reality, however, was that *he* was the company. Undoubtedly haunted by his own family's fate when his father died, he understood that if anything happened to him, Barbara and the seven children were in serious jeopardy. That said, *NCR* was no secure haven; it was in shaky financial condition. Ultimately, in late 1965, Thorman moved to Kansas City as *NCR*'s second publisher.

In February 1966, the rest of the family arrived and settled permanently in Kansas City. Peggy was in eighth grade; Damien, the youngest, was four. Years later Peggy commented, "We found it strange he was coming home for dinner. That had not been the norm."

At 115 E. Armour Blvd., Thorman was not welcomed with open arms. He began by setting up proper business procedures. This was why Herr, described by Barbara Thorman in 1988 "as a hard-nosed businessman," had wanted him. She said,

> Bob Hoyt came from a Catholic Worker background where everyone threw the money into a pot and took out what was needed, including he and Bernadette. Don established a bank account, made people responsible. There was a great division between the so-called editorial side and the business side. Don had the task of bringing these guys down to some sort of functioning organization that was responsible for what was going on, what was happening in the business world. If they couldn't function as a business, it would fold. There was a kind of elitist snobbery. Anything proposed to make it a going financial concern was kind of dismissed, with disdain from Blackburn and the other editor [Olmstead], and I think Don felt it very strongly—constantly fighting Hoyt.

As a result of the constant disdain and disagreement, "totally un-businesslike, I saw, as the years progressed, a kind of cynicism in Don that I didn't like."

"Of course," Barbara continued,

> the board was hand-picked and pretty supportive. But the board meetings only happened four times a year. There was constant tension [between Thorman and Hoyt]. For example, the editors wouldn't start putting the paper to bed on Friday night until, well . . . at 6 p.m. they'd go out and eat, drink and be merry and come back and be working until 1:00 and 2:00 in the morning. Don thought that was pretty horrendous.

Hoyt said the board had stressed to Thorman that the publisher was the publisher and the editor the editor. Thorman said he had no interest in the editing. "Let me say first," Hoyt insisted in a 1988 interview, "that from the day he came he worked his ass off. He worked very, very hard. He was a very intelligent man and a good businessman. I differed on matters of policy. I thought we paid ourselves too much [Hoyt and Thorman received the same salary] and people like Blackburn, Olmstead and Winter too little."

Hoyt recalled Thorman's layman courage on the day in 1966 when Bishop Helmsing was at 115 E. Armour to bless the offices. Once the ceremony was concluded, champagne and nibbles were served. Helmsing promptly produced a statement and read it. He attacked *NCR* for its "imprudence and rash sensationalism." Said Hoyt, "This was Don Thorman's finest hour as far as I was concerned." Explained Hoyt,

> Not in these words, but Thorman told Helmsing, "Bishop, you don't know what you're talking about. You don't talk to the people we talk to. Or the people we talk to don't talk to you. Or, you're not listening." Thorman was not insulting. He didn't sound angry. He was very straightforward. I really admired that because despite what I could do at the typewriter, I had too many years as an altar boy to do that. In the presence of an episcopal ring I tended to turn back into an altar boy and become deferential.

Art Winter, too, came away with a lesson. "I always remembered that scene and carried the image with me—laypeople standing up to a bishop and his staff. That was something new for me. As a subscriber from the first issue, I knew *NCR* had staked out its role as a newspaper independent of the church. But this brought it home to me. I knew I had arrived. I was where I really wanted to be. I thanked God for it."

Of the editor-publisher relationship, Winter said,

> From the time I came, I sensed bad blood between Hoyt and Thorman. I don't know why. Two egos? My understanding of the *NCR* structure was they were equals. The editor wouldn't bow to the publisher; the news would always be pure, untainted by the realities of the world Thorman had come from. He'd written *The Emerging Layman*. It was quite successful and taken seriously. I don't think Hoyt respected Thorman very much. Circulation started going down and that created more tension I think.

The news was not good behind the scenes at *NCR*.

Circulation was falling and board member Jesuit Fr. Joseph Fichter regularly drew attention to the fact. Understandably, the board was restless. There were other reasons.

Hoyt had separated from his wife and left the family home. When he finally told his wife about his affair, he did it in a letter. "Bernadette had no idea, none," Barbara Thorman said, "which knocked her out of the water. It was pretty cruel not to face her. Don was just totally disgusted with the whole thing."

The Hoyt-Thorman relationship, never particularly warm, turned frostier. Hoyt might have to go. An unaired bone of contention on ex-Marine Thorman's side was his anger at the newspaper's (that is, Hoyt's) condemnation of the Vietnam War.

By 1970, four of the earliest board members no longer served. In 1968, John Fallon, the first chairman, had resigned, not because of Helmsing's condemnation, he wrote, but "proud of what *NCR* has done. . . . On the other hand the tone and style of *NCR* do concern me . . . constant emphasis on the issues which divide us in the church . . . it hardens attitudes and makes further dialogue most difficult. The time is past [for] a thirst for the fray."

What was to be a climactic board meeting in Chicago in September 1970 to solve the Hoyt-Thorman dilemma (by firing one of them) was halted part way through. The brother of a board member had had a serious heart attack. Board members Bob Burns, Dan Herr and Martin Marty decided to resign.

That left a five-person board: Fichter, Hoyt, Thorman, Joseph Cunneen and Brennan. In January 1971, Thorman told Hoyt that Fichter had again written regarding the still declining circulation and another board meeting was called for May. That same month, Hoyt wrote a well-crafted article on "the politics of celibacy." It did not read as if, in that first week in May, he had written it knowing that the following week he would be fired by *NCR*'s board of directors.

At that board meeting, Hoyt later explained, as board secretary he kept writing the minutes up to the point when he refused to offer his resignation. They voted to dismiss him, three to two—Brennan, Fichter and Thorman in the majority. Hoyt was crushed and felt betrayed.

Hoyt's name was removed from the paper's masthead in the following issue, May 14, 1971.

Vickie Breashears, currently *NCR*'s longest-serving employee, said she knew Hoyt from passing him in the corridors and exchanging greetings. He was "reserved, pre-occupied and hard-working," she said, but "there was something of the elf about him. When he knew he was leaving, the 'elf' went out of him."

Of the inner "elf," Hoyt's eldest son, Mike, said,

> I do think he was devastated by the firing; he had built the paper into something that mattered, and leaving it was extremely hard, and I believe that did stay with him. But other things were going on in his life at the time, including the break-up of his marriage. He also soon left Kansas City, leaving six children behind, the oldest in their teens, with my mother—who was debilitated for a while by the divorce. So I expect he was deeply hurt by the firing, but he was spreading around some of that hurt.

"No, I don't think [Bob] got over it," Tom Blackburn said about the firing, "but I never could figure out how a Catholic editor could think he could get divorced and remarried without there being repercussions, including repercussions in the circulation department. I never did ask him."

In 1988, Hoyt said Herr never again spoke to Thorman and refused to give Thorman a tribute when he died, though Hoyt himself had. Hoyt later told Blackburn, "Thorman blindsided me, but saved the paper."

"What Thorman had in mind," Hoyt contended, "was evident from the first issue when he took over as editor and publisher. He ran a series of columns in which he said NCR would seek reconciliation with the bishops, the paper would seek to guide itself by the mind of the church."

To most NCR readers and Catholics in the know, news of this shattering development—Hoyt's dismissal—was eked out. In NCR itself, Thorman wrote neither an editorial nor a column commenting on or explaining Hoyt's firing—despite the fact that to NCR's readers, Hoyt, through his editorials and newsgathering direction, was NCR.

Instead, in a lengthy column in the issue following Hoyt's dismissal (May 14, 1971), Thorman wrote, "Is the National Catholic Reporter changing? Friends ask us this question often nowadays. The answer is yes and no. Our main thrust has not changed. The NCR will continue the struggle for greater freedom and openness in the church."

It was a keen-eyed reader who would have caught a short, five-paragraph article tucked into the bottom left-hand corner of page 5. The reader may or may not have been drawn there by the innocuous, minimalist three-word headline: "NCR announces changes." It was the briefest possible report on the just concluded board meeting. The second paragraph merely stated that board chairman "Brennan also expressed deep appreciation for the contributions of Robert G. Hoyt, founding editor, whose services were terminated."

Once the news was out, readers' letters were scarifying, though kept to a bare minimum of four in NCR itself. Cartoonist Joe Noonan, a mainstay of the Hoyt years, tried to organize a national petition or boycott. Nothing came of it.

The top U.S. Catholic news story of the year had been ignored by the top U.S. Catholic newspaper. The reasons behind the decision were never publicly explained. Thorman's handling of the firing in NCR was shabby, and he quickly understood that. But it was too late.

Winter had worked for Hoyt for five years when Hoyt was dismissed. Winter said he and his wife, Betty, "regarded Hoyt and Bernadette as Joseph and Mary, we were young then." When Hoyt and Bernadette divorced, said Winter, he and his wife wondered, "If they can't make it, how can we?"

Winter said he knew he'd never be a Thorman favorite, "and I wasn't. [Thorman] was not a particularly good news person—didn't have the background—but I would say he probably did save *NCR*."

Whatever the mix of facts and motivations behind Hoyt's firing, it now fell to Thorman to prop up the financially ailing, and sadly bereft, *NCR*.

The final word that year on Hoyt's departure appeared in *America*. Msgr. Salvatore Adamo wrote in his "Media" column in *America*,

> It's a puzzlement. What is? Why and how a board of directors came to fire the founding editor of the *National Catholic Reporter* early in May of this year. That such a move took courage is unquestionable . . . how do you lay an axe to the trunk of the Cedar of Lebanon of the Catholic press? And how do you muffle the thunder when it goes down? Yes, it's a puzzlement. So little comment on so drastic a demise.

5

CIRCULATION WOES; DJT INITIATIVES

Don Thorman was now editor. The title was more honorific than descriptive. Tom Blackburn and Art Winter said Thorman rarely entered the newsroom. He ran the company from his fourth-floor office and wrote his columns there. There were no editorial meetings. During the next few years, there were a couple of executive editors and managing editors. Thorman's time was far from wasted; it was spent trying to save the company and then balance the books. Equally, his editorial stance—as reflected in his writings—was his continuing attempt to balance what he considered a lopsided relationship between *NCR* and the bishops.

In the Catholic news years immediately ahead, as if reflecting Robert Hoyt's ouster, push was turning to shove. Belgium's Cardinal Leo Suenens was pushing hard to persuade Pope Paul VI to ordain married men while keeping celibacy as an option. More, the U.S. political season loomed, and Catholic priests and religious hoped to shove aside established figures and make their way into political office. Jesuit Fr. Robert Drinan was seeking election in Massachusetts; right-wing pundit Jesuit Fr. John McLaughlin hoped to oust a Democratic senator in Long Island, New York; St. Norbert College history professor Fr. Robert J. Cornell hoped to upset a Republican congressman. There were priests and nuns competing for elected posts at the state level too. A nun in Spokane lost her bid for a seat in the Washington state legislature. Among the Jesuits, Drinan was successful; McLaughlin was not. McLaughlin's consolation prizes included a position as adviser/speech writer to President Richard Nixon, two marriages, and a stint as a television political talk-show host.

In 1970, the Catholic Theological Society of America recommended that Rome be open to ordaining women deacons, and at the following year's synod, Archbishop Leo Byrne, coadjutor archbishop of Minneapolis–St. Paul, spoke in favor of the promotion of women: "No argument should be used to exclude women from any service to the church if it stems from male prejudice, blind adherence to merely human traditions rooted in other times, or questionable interpretations of Scripture." In 1974, the six-hundred-plus attendees from 370 congregations at the Leadership Conference of Women Religious (LCWR) meeting overwhelmingly approved a call for all church ministries to be open to women.

In fact, women were being taken *very* seriously. In 1972, Duquesne University had found "pervasive" bias against women. A six-month internal inquiry could find nothing else to explain the $3,000 pay differential between men and women in the same department with the same credentials, nor the $10,400 difference between the highest-paid full professor, a man, and the lowest-paid full professor, a woman. Duquesne established a $90,000 fund "to redress inequities."

The following year, in 1973, a Boston conference attended by 150 in ministry turned the women's ordination proposal on its head. Dominican Sr. Ann Kelley, Harvard-Radcliffe campus minister, said they should not focus on whether women ought to be ordained. Her argument was that ordination to the priesthood was not desirable for women or men—"There must be a better way of exercising ministry." (Forty years later, that is a question that's lost none of its sting—or sensibility. Even the conservative Garry Wills has written a book titled *Why Priests?*)

Sexist terminology was a growing issue. *NCR* contributor Leonard Swidler, Temple University professor of Catholic thought, was praised by *NCR* reader Joan Walsh Ludati of North Carolina for calling for an end to it while banning sexist terminology from his own writings and publications.

U.S. bishops asked for a study on the ordination of women; the National Coalition of American Nuns called the proposal "self-defeating." They urged the bishops instead to listen carefully to American women scholars on the issue while subsidizing their research and to invite women theologians to their meetings. A joint committee of Organizations Concerned with the Status of Women in the Church jumped in: "Saying a study is needed on the matter of ordination is the same as saying a study is needed on the matter of women being treated as equal human beings—an insult and humiliation inflicted on more than 50 percent of the children of God."

It was an era when young nuns from India suffered a cruel form of humiliation. *NCR* broke the "nun-running" story of young nuns sent thousands of miles from home to vocation-depleted European convents "to work as skivvies." The Indian priest running the program denied the young sisters were mistreated. The Vatican said it would study the matter. The Changanachary archbishop told the priest to stop the practice. (Twenty-plus years later, *NCR* broke open the story of young African nuns being seduced or coerced into sex or raped by priests because the nuns were HIV/AIDS free on a continent that wasn't.)

During this same five-year period of Pope Paul VI's reign and rule, the pope strongly condemned war and torture; he heroically worked at peacemaking, meeting both sides in the Vietnam War. He did not seem to be trying quite so hard with both sides in the church. Paul clearly understood the overall Western church's preferred post–Vatican II direction and was clearly discomfited by it. He eyed the 1971 World Synod of Bishops warily.

NCR Rome correspondent Desmond O'Grady wrote that the pope's

> extraordinary opening statement ordered the bishops to regard themselves as the exclusive voices of their respective churches and to ignore the input of public opinion. In an amazing piece of rhetoric, he pictured the church as surrounded by hordes of schemers seeking to stampede the bishops into decisions in doubtful conformity with the faith, contemptuous of decision, opposed to authority and tainted with secularism. Even the charisms of which the council had spoken to sympathetically were consigned to the same trash can.

"Whenever a speech challenged the 'official' position," continued O'Grady, "it quickly provoked a saturation response. When Suenens pleaded for a modest opening in the celibacy legislation, he was immediately shot down by five cardinals" in a row: Thomas Cooray of Ceylon; Peter McKeefry of Wellington, New Zealand; Joseph Parecattil of India; Anthony Poma of Italy—and John Krol of Philadelphia. These same traditionalists closed the possibility of ordaining married men. O'Grady said "the exasperation of the delegates was well expressed by Bishop Joachim N'Dayen of Bangul, Central African Republic: 'I did not travel thousands of miles to Rome to dance the tarantella. This formation (re: ordaining married men) is almost identical to the previous one. What happened to our amendments?'" Dom Helder Camara jabbed the institutional conscience when he asked, had not the church given a genuine reason to Marx to describe religion as "the opiate of the people?"

The synodal charade of independence was completely exposed when U.S. Cardinal John Wright simply said there would be no final vote on the issue: The pope would decide.

The task of formulating the final synod conclusions in secret was handed to the curial bureaucrats. Synodal coverage since has recorded the rapid deterioration of the freedoms initially intended for these bishops' meetings. Adding insult to injury, Taize's prior, Roger Schutz, warmly praised the bishops' synod for reaffirming priestly celibacy. The synod's theme had been justice.

In an anticlimax, the synod safely passed a resolution calling for an end to the war in Vietnam.

Two weeks later, when Krol was elected president of the National Council of Catholic Bishops (NCCB, predecessor to the USCCB, the Vatican-mandated and neutered U.S. Conference of Catholic Bishops), a moderate bishop described Krol's statement to the press as "triumphalistic." One of the triumphs was that Krol's extra visibility led to his role as an ally to Nixon. A gain for the public was that the bishops agreed to open their meetings to the press. Given the large number of bishops who had always been willing to tell the press what was happening behind closed doors anyway, the bishops were simply making an omelet from already-cracked eggs. But the "open door" principle was a good one.

It was during this period that the Vatican decided to renegotiate its concordat with Spain, where the dictator General Francisco Franco warned that under his rule, there was no room for dissent by progressives, including priests, and that church and state must cooperate. The church had been an ally for all of Franco's thirty-three years in power: "two powerful and vital forces that have the same goal," Franco said, "and contradiction in those goals would lead to a regrettable crisis. The state cannot stand idly by in the face of certain attitudes of a temporal order shown by some churchmen. Thus the state will oppose any inter-ference whatsoever in its sovereign functions." Spain's church was mov-ing slightly to the left, and Franco was worried about loss of support.

Before the end of 1972, the Vatican took control of the Italian Cassi-nese Benedictines in order to gain control of Saint Paul Outside-the-Walls. The outspoken Vietnam War critic and social activist Abbot Gio-vanni Franzoni, who criticized the church's widespread holdings throughout the city of Rome, was being pressured to abandon his pul-pit. He resigned to live with the poor, which many of his monks were already doing. (St. Paul was the place where John XXIII announced he was calling the Second Vatican Council.)

In America, the presidential race was seriously underway. Candidate George McGovern was unsuccessfully seeking Catholic support, and Cardinal Krol was in photo ops with Richard Nixon. The cardinal was also in the news because the archdiocese had taken on the Girl Scouts, persuading them to drop their merit badge "To Be a Woman" or the church wouldn't sponsor Scout troops. The merit badge would have taught the girls about contraception, abortion, venereal disease and sexuality. The Scouts backed down.

Lighter notes: The first Catholic lectors strike took place in Brook-lyn, New York, in 1972 when a married couple, the Zirkels, refused to read certain passages by St. Paul on marriage at their 11 a.m. Mass. In 1973, Miami Catholic People United demonstrated outside the cathe-dral, organizing a series of "Don't Give Sundays" until Archbishop Coleman Carroll altered his policies on the suspension and transfer of priests, the lack of public accounting and his decision that Miami Cath-olics must abstain from meat during Lent.

Unhappily, in 1973, there was a whiff of anti-Catholicism in the air, too, when for the eighth time, the University of Chicago refused tenure to forty-five-year-old sociologist Fr. Andrew Greeley. Greeley, who had brought millions in research grants to the university, quit. A Hyde Park, Chicago, newspaper commented there was "strong and convincing evi-dence he got shafted, especially because he is a priest and has a propen-sity to step on toes."

For the pope, as the first five years of the decade closed, there never seemed to be any praise even for his best efforts. His Vatican Museum of Contemporary Art opened in the summer of 1973. Many observers thought it a worthy effort to reestablish the church's ties to the art world. Paul, in his attempt to stimulate an interest in creating modern works with a spiritual dimension, had called artists "a highly sensitive mirror of the contemporary soul." That was not the verdict of the critics who began to study the museum's acquisitions. Said one, "If some mischievous curator has been asked to assemble a collection of rhetorical sham displaying all the clichés of modern art at the meridian of pious frivolity, he could hardly have done better." Pope Paul was sold "a bill of goods," said Portland, Oregon, Archbishop Robert J. Dwyer in the Catholic newspaper *Twin Circles*. He attacked the "ignorance, ineptitude and blundering of those confided with the selection."

Otherwise, Catholics and Protestants criticized President Gerald Ford for immoral CIA interference in Chile, destabilizing the government of Salvador Allende. Archbishop Joseph Bernardin of Cincinnati in a nice turn of phrase said, "Mankind is locked together on a limited globe, vulnerable to each other's actions and therefore responsible to one another, and called to an international social justice as a constitutive element of our evangelizing ministry."

Five thousand Korean Catholics protested President Park Chung Hee's government as the imprisoned Bishop Augustine Kim Jae Doek of Chonju noted that Park had asked South Koreans to give up small freedoms to maintain the larger freedom. "But there is no such thing as small freedoms or a big freedom."

Catholic women's colleges experienced dramatic enrollment increases as campuses were bolstered by older women seeking advancement.

In Kansas City, Missouri, De La Salle Academy in downtown closed, and the brothers opened an alternative school in the neighborhood. Hoyt, at then-Brother Victor Moeller's invitation, had once addressed the academy's students.

In *NCR*, Don Thorman wrote that lawyer John J. Fallon, insurance executive Frank Brennan and *Kansas City Register* editor Michael J. Greene were those who originally conceived the idea of a national version of the diocesan *Catholic Reporter* "so ably edited by Robert G. Hoyt." Hoyt replied he did not wish to minimize the contributions made by others, but Thorman had "cast supporting players in leading roles. Ten years from now this may not bother anybody, this year it still matters to me and a few other people."

Looking ahead, Greeley predicted, "Catholicism as an ecclesiastical institution in the United States will continue in the course of its precipitous decline. At the same time however, American Catholics as a community in our society will experience a dramatic increase in healthy self-consciousness and self-awareness." This was part of an unbelievably lengthy Greeley essay in *NCR*. It was 9,000 words. Except for the scholarly types, the readers must have groaned as the paper regularly sopped up space with 2,000- and 3,000-word documentation articles.

Worth noting at this point, 110 Catholic theologians, writers and educators called for the ordination of women to the priesthood. On the materialism front, in *NCR*'s "Mortgaging America: From slums to suburbs—40 years later," Martin Marty wrote that Americans had made their homes into "'idols,' and ends in themselves." Four bishops attending an NCCB meeting refused to stay at the Washington, DC, Statler Hilton Hotel because of the cost and instead settled for rectories, convents and a religious brothers' residence. At a future bishops' conference, the bishops, in a deliver-us-from-temptation mood, switched accommodation entirely. That was because some bishops protested that the prime Washington hotel they were using had an "adult" (i.e., pornographic) movie channel on its list of offerings.

In the ups and downs division, Cardinal Krol's term as NCCB president ended; the Campaign for Human Development was down $1.5 million in contributions; and Dusquesne University chaplain Holy Ghost Fr. Joseph Healy learned his priestly faculties would be withdrawn if he continued to permit distribution of Communion in the hand. That prompted accusations of partiality from Holy Ghost Fr. Leonard Tuozzolo, assistant chaplain, who protested his exclusion from the edict by Auxiliary Bishop Anthony Bosco of Pittsburgh. Tuozzolo made the point that he also presided at Mass where Eucharist was received in the hand.

Newly appointed Washington Auxiliary Bishop Eugene Marino told how he and his sister were once evicted from a laundromat because they didn't see the "Whites Only" sign. Patrick Crowley, sixty-three, founder with his wife, Patty, of the Christian Family Movement, died of cancer. The bishops elected Bernardin NCCB president. The Jesuits began their 32nd general congregation in their four-hundred-year history with Fr. Pedro Arrupe criticized by Pope Paul, who warned that "certain shadows" that hung over the previous congregation had not been fully dissipated. Maryknoll Fr. James Sinnott was arrested in Seoul by South Korean riot police as he joined relatives protesting thirty-five family members who had been arrested under an emergency measures decree, while Bishop Daniel Tji, in a letter smuggled out of prison, told his fellow South Korean bishops to continue their opposition to the Park regime. The parish of the Good Shepherd in Mount Vernon, Virginia—where Arlington Bishop Thomas Welsh forbade women serving as lay ministers—was ordered not to distribute a newsletter containing a summary of parish council actions and copies of correspondence between the council and the apostolic delegate. Welsh rebuked parish council officers for discussing the controversy with reporters. The newsletter continued to be distributed at all Masses.

6

1974: ARTHUR "WHO?"

Don Thorman's December 27, 1974, announcement in *NCR* that I was the new executive editor did me no great favors. There was no mention I'd previously worked for two well-known Catholic editors, Msgr. Salvatore J. Adamo of the *Catholic Star Herald* in Camden, New Jersey, and Desmond Fisher, editor of the *Catholic Herald* in London, a highly regarded journalist with a strong Vatican II background. Thorman did not say I'd worked for secular newspapers in the United States or that I'd reported from Cuba—the only Western journalist there in 1963— on the suppression of the church under Fidel Castro.

Consequently, all that the *NCR* readership, the "Catholic literati," the *NCR*-watchers, the *Sun Herald* or *NCR* communities in Kansas City, Missouri, and the staff in the newsroom knew was the new executive editor was a former *Forbes* financial writer. And British. They didn't know I was married and had three children. Or even that I was a cradle Roman Catholic.

Did it matter to making a good initial impression with the readership and getting off to a fast start? Oh yes. Five years later, the *Kansas City Star*, which was just down the road from the office, could still inaccurately describe me as "a cocky British journalist of Anglo-Catholic religious sensibilities . . . who had no roots in the American church." ("Cocky" did come close, but it missed the "cheeky chappie" merriment that offsets it.)

I was born in Liverpool. Liverpudlians, according to Stuart Maconie in *Pies and Prejudice: In Search of the North*, are "warm and funny and hugely entertaining . . . with a gentle, wry artiness and brashness, as well as, yes, devious, truculent and arrogant. Just like the rest of us." For Liverpool's impact on my work, just imagine the Beatles as boy journalists.

I was from a happy, musical family, yet I was formed by war. We were four children, but in 1941, Cyril, the brother between my oldest brother, Roy, and I, died at age seven from brain injuries suffered at birth. My sister, Margaret, is two years my junior.

During 1940–1941, there were two hundred bombing raids on Merseyside across three hundred days. They blasted the wooden shutters off the windows, shook our red-brick Victorian chimneys, and filled our steel Anderson shelter in the second kitchen with soot and dust. When the air raid warning went off, my twenty-nine-year-old mother, Alice, headed for the shelter with her three kids. Cyril was hospitalized; my father, always on duty at his own hospital. We knelt beside bunk beds to pray,

> Our Lady of Mount Carmel
> Watch over us and pray for us
> This long night through
> And keep us safe
> From all harm and danger.

We didn't know where Mount Carmel was or why it was significant. But we knew where Our Lady was: directly across the road in the red-brick-and-tile St. Joseph's Catholic church.

In May 1941, the month I turned five, there was the "May Blitz," a three-day period of almost nonstop bombing. More than 1,700 people were killed within a four-mile northern arc of the house. More than 500 were buried in a common grave. My father was home from the hospital one of those nights. After the all-clear siren, Dad took Roy and me to the rear of the house. We lived on a hill. Right across the horizon, half the sky was filled with the furious yellows and red of Liverpool burning. My father said, "Never forget this." Nor, that our brother Cyril died.

By this point in 1941, my dad's youngest brother, Uncle Cyril, a Fleet Air Arm pilot, had been killed. Then his next youngest brother, Uncle Norman, in the Reconnaissance Corps, was killed, his body never found. (My grandmother put a light in her front window every night for the rest of her long life in case he wandered home.)

My father volunteered, though he was exempt from military duties because he was in the hospital service. My father's parents, his wife, and we three kids all assumed my father, too, was going off to be killed. Thanks be to God, he was not killed. He was commissioned into the Royal Engineers and seconded to a regiment in Egypt.

For the duration, we moved to my maternal Scots-Irish grandparents' home in Warrington, Lancashire. They were Irish-born, Scotland-raised. Warrington was the second-most Roman Catholic town in England—a country where "RCs" were a distinctly small minority, less than 10 percent. The most Catholic town, St. Helens, was eight miles to the north. Lancashire was "Good Catholic Lancashire" for the way it held fast during seventeenth- and eighteenth-century persecutions.

My grandparents' home was periodically overflowing with visiting first cousins from Drogheda whose first language apparently was Irish. They had come from neutral Ireland to work the farms and the mines because so many Britons were in the military. (Thanks to those cousins, when I met for the first time the woman in America who would one day be my mother-in-law, we—very briefly—exchanged greetings in Gaelic, then both had to switch to English.)

Women such as my mother and her sisters and sisters-in-law kept the home front of the war-torn nation going despite constant shortages. Food was short; rations were minimal. Per person per week: 2 ounces of tea, 2 ounces of butter, 2 ounces of margarine, one egg, 4 ounces of cheese, 4 ounces of bacon, 8 ounces of sugar, 3 pints of milk. Clothing and shoes were rationed. There was no leather or thread to repair falling-apart shoes. Light bulbs were rare. Everything in wartime households became worn out. Light switches went, door locks broke, but all were patched together and kept working. I became a fix-it man very early.

The world I knew was one of cooperation and sharing. Certainly there were "spivs" (shady black marketeers) and grocers who took bribes to make more food available than the ration coupons allowed from "under the counter." But generally, people helped one another out.

The government worked hard to guarantee fairness.

In late 1945 and early 1946, the men returned home. I watched as innovative women who'd kept the home fires burning and the light switches working for six years suddenly—overnight—were reduced to second- and third-class status. Mind you, I was probably at least eighteen or nineteen before I realized precisely what I'd witnessed.

We settled as a family once more in our own home. My parents, my father in particular, raised us to ignore the prevailing class system, to treat all individuals the same and measure them only by who they were. In a nation known for anti-Semitism, we were not. That was my paternal grandfather's influence. He could have been chief constable of Liverpool if he'd given up his "theatrical friends" (i.e., Jewish friends).

He'd thunder, "Give up Fitch [his Shakespearean actor friend]? Never!"

My brother and I—both originally destined for Catholic boys' schools—were sent instead not to St. Anselm's but to the sixteenth-century Anglican boys' school founded in 1526 by Sir Thomas le Boteler. It had Boteler's motto as its own: *Deus Spes Nostra* [God is our hope] (more loosely translated in my years as "God, this is hopeless"). The headmaster, Nathaniel L. Clapton, brilliant academically at Oxford, was a brute—Wackford Squeers of Dotheboys Hall reincarnated. He had a "double first" from Oxford (first-class honors in two subjects). His Boteler reputation was he had a "double first in sadism." He made my life hell, and I was a minor irritant in his. I was well caned and often detained. The pain and punishment was payment for a superb education. Lewis Carroll (Charles Dodgson, 1832–1898) was a Boteler boy. Was his headmaster the Red Queen or the Mad Hatter?

Clapton in the raw was best captured in a "Boteler Oldboys" online blog remark from Harry "Tadger" Hayes. Hayes was in my older brother Roy's year.

> We used to "stop pies"—one or two of them from Currall's (a nearby pie shop), take them into the dining hall if you didn't like school dinners. Think that is not allowed now. The wealthy used to go off to Greenwood's (fish and chips shop) in Sankey Street. One or two pupils shop-lifted in town, to order, in their dinner hour. One lasting memory is the first day there. We all gathered in the hall and the headmaster, Nat Clapton, strode onto the stage and his first words were "Shut-up you pigs."

There was morning assembly and prayers with the Anglican chaplain, and religious education. Catholics went to Mr. Scudamore, the Catholic art master. The two Jewish boys in my year were grandfathered in as honorary Catholics. Outside the school, we were in the hands of the Benedictines.

Looking back now, I see that confused, searching twelve-year-old. My instincts, based then purely on experience and family attitudes toward the poor, would later have labels: feminist, ChesterBelloc distributist and Christian socialist. I knew nothing of those. That boy was a jumbled mix of fear, uncertainty, compassion and—deeper—anger at the deaths, the injustices and the unfairnesses of the war, and anger against Germans especially. In seventy years I have never sat through a World War II film or a movie or television documentary about the war or about the Nazis or the Holocaust. If any hint of that appears on the screen, I walk out.

At the Boteler I was a good if uneven student (always first in one subject but never the same subject two terms in a row). At fifteen, I fell in love—with economic history. No topic ever came so easily to me. Yet at sixteen, I turned into one of those least comprehensible of human beings: an off-the-rails teenager. In the classic manner of a sixteen year old cutting off his nose to spite his face and cutting class to go motorcycling, I decided to take my revenge on Clapton's Boteler. The school prided itself on its examination successes. For each of my nine subjects, I went into the examination hall, wrote my name and topic on the paper, handed it in, and walked out. At the conclusion of the examinations, I had walked myself out of school—and into an apprenticeship as a journalist.

In those years, the medieval city and guilds system of apprenticeships still governed most of Britain's working world. To be a lawyer or a surveyor, a journalist or an engineer, a baker or a carpenter, it was necessary to "sign papers." For a male of my era, that meant apprenticeship, followed by military conscription and, in my case, in my twenties, college. I'd known at fourteen which college I'd attend.

I was indentured to the *Guardian* series. (Not the *Manchester Guardian*, now the London-based *Guardian* newspaper. That was just up the road.) My *Guardian* was an 1854-founded chain of weekly newspapers in Lancashire and Cheshire. I was a junior newspaper reporter. At eighteen I was conscripted into the Royal Air Force. Given the traditions still in place at that time, I could have been commissioned into my father's old regiment. Not for me. I was drafted into the Provost Marshall's Corps as a noncommissioned officer specializing in security, a policeman by any other name.

In three years in the Royal Air Force I learned three things: how to pilot a glider, that there is no such thing as security, and how to spread extremely cold butter on extremely cold bread on an extremely cold winter morning in northern Germany. (First, stick the knife blade in the teapot for a couple of minutes.)

My first visit to America, 1958–1959, was to meet my pen friend, Robert E. Hopp, who lived in Warren Township, New Jersey. Bob was, by 1958, a sophomore or junior studying architecture at Pratt Institute in Brooklyn. The two of us had corresponded faithfully for eleven years. He was a warm and friendly fellow in person and we remained in close contact through the earlier years of our marriages but later lost touch. His family welcomed me with open arms. In time, both sets of parents met, in England and America.

During that year, through her brother, John—we both drove English sports cars—I met a New York nurse, Margie O'Brien. I went back to England on schedule. But Margie and I were in love (it's lasted fifty-two years). I returned to America, and we wed in 1961.

Thanks to the fact that I left secular journalism for the *Catholic Star Herald*, from then on I was a Catholic en route (as yet) to becoming a Christian. My guide into the world of the social Gospel was Fr. (later Msgr.) Salvatore J. Adamo. Adamo put that social Gospel meat on my "feminist, distributist, Christian socialist" et cetera bones.

It was some era: John XXIII was pope; John F. Kennedy was president.

There was the March on Washington for jobs and freedom, the experience that gave me hope in America, hope that racism from then on would be on the wane. In 1958, American racial bigotry had startled me then seared my soul. It was worse than the same wink-and-nod, silently metaphored and openly exhibited English class system to which my family was hostile.

I had unusual connections to the black community for a visiting Brit. In 1960, three of us working the night shift at the *Courier-News* in Plainfield, New Jersey, started possibly the first U.S. city magazine of its type, *Four Corners*, in Newark. Through *Four Corners* and my coeditor friend Derek Winans (coeditor Frank Jones, no relation, was funding

Four Corners), I was drawn deeply into the city's black community. I came under the tutelage of one its leaders, Tim Still.

While I was at the *Star Herald*, Margie and I lived in a poor-white area of Mantua, New Jersey (we paid $4,900 for our house), where not all the neighborhood children had shoes. Margie and I became friendly with local black Catholics. Regularly, we had the Robinsons, an African American couple, over to play pinochle. This was in 1962 and 1963. The white neighbors' eyebrows never lowered, but they said nothing (and our pinochle opponents invariably won because Ms. Robinson always knew where every card was).

After the March on Washington, I went into the migrant world and wrote about a Puerto Rican family left behind when the picking season ended. They were George and Juanita and three children, not all of them George's. Adamo said to put their groceries on my expense account. I had a friend who knew a mayor, and we had the unwed George and Juanita married so they could collect benefits.

In the interim, I researched and wrote out two broadsheet pages filled with Pius XII and the Jews. The investigation was pegged to the opening in London of Rolf Hochhuth's Pius XII and the Jews play, "The Deputy." That gained me some notoriety and Adamo a regular spot on an all-night Manhattan radio talk show, the "Long John Nebel Show." With a photographer in tow, I covered the play's opening night in New York.

In October 1962, Adamo agreed I should go to Cuba to write about the suppression of the church there. I was turned back at Miami airport—Bay of Pigs. So I did an article titled "Last refugees out." The next year, I was the only Western journalist in Havana, filing for the *Star Herald* and Ben Bassett, foreign editor at the Associated Press. I have always freelanced. I was back in Cuba again in 1964.

One day, Adamo asked me to drive Redemptorist Fr. Francis J. Schlooz to Idlewild (soon to be John F. Kennedy International) Airport. Schlooz was a Dutch missioner who worked in India. He'd been sent to America to raise money and was hopeless at the task. As we drove up Route 1 in New Jersey, he saw a huge modern building set back on acres and acres of freshly mown lawn.

"Stop! Stop the car," Schlooz pleaded. I did, and he got out. I followed.

"What is it?" he asked.

"The headquarters of Johnson & Johnson, a pharmaceutical company," I told him.

He shook slightly then burst into tears. Heck, I was in my twenties,
and he was not much older. I put my arm around his shoulders as he
cried and cried.

Finally, he was able to say, "I could have enough sheep and goats on
that grass to support a dozen families."

Something clicked. I suddenly saw the world in a different way. I
understood directly something about the world I previously hadn't, except theoretically. Though as a teenage hitchhiker I'd seen rural poverty
from Denmark down to southern Italy, I hadn't truly realized the
depths of the crushing poverty of those living on the margins. Schlooz's
tears washed the scales from my eyes. I'd met my first holy person.

A Damascene moment on Route 1, New Jersey? I hope so.

Schlooz's brother in Holland sent me a little table lamp, a small
galleon in full sail with an ornate and colorful Maltese cross on the
mainsail. Francis and I remained in touch for years. He remained with
the poorest of the poor.

Paul VI was pope.

My early career as a young reporter was marked by long- and short-
term periods on several newspapers. During my initial visit to America,
I was fired by my first New York newspaper after five weeks, then
Gannett fired me twice but hired me three times. I was not an easy
employee, but I was a good reporter. Each firing was for challenging an
editor. If I didn't respect an editor professionally, I quit—or was fired
before I could quit. Or I said my piece and we came to terms. My mark
of a good editor: striking a balance with a reporter the editor wanted to
keep.

Adamo I liked. Ours was only occasionally a stormy relationship.
When it was evident I'd return to England and college, I gave Sal four
months' notice because I didn't feel like being fired too early.

After the *Catholic Herald* in London under one of my favorite editors, Des Fisher, and college, Margie and I, now with two children,
returned to America. At college, I'd had two tutors who taught history
from diametrically opposed positions. Victor Treadwell, known in Oxford as "the historian's historian," wrote and believed in minutely detailed "top-down histories" (think presidential, political and papal histories). Raphael Samuel, by contrast, helped create the discipline (to the

master's level) of "people's history." He wanted history thoroughly researched from the bottom up (think liberation theology). It stood me well at *NCR*.

Still freelancing, I burrowed deeper into U.S. society by signing on for two years in the Office of Economic Opportunity (OEO)—the War on Poverty. My three beats were Newark, Trenton and Washington, DC. Once more, the world from the bottom up. OEO had so many ex-ministers and ex-priests (think *NCR* columnist Colman McCarthy), it was known as the "Office of Ecclesiastical Opportunity." It was Ivy League at the top, with graduates from places such as Rutgers University and the University of North Carolina. UNC was still known then as a last redoubt for Ivy Leaguers who'd been kicked out of the league's colleges.

In 1967, I circulated my gently satiric Catholic pamphlets, *The Arrogant Sheep*.

My OEO poverty warrior-ing ended in part because of the Newark riots—and in part because of my OEO samizdat sheet, *Info*.

When I wasn't in Washington or Trenton, I was in Newark, my main focus some 60 percent of the time. Home turf. With a colleague, Cliff Goldman, I wrote a report for the governor (Democrat Richard Hughes) that explained why there would be a riot in Newark. We had it firsthand from folks like Tim Still, the Black Panthers, welfare mothers, priests and project tenants. It was a tinderbox situation in a city deliberately segregated by highways where ambulances wouldn't go into projects, where housing clearance for a New Jersey College of Medicine was causing an uproar, where resided a quartet of official and street-level racism, joblessness, poverty and hopelessness. Any spark could set it off. (What did, according to the official investigation, was the arrest of a black cab driver, roughly hustled into a racist police headquarters.)

During the riot, the governor went on television and attributed the cause to outside agitators. I was furious. My boss, Commissioner Paul Ylvisaker, was in Washington, DC, at a meeting. I persuaded some colleagues to sign a cable with me urging Ylvisaker to go on television and explain that it wasn't outside agitators. The causes were known; almost anything could have been the spark. Ylvisaker didn't challenge the governor, though when Ylvisaker returned to Trenton, he did challenge me and suggested I might want to consider moving on. I stayed.

There was my section of the riot commission report to write, the welfare section, but now I insisted my name not be on it.

The occasional *Info* was still being circulated, and one tipped Ylvisaker over the brink. Most of the illustrations were lifted from a mid-nineteenth-century English magazine called *Once-a-Week* magazine. I had the bound volumes.

In one illustration, a charming, obviously well-born young man in his early twenties appears as a supplicant to a man of undoubted wealth and influence. "My dear sir," the cutline read, "I'm thinking of making a career in poverty. Do you advise it?"

Bye-bye, OEO, and hello, Rutgers. I was still on the trail of America.

I worked in the community and taught at Douglass College, the women's college at Rutgers University. With OEO's Tom Hartmann, I cowrote and taught at Douglass a course on the causes of the city riots. In academic-speak: "Contemporary City Dynamics." Hartmann taught it at Sarah Lawrence. Most of my students were young black women. When they began their protests—turning over their lunch plates in the dining hall rather than eating—they were standing up against what they saw as the university's institutional racism and whites calling racism and riots "a black problem." The black students rightly contended it was really "a white problem." For the campus-wide community meeting with faculty, the black students asked me to be their faculty spokesperson.

I found the university environment stifling. Next, *Forbes* magazine, the "Capitalist Tool": What better place from which to view the world from the top down? Two years later, Margie and I were back in England, where I was *Forbes* European bureau chief. My left-wing friends could never understand why I wrote on finance and economics; my *Forbes* and *Financial World* and *Financial Times* friends, why I favored radical Catholicism. One of those journalists, Peter Jay, likened me to "a Venetian whore working both sides of the canal between God and Mammon." I countered I only *visited* Mammon's side; I lived on the other bank. Nonetheless, Jay's was an apt jibe, and not without merit later on. (In 1981, future *NCR* editor Tom Roberts wrote to Tom Fox applying for a Washington job. Fox told him *NCR* couldn't afford to pay enough to support a family there—*NCR* pay was pegged to Kansas City's much lower cost-of-living. Nonetheless, Fox invited me to take the Washington job. The quid pro quo was I'd also have to freelance.

That was fine because we cut a deal with me piggy-backing *NCR* stories in places around the country I was visiting for others, Fox and I working out what we most needed for *NCR*, and from where.)

In 1974, while I was still in England, *NCR* advertised a "Senior Editorial Position" was vacant. I flew out to Kansas City (at *Forbes'* expense—after meeting *NCR* publisher Donald Thorman, I flew on to Texas to do a *Forbes* story). In his letters, Adamo had always enthused about *NCR*, as had the *Kansas City Star*'s Jim Johnson during *Catholic Herald* visits, interludes from the Vatican council he was covering.

And so it was, with Margie and the children, Christine, Michael and Ian, still in Henley-on-Thames, that on Monday, January 5, 1975, I walked into 115 E. Armour Blvd., Kansas City, pushed the button and took the fabled-in-*NCR*-lore elevator to the third floor.

7

FINALLY, A REPORTER'S *REPORTER*

I was in early. So was Thorman. We had a quick chat. I went down-stairs.

Mrs. Jean Blake, my saving grace in so many ways, had persuaded Thorman that I must have a tea service for my morning "elevenses." That first morning, she told me in all seriousness that the first word in secretary was "secret," and that if I kept secrets from her, she couldn't function. I assured her she would know everything. In turn, I never wanted to hear any gossip, and I explained my daily "yellow pad" track-ing system so that phone calls, ideas, meetings and letter answering wouldn't get lost.

We agreed elevenses would be when I'd answer the readers' letters. We worked in perfect harmony for the next five years and remained close friends for four decades beyond that.

I met Terry Brock, running the *NCR*'s *Celebration*-cassettes-news-letters Division across the corridor on the same floor. He'd once been an executive editor under Thorman.

My immediate predecessor as executive editor, Fr. Jack Joyce, stopped by. I had no questions for him when he asked. He shifted around on his feet, made a particularly cutting remark about one mem-ber of the minimal staff before I'd even met the staff, wished me luck, and disappeared to talk to Thorman. The guard was changed.

Half an hour or so later, there were three more people in the news-room: Dawn Gibeau, Jane Peckham and Albert de Zutter, none appar-ently with secular journalism experience. I introduced myself to the

trio, rested my backside against a desk edge, and enthusiastically outlined my admittedly rudimentary plans for a rejuvenated newspaper so
enthusiastically that de Zutter later said he thought I was going to jump
up on the desk. De Zutter informed me that all decisions were made
collegially. I forcefully retorted that collegiality had to be earned. I
needed a measure of their capabilities first.

My unexpressed view, at that point, was the Catholic church in the
United States was obviously fracturing. There was little sense of
"church" as one church. I wanted to cover two areas where "church" as
"church" was standing up against state oppression. My twin focus was
Poland and Latin America.

I told the threesome I was not some big-time writer come to sop up
the money. I said I'd been hired at $22,000 a year, before taxes, a
considerable drop from my previous pay. With a staff of three, we'd
have to work hard and fast to turn the paper around and get some
important reporting done. My mantra was "faster, faster." They soon
realized I meant it.

Newsrooms are not big on dignity. I'd been at *NCR* about four
months when the staff made a formal presentation to me. It was a T-
shirt. There were two turtles copulating. The one on the bottom was
looking up at the one on top urging, "Faster, faster."

I admired them for doing that. I was all for going eyeball-to-eyeball
with editors. Newsrooms function best when an editor has a staff that
stands firm to argue its case.

(A future Washington bureau chief, Mark Winiarski, was furious
because his lead Washington stories were twice bumped off the front
page by "bare-assed babies and bishops"—it was June Carolyn Erlich's
El Salvador coverage of Archbishop Oscar Romero. I explained the
significance. Winiarski sent me a beautiful card. It was all stained-glass
church windows. The leaded panes spelled out, "Go [naughty word]
Thyself.")

I wanted a woman as second in command. Gibeau became managing
editor; de Zutter, national affairs writer. There was a part-timer in
Washington whom I'd not yet met. Peckham was Opinion Section coordinator; Desmond O'Grady (whom I'd also not yet met) was part-time
Rome correspondent.

Gibeau was a copy editor, and a good one. She had her moods and
quirks. She detested the gooey pop-sociology-speak entering the Catho-

lic lexicon. She cut out the word "needs" in felt and pasted it to her desk with the warning notice: "This is the only 'felt needs' in *NCR*."

Peckham was intelligent and imaginative. I tried her out as a reporter. After she wrote up her first meeting story, I commented, "I might as well have sent the bloody tape recorder." Then I showed her how to go about it and why. She was talented, quick on the uptake.

My intention as editor was to lure first-class reporters to Kansas City by telling them I wanted them for a minimum of two years, a maximum of three; after that, I'd either give them a bureau or help them get a job on a daily newspaper. I wanted the reporters to be so good my peer editors would try to hire them away from *NCR*.

I also believed in hiring interns. *NCR*'s first, a local nineteen-year-old French and music major, still in college, was Patty Edmonds. She later became the lead front-page writer for *USA Today*. She was typical—a sharp mind when she arrived, an even sharper journalist when she left.

In the second week of January 1975, we sprang into action again.

The *Sunday Times* in London was about to run a two-part series on the Vatican bank, formally known as the Institute for the Works of Religion. Topic: its scandalous involvement with Sicilian financier Michele Sindona.

I telephoned O'Grady in Rome and told him to get an interview with Vatican bank head Bishop Paul Marcinkus. O'Grady called back and said Marcinkus had refused. I told O'Grady to call Marcinkus again and tell him I was buying the North American rights to the *Sunday Times* articles and they could run either with or without any comment from him. Marcinkus knew the *Sunday Times* would not cast him in a favorable light over his connection to his sometimes-golfing-buddy Sindona. He agreed to the interview. I flew to Rome, budget be damned, and with O'Grady went to see Marcinkus.

We ran a four-part series. The larger point was that the readers realized the newspaper was waking up.

My byline had appeared in *NCR*. That had never been my original intent. I had no desire to be the front man for the publication—Thorman could do that, and he did it well. I wanted no part as a journalistic lay guru for the U.S. Catholic church.

In the next two years, my byline appeared four times, either because I was the only one to write the article or because I needed to handle as editor the topic identified. Other than on the masthead, I didn't want my name or face in the paper. I had no intention of giving talks or writing "Catholic" books. My economics book, *The Decline of Capital*, was about to be published. Later, I did deliberately write two sizeable pieces for the paper, frankly because I considered it an area where I could make a contribution. The first, on the economic Jesus, ran as a "Christ as Economist" series.

I believed what I should also provide for the readers was some way of bringing that series down to the everyday. My attempt was "Reassessing: A piety of possessions and relationships." I used the rosary as the format and made every bead the symbol of some essential possession or relationship.

Happily, my wife and children finally arrived from England.

We were spiritually centered in the Shalom Community in Kansas City, Kansas. Fr. Richard Wempe was a diocesan priest who'd established a full-time peace center in a storefront. Upstairs, it was a Catholic Worker house for men. The modest altar was made from railroad ties, three across and four for the pedestal. One Sunday, a mouse peeked out from the pedestal.

It was a modest community. The eucharistic wine was whatever was left over from hotel banquets—one of the members was a banquet manager. We wrote petitions, helped the men—my visiting-nurse wife checked their feet—and had picnics.

The liturgy was beautiful. It kept to the canon, but there were long spells for meditation.

Occasionally, there'd be visiting families with small children, at first rambunctious. If the visitors returned more than once, however, by the second and third time, the children had adjusted. They, too, almost regardless of age, were silent.

For us as a family, it was our anchor, our formation.

Under my editorship, *NCR* editorials were rare. I settled mainly for a form of commentary, called "Notebook," a mini-editorial positioning the paper—unless it had my byline on it.

Our Good Friday issue was *NCR*'s first "special." The entire issue dealt with hunger. The front page carried no words other than the masthead. There was the outline of the cross, and inside the frame, a child at the breast of a skeletal mother, an elderly woman, an emaciated man and a dying baby. It introduced the readers to writer Sidney Lens, who coordinated many future probing specials, from militarism to criminal justice. The latter dealt in America's predilection for incarcerating as many citizens as possible, preferably minorities. I hired a full-time labor writer, the energetic Steve Askin. With Askin and Lens, I'd moved the paper slightly further leftward.

The "Criminal Justice" special was triggered by an *NCR* article on Fr. Ronald Marston, chaplain at Rhode Island state prison, who refused to say Mass there because he would not accept restrictions placed on him by city officials. He insisted that in order for his ministry to be truly Christian, it must include advocacy for justice for the prisoners.

Some stories we ran defied belief. Kansas City Archbishop Ignatius Strecker denied that money was the issue when two children were expelled from a Catholic school for not selling enough tickets to the school play.

The news flowed in streams and swirled in eddies: Mexican-American Catholics picketed the 60 percent Latino Monterey, California, diocese to protest its failure to adequately serve their needs with Spanish Masses. Another headline: "Women in campus ministry once administrators, now program shapers." Henri Nouwen wrote on the movement "from loneliness to solitude." One headline warned about serious changes in the U.S. Catholic presence overseas: "U.S. missioners fewer; more put life on line."

Apart from a morning chat with Thorman and editing copy, I lived in the newsroom. Thorman and I found we liked one another and could work well together. He was comfortable with me because I understood his language—business, management imperatives, organization. (It may have been the reason he hired me.)

The continuing news flow included *NCR* commissioning Moises Sandoval to write a two-part series on the Spanish-speaking church and on national budget director (under Nixon and Ford) Roy L. Ash—who publicly worried on behalf of the administration that "if present trends continue the U.S. would be socialist by the year 2000." *NCR*'s Notebook said, "We're concerned because so many people (like Roy L. Ash) don't seem to know the difference between 'socialism' and 'democracy.'"

Sr. Shawn Copeland was asked to write a piece on black nuns. In the readers' letters section, Repartee, reader Glenda Barbre of Soquel, California, urged, "Open full ministry to women." Writer Mary Fay Bourgoin attended a service where there were five Episcopal women priests. To experience what the Episcopal women had experienced—looking out from the altar into the sea of faces—Bourgoin in her own parish became an acolyte. She wrote about sharing the altar with three priests and a nine-year-old altar boy. She could see her dentist in the congregation. "What should I do with my hands?" she wondered. "I could take a cue from the priest next to me and crack my knuckles."

On the women priests issue, Winiarski accomplished a magnificent first. In St. Paul's Chapel at the University of Wisconsin, Madison, he took four photographs for *NCR*'s front page that showed Episcopal priest Sr. Alla Bozarth-Campbell co-celebrating Mass with Catholic priest-assistant chaplain Fr. Thomas Coyle. The local bishop erupted like Vesuvius; the senior Catholic chaplain supported the bishop; Coyle apologized.

The *NCR* readers loved that front page: "A sign that the Spirit— which transcends our institutionalism—is alive and working in the hearts of men and women today," wrote Richard Boyd of Clinton, Iowa. "The pictures spoke quite artfully to the spirit and vitality of the contemporary church, and the singleness of purpose of the people of God will replace the division of labor currently determined by sex roles and man-made historical differences."

In the same issue, O'Grady in Rome quoted Dominican Sr. Catriona McLeod: "I doubt if the Pontifical Study on Women in Society and the Church will continue after its next meeting . . . it hasn't achieved anything but I hardly expected that it would." Still in 1975, de Zutter was at a Detroit meeting where the 1,200 attendees supporting women's ordination included priests, religious brothers and other males, while a few pages later, Hans Küng commented, "As a theologian I must repeat that there are no serious theological or scriptural obstacles to the ordination of women to the priesthood."

As with women, so increasingly for coverage of gays. The 1975 news year would close with the lifting of the two-year gag on Jesuit Fr. John McNeill that had been imposed for his writings on homosexuality. The Vatican had ordered his silence until experts could examine his writings.

The Vietnam War wound down. The Saigon baby airlift was underway. Sister of Charity Anne Darlene and the first planeload of orphans, all with legal papers, landed in Los Angeles. Catholic Relief Services (CRS) in Vietnam was preparing to feed an additional 500,000 more refugees daily, and Vietnamese bishops had pledged not to leave their dioceses. Soon *NCR* had an investigative reporter, our new Washington correspondent, Richard Rashke, probing CRS's earlier role supporting various U.S. military pacification projects in the Vietnamese country-side.

Tom Fox was back in America, working for the *Detroit Free Press*. I invited him to write for us.

We needed a brighter, more attractive newspaper with quality photographs, plenty of illustrations and editorial cartoons. Graphic art-ist Rollie Swanson was a joy. His illustrations deserve their own chapter in this book. (I also asked Henry Martin, the *New Yorker* cartoonist, if he'd cut *NCR* a deal—letting me choose from his *New Yorker* rejects. He agreed but nearly died when I told him he'd only get $25 per cartoon.) My friend Tennyson Schad was another New Yorker I invited to serve *NCR*. He was *Forbes* and *TIME* magazines' libel lawyer, and I asked him if he'd take *NCR* on as a permanent client, more or less pro bono. He cheerfully did so. To this day, his firm represents the news-paper.

NCR began using incisive cartoons by Paul Conrad and Tony Auth along with Hoyt's old standby, Jules Pfeiffer. Swanson did cartoons to order once I'd decided on what I wanted; for example, a cartoon of *L'Osservatore Romano* rolling off the Vatican presses with only the word "No" on its front page.

I pressed hard for first-class photographs and photo spreads. Photographers were sometimes rewarded more by the space we gave their photos than the money we paid them. Across two decades, Rick Reinhard in Washington became a key *NCR* photographer.

In January 1976, Thorman equivocated over his promise to name me editor after a year. He wanted to delay it "until later in the year." I said nothing. Three weeks later, I handed him a letter. It was a job offer from an East Coast publication offering me $40,000. I was promptly named *NCR* editor. I'd also negotiated that three weeks without pay be added to my three-week vacation so I could get the family out of the Midwest for a month or so each year. But I told Thorman I'd be gone within two years because he'd failed to deliver on his word to name me editor. (His son, Jim, a long-term *NCR* employee, smilingly told one interviewer, "Arthur Jones was always threatening to quit." Not quite always.)

The Thorman-Jones working relationship remained easy. We still liked one another.

To mark the 1976 U.S. bicentennial, *NCR* called all around the country asking folks what their birthday wish for America was. The staff dialed diner waitresses and politicians, bishops and women religious. They filled four pages with greetings. Arlo Guthrie sang his interview to Patty Edmonds. Dorothy Day had one word: "Repent."

The bishops' bicentennial program was six 1976 listening sessions around the country. Here's a snippet from *NCR* columnist Rick Casey at the final one on ethnicity and race:

> Three days and three parishes. The first day was held in urban Italian St. Lucy's (spaghetti supper in the parish cafeteria, complete with festive organist, reminiscent of an Italian wedding); the second at Queen of Angels in a deteriorating black section of Newark (fried chicken, sweet potatoes and greens) [and the third at Our Lady of the Lake Parish in suburban Verona]. Some 60 speakers presented the two dozen bishops, and about ten others on the panel, with a sort of post-Thanksgiving cornucopia of needs and demands. . . . The black Queen of Angels Parish the second day was equally homey, the testimony considerably angrier. Heated testimony was sometimes reinforced with "Amens."

Casey was a superb you-are-there writer and columnist. His article deserves to be read in full to appreciate how well it was written. The same could be said of Winiarski's coverage of an event that boded well for future evangelization but brought the Vatican hammer down.

In December 1976, Memphis Bishop Carroll Dozier after three months of diocesan-wide "indoctrination" (used in its purest sense as regards doctrine) attracted twelve thousand Catholics to the city stadium where, after a service, Dozier gave them a general absolution.

Dozier had followed all the norms. Then he had to face the storms.

Attendees knew they must go to confession within a year, and there were confessionals at the stadium. But the church-in-Rome wasn't about to tolerate forgiveness made easy. Jesus could forgive easily, but not the church-in-Rome. The Congregation for Divine Worship and the Discipline of the Sacraments attacked Dozier's act.

That attack generated more than 2,500 letters of support for Dozier from around the nation and the world. The bishop received literally thousands of telephone calls and hundreds of personal visits. Dozier had touched an important reconciliation button. The Vatican declared it a hot button, and the evangelization momentum was lost. *NCR* soon followed with a two-parter on evangelization—which I greatly cared about—but the damage was done. Forty years later, Catholic evangelization has dwindled down to a few plucky souls, primarily Paulist-centered.

Deserving of a reprint too was Edmond's reporting. She was the one who put the night earnings for a Filipina prostitute on her expenses. Writing in a sidebar about the "servicing of the fleet"—the U.S. presence in Subic Bay, the Philippines—Edmonds interviewed "Luz," a young prostitute who had almost completed her five years of civil-engineering studies. She was paying her way through her prostitution because two years earlier, she'd lost her job selling encyclopedias. "[She] starts at 8 p.m. each night in The Spider's Web, a dingy bar with a red-lit tinfoil ceiling and a papier-mâché spider lurking in a dusty web over one booth." A night with Luz cost $7, "but the next morning the man might leave a 'Thank you' (a tip)."

Step by step, through news and analysis, the newspaper expanded its coverage and critique.

There was a sharper edge to the writing than previously.

Apostolic delegate Archbishop Jean Jadot declared the policy of the Holy See (Paul VI) was to look for bishops who had a very wide and pastoral experience. I interviewed Jadot and wrote an editorial, "Jadot: Urbi et Orbi" (the title of the pope's annual address).

The senior Jadot-hating U.S. hierarchy (Cardinals John Carberry of St. Louis, John Krol of Philadelphia and John Cody of Chicago) were incensed.

Two years down the road, *NCR* was moving with greater certainty into covering the church-in-Rome's initial dithering over homosexuality and Catholic gays. *NCR* was strongly supportive of gay Catholics and highly critical of institutional reaction. Even so, it was new territory for newspaper pages. (I was learning, too. Not about the existence of homosexuality, but about the quality of my conversation concerning it. It wasn't keeping pace. I'd hired Bill Kenkellen as news editor and future San Francisco bureau man. He was gay but not yet fully publicly. One day I made an offhand remark—not about him. Deeply offended, he sharply rebuked me. He was correct to do so.)

The headlines included Jesuit Fr. Avery Dulles saying church reform was at a standstill. In Rhodesia (Zimbabwe), courageous Bishop
Donal Lamont took a stand that pitted the church against the terror
reign of Ian Smith's white supremacist government.

I welcomed Fox's freelance coverage of a six-day North-South liberation theology conference in Detroit. However, by this point in my
editorship, I'd become quite aware of something else. I was an
American (by citizenship) and a Catholic. Yet I realized, and believe it
still holds true today, that *NCR*'s uniqueness requires it be edited by an
"American Catholic," by someone who has grown up breathing the
same Catholic vapors as the readership and wider audience. I was an
America observer. Not so bad at it, and a church-in-Rome "Leveller,"
and I loved it. (Levellers were seventeenth-century Christian and social
radicals.) But it still wasn't the same as having an American-born-and-
raised Hoyt, Thorman, Fox, Tom Roberts, Pam Schaeffer, Joe Feuerherd or Dennis Coday at the helm.

Back to the news. Josephite Fr. John J. Tyne concluded a tour of
U.S. cities. He wrote the Catholic church was the only U.S. institution
that could speak to the rising black-white tensions because "it was the
only one with a presence in both communities, and because of its pro-
nouncements. But the Catholic Church, too, looks as if it is ready to
leave the cities." For the rising number of Latino Catholics, a continuing and serious complaint was the lack of Spanish-speaking priests; a
minor complaint, the high cost of funerals. Latin America was still on
my coverage horizon.

June Carolyn Erlick was still covering Central America for us. Many
of the women writers and columnists *NCR* had were journalists Gibeau
knew through a women-in-communications organization. When Gibeau
mentioned a Penny Lernoux, who was living in Colombia, I immediately contacted her.

Lernoux, a graduate of the University of Southern California, was
freelancing for *Business Week* and *Newsweek* while completing her
soon-to-be-famed *Cry of the People* on the church and human rights in
Latin America. Courageous and industrious, Lernoux's reporting and
assessments penetrated their subjects like gimlets, deep into the meat
of the topic. Her books mightily offended the comfortable, whether
clerics, cardinals, bankers or political leaders.

Peter Hebblethwaite succeeded O'Grady in Rome and became *NCR*'s first full-time, in situ, Vatican correspondent. He was a former Jesuit and editor of the British Jesuit journal the *Month*. However, Hebblethwaite's initial *NCR* assignment had come earlier. I wanted Poland covered; he reported from Poland and other parts of Central and Eastern Europe. Hebblethwaite was an excellent English reporter of the essayist mode. (One reader suggested Hebblethwaite limit himself to writing editorials "because that's what his reports are.")

The newspaper generated more of its own news through an expanding network. *NCR* selected college kids situated in places where they had access to two or three different city dailies in their college libraries. They were paid $5 for calling in anything "Catholic," $10 if it was used. If the item needed development, the student would do it, and we'd have another novice reporter out there. A young fellow at Ohio Wesleyan, Jim Michaels (son of a *Forbes* editor), later served as our Southern correspondent. He became *NCR* Washington bureau chief and for decades since has written for *USA Today*.

Other reporters began calling in with story ideas. Terry Malone from the *Advocate*, the Newark archdiocesan paper, asked if she could write about Franciscan Fr. DePaul Genska, who had begun a ministry to prostitutes in New York. He wanted prostitution decriminalized. I said yes, provided she asked him how he handled his own celibate sexuality—was he getting some sexual kick out of it? Genska admitted to Malone, "Some of these women are beautiful, no question about it. I can't say I've never had a fantasy. But the Lord's been good."

The women religious were always on the front line, lined up on the Vatican's firing line, or both. Sister of St. Joseph of Carondolet Ann Gabriel Marciac and three other counseling center workers were indicted for aiding "illegal aliens." Never a word of support from the U.S. bishops or Rome.

The news drumbeat rarely faltered. We never played a customer's game. If the reporting cost us an advertiser here or there, so be it. Nor was *NCR* kissy-kissy toward those it admired.

When the paper did an eight-page Küng retrospective—and we admired him—Patricia Lefevere opened it by asking Küng,

> Why is it that Edward Schillebeeckx told an interviewer that Küng once jokingly said, "70 to 80 percent of his books are written by his

students"? I handed the article to Küng who momentarily seems to have shed some of his summer color. He reads it . . . on his feet now he stammers: "I am disgusted . . ." Suddenly, however, his adrenalin begins to circulate German through his system: "Herr Kuschel, Herr Kuschel, kommen sie hierher bitte . . ." Sounds of Sturm and Drang pollute the air. A theological dogfight is underway. In English Kung said, "I never said any such thing. Even if it were true I would not be so stupid as to say it."

The retrospective's assessments of Küng were written by Yale's Jaroslav Pelikan, St. Michael's College's Harry McSorley, Avery Dulles, Outler and Chicago Divinity School's Joseph Sitler.

It was at this point, on November 30, 1977, that publisher Donald J. Thorman died. He was only 52. I wrote an appreciation, excerpted below.

He slid the letter across his desk and said in his deepest, now-we're-in-trouble-again tones, "You'd better read this." He was so solemn about the letter it was obvious he was pleased by it.

He leaned back in his huge, black chair—it had to be huge, he was a giant of a man. As a diversionary tactic he had the habit of picking at his teeth with his thumbnail—even if there wasn't anything to pick at. He did this then, his eyes trying not to reveal how much he was enjoying the scene.

This was just ten days before his death. The letter was from Father Hans Küng and, for Don Thorman, it became a treasured possession in the week-and-a-half he had left. "Dear Don," wrote the Swiss theologian, "this is not a letter to the editor or to the publisher, but a private letter of gratitude. It is certainly a very special honour to be presented in the *NCR* in such an extraordinary way. I am sure that such an issue will help Catholic theology in general, but will of course also help my own theology to be understood better . . . I also found it correct that you published a very critical article. I shall have the opportunity in the next few weeks to study all the articles very carefully in order to make 'an examination of conscience' for a confession on my 50th birthday next March!"

To Don Thorman, the letter signaled more than just a successful issue of *NCR*, however, it was a bold next step in seeing the newspaper report on the major figures, and major thinking. He saw it, too, as a good and decent response to the newsroom's determination to take the issues to the people.

For weeks, as Jones and the news team had pulled the Küng material together, an eager Thorman was constantly asking when it would appear. He was drafting and re-drafting his own thoughts for a column in the same issue. For "DJT"—as he was known around the old redbrick—the column signed "Finis" to his own writings:

"Most of us who still believe in the institution (the church), its ultimate values, and our spiritual heritage must learn to make do. We don't have enough time left in our lives to wait for the theologians and the official magisterial forces to work out a modus vivendi. The 'now' we live in demands that we live as best we can, making our own decisions based on the best information available to us and the formation of our own consciences."

Thorman had engineered *NCR*'s moves into other fields as hoped-for profitable ventures to help sustain the newspaper and allow it to grow. These included the *Celebration* liturgical service, newsletters and cassettes. The diversification worked, sufficiently so that the newspaper was able to continue, then to finally begin to move slowly toward the black ink and a reviving circulation [that would reach just under 50,000—its final peak—in the 1980s].

The diversification grew into a major division of its own, the Media Department, connected to the newspaper only by the common umbrella of the National Catholic Reporter Publishing Co., Inc. His death was a tremendous blow to his family and *NCR*, but his passing also meant a "connector" had been pulled like a thread removed from a tapestry woven of Catholic liberals and progressives.

Don Thorman would be pleased we didn't knock all the news off the front page to announce his death. And he'd be miffed by the number of typos in this issue.

He was a good man.

In the 1976–1977 period, Thorman traveled more. Occasionally when he and I chatted, he worried what might happen to *NCR* if he died in a plane crash. Time and again, he'd warned me there were Catholic consultants, predators, quick to skim the bit of cream off small businesses like *NCR*. I provided a solution. I suggested he write a letter naming me publisher/CEO in the event of his death and give it to board chairman Frank Brennan. Simultaneously, I'd write a letter of resignation, undated, for Brennan. Nothing could happen until the board was able to decide on a successor. Thorman was at ease.

When he died that November, I was automatically editor and publisher. I told the hastily called board meeting I wouldn't let the paper down. I'd stay long enough to bring in an editor and publisher and then be gone. The process took two years.

Newspapers need a public face. Now it had to be mine. My face appeared, but I fooled around with my teacup in the photographs. If the readers were looking for gravitas, they wouldn't get it from me. I wrote a column. I disliked being center stage, but I knew how to entertain an audience.

In the 1970s, opinion editor Kenneth Guentert brought first-class writers and themes to the newspaper. When *The Road Less Traveled* by M. Scott Peck was published, *NCR* was one of only two papers to review it in the book's first six months. For its next 7 million copies, the book carried on the front cover a quote by the *Washington Post*'s Phyllis Theroux and on the rear cover a quote from psychiatrist Gerald May's review in *NCR*. It didn't seem to do anything to increase our circulation, though.

By now the paper was covering and applauding each step in the women's ordination movement. In a 1978 Notebook, almost four decades ago now, *NCR* formally endorsed women's ordination.

> Ordination of women is a matter of justice. . . .
>
> The male-only rule . . . excludes a whole category of human beings from ordination.
>
> Here the church rule is a close kin to racism, no different really than a rule which would exclude blacks or people with red hair from ordination.
>
> It does not matter if women would make better priests than men—or worse.
>
> It does not matter if women would make the priesthood more clerical—or less.
>
> It does not matter if women would make the priesthood more cultic—or less.
>
> It does not matter if women would make the priesthood more pastoral—or less.
>
> It does not matter whether ordaining women would solve the priest shortage—or create new and worse problems.
>
> What matters is justice. And Catholic women are not getting it.

For women, women's ordination and other reasons, 1978—and not necessarily for the better—would be the most significant in global Catholic history since the year the Second Vatican Council opened. It was the year of three popes: Paul VI, John Paul I, John Paul II. Pope Paul died. Excellent analysis from *NCR*, but somehow the front-page headline dropped off at the printers.

The patriarchate of Venice, a small but prestigious post, had now given the church three popes in one century, for it now gave the church Albino Luciani as Pope John Paul I. The other "pro tem" Venetian patriarchs (all born elsewhere) were Pius X (1903–1914) and John XXIII (1958–1963). John Paul I was a simple man, a pastor with a merry spirit, a writer and the choice of the elderly Vatican II cardinals who wanted their council back.

Hebblethwaite, Fox (for the *Detroit Free Press*) and I covered the conclave. Hebblethwaite immediately spotted the Vatican Curia's games when *L'Osservatore Romano* offered Luciani up as a conservative. He wasn't. But it scarcely mattered, for thirty-three days later, John Paul I was dead.

John Paul I was not murdered, but a charge of negligent homicide could have been leveled against those Vatican officials who failed to ensure that his basic medicinal regimen was maintained in his shift from Venice to Rome. (See John Cornwell's book *A Thief in the Night*.)

In 1978, Polish cardinal Karol Wojtyla, unknown outside the Vatican, quite well-known to some conservatives within it, including Joseph Ratzinger, was elected and given the benefit of the doubt by Vatican II cardinals willing to give an outsider non-Italian his chance. Enter Pope John Paul II.

I warned the readers an autocrat was en route: no annulments, no laicization. A "no" pope. I wanted to give him some benefit of the doubt, so I omitted my other cautions in the final draft.

Part of my mid-to-late teenage years were spent with émigré Polish intellectual Catholics. They were part of the parish I attended. They were fun, gregarious, openhearted, intelligent, caring and intellectually rigid. Their formation, like Wojtyla's, was nineteenth-century.

John Paul II's autocratic style inside the church was his pedagogical experience as a student and professor.

Asked to summarize John Paul II's pontificate's effect on the church, I'd turn to Belloc's frequent reference to "Mother Rome" and note that under Wojtyla, "Mother Rome" was closer to the "Mother Ireland" of John Boyle O'Reilly and James Joyce: "A fruitful mother of genius, but a barren nurse," "an old sow that eats her farrow." The Wojtyla era attempted to turn back the Vatican II church, and it came very close to succeeding.

The public John Paul was a fascinating and admirable character. His public courage—indeed, audacity—was, at times, very refreshing. (I found particularly endearing the fact that he died broke. A pope is paid a lump sum of an unrevealed amount once a year. John Paul had nothing of material value to mention in his will.)

Inside the institution? He was its monarch. It came as no surprise that his first action, seventeen days after being elected, was a flexing of his monarchical power.

The 1953-founded Shrine of Our Lady of Czestochowa in Doylestown, Pennsylvania, brainchild of the Polish Pauline Fathers, was in trouble. The cause—at a minimum—was mismanagement and $7.9 million in debts. *NCR* bought reprint rights to the Gannett News Service series on the Pauline Fathers.

The shrine's bondholders were demanding their money. Philadelphia's Cardinal John Krol had $720,000 tied up in the project and had persuaded some powerful Pennsylvanians to buy the bonds. The SEC was investigating. The Paulines were refusing to cooperate.

By the time Wojtyla was elected in 1978, the Vatican "visitators," winding up a five-year investigation by Fr. Paul M. Boyle of Chicago and Bishop George Guilfoyle of Camden, New Jersey, had completed their report. Its twenty-five recommendations concerned finances, religious life at the Pauline shrine and disciplinary action against certain monks. Pauline Fr. Michael Zembrzuski, who'd founded and headed the U.S. order, topped the list of those recommended for dismissal.

Two-and-a-half weeks after being elected, John Paul II summarily placed the shrine under the patronage of Poland's Cardinal Stefan Wyszynski, ignored the Boyle and Guilfoyle's recommendations, reappointed the ousted, and declared the matter closed.

This was the new pope.

Wojtyla's abrupt assumption of papal power and the wielding of it, despite what anyone else said or recommended, stamped his papacy. A Vatican quilt was quickly spread over the entire Doylestown affair to muffle it, a comforter undoubtedly hand-stitched to order by the Vatican bank and Krol.

The pope's first full year, 1979, belongs to him, to Mercy Sr. Theresa Kane, to Mary Fay Bourgoin, to Penny Lernoux and to Peter Hebblethwaite.

John Paul II first visited the United States as pope in October 1979.

My favorite papal visit story concerns the photographer I'd assigned to get a first-class close-up of the pope. I told the photographer I wanted him so close, I'd be able see in the photograph the follicles in the pope's nose. On the relevant day, the photographer called me. "I got it, Arthur. I got it. I had to go to Communion three times, but I got it." He was Jewish.

The pope's visit was a triumph—unless one was a Catholic woman or wanted Communion in the hand from the pope. John Paul was—throughout his pontificate—a wizard at conjuring up enthusiasm in enormous crowds. He was always the young priest-playwright from Wadowice either on stage or mixing with his students, but playing to an audience on a grander scale than previously witnessed.

A fresh element in papal-lay relations came to the fore in the Basilica of the National Shrine of the Immaculate Conception in Washington, DC. For the first time in public, a pope was asked to ordain women.

Kane, president of the Leadership Conference of Women Religious (LCWR), asked the pope that women be included in "all the church's ministries." The fallout unfolded in the predictable pattern. The curial hierarchs were horrified at Kane's *lèse majesté* (a social gaffe, violating "majesty"), and if the Vatican's Congregation for the Doctrine of the Faith keeps a hit list, Kane and LCWR are still on it thirty-five years later. All she had said—all she had needed to say, in fact—was this:

> As women, we have heard the powerful messages of our church addressing the dignity and reverence for all persons. As women, we have pondered these words. Our contemplation leads us to state that the church in its struggle to be faithful to its call for reverence and dignity for all persons must respond by providing the possibility of women as persons being included in all ministries of our church. I urge you, Your Holiness, to be open to and respond to the voices coming from the women of this country who are desirous of serving in and through the church as fully participating members.

Catholic women who saw, as Kane did, a need for women in all the church's ministries applauded the plucky nun. Pro or con, everyone, or so it seemed, wrote to *NCR*. The headlines over the letters included "Kane shamed us," "Kane: Disown her, or clone her?" "Theresa Kane wins support, but not in Rome."

Behind the church screen, Hebblethwaite reported, when the pope addressed 350 U.S. bishops, he "revealed clearly for the first time what the strategy of his pontificate will be. It will be collegially conservative, socially progressive and doctrinally restorationist." Hebblethwaite was right on the mark. He was present again a year later when once more John Paul was told, this time in Germany in November 1980, that the institution totally misunderstood Catholic women.

"Young people have the feeling," declared Barbara Engl, president of the Munich Association of Catholic Youth,

> that the church is more interested in divisions with the evangelicals than in what brings us together. Young people find that their concerns for friendship, sexuality and partnership receive only negative answers. Many young people cannot understand why the church should insist so strongly on celibacy for its priests when there is a manifest lack of priests and a lack of young chaplains in the universities and high schools.

Engl continued, "Nor can young people understand why a greater sharing of women in the ministry of the church should be ruled out. We know perfectly well that the Gospel challenges us, but we do not feel oppressed by neuroses and a lack of courage since Christ has promised us the fullness of life." If the pope had an answer, it did not come. The slightly pained expression on his face differed little from that expression seen year after year when, leaning on his silver evangelist's cross, head down, eyes closed, he was shuttered to the world in his own private pondering.

Elsewhere in the paper, a fine photograph showed Cesar Chavez autographing a supporter's coat during a strike.

Headlines noted that Msgr. Reynold Hillenbrand, the father of Young Christian Workers in the United States, had died. A Philadelphia pastor was fired for "being obnoxious"—the result of an anonymous parish complainant, name never revealed. Peter Steinfels's magisterial *The Neoconservatives: The Men Who Are Changing America's Politics* was reviewed. "Hispanic ex-seminarian says bias drove him out" referred to a story about St. Patrick's Seminary in Menlo Park, California.

The actual U.S. seminaries story *NCR* investigated was far larger.

Two Latino seminarians telephoned from San Antonio to ask if I'd see them. Of course.

A day or so later, after changes of buses, they arrived in Kansas City. They were pleasant young men with a sound complaint: "It's bad enough being a Latino in the seminary, but we're expected to be gay too." The result was Mary Fay Bourgoin's probing, wittily written, frank, four-part "Saturday Night in the Seminary" series.

The howls from the offended were loud and prolonged. The series generated more letters and columns, more angst, admiration and condemnation than space here can even suggest. The letters pages were filled week after week. Bourgoin had struck a raw nerve in the same manner Robert Hoyt's *NCR* had with the very first *NCR* article questioning celibacy.

Otherwise, upbeat stories abounded: "Church music thrives in Chicago," under Richard Proulx; "It's not chauvinistic to note U.S. growth in biblical studies"; "Toward a genderless God"; "The rise of the ministerial church." And, always, the downbeat: "John Paul urges brakes on annulment process" (a short time later, it was the laicization process).

But my time as editor was ending. Certain appointments still needed to be made.

In 1979, I'd turned over some marketing and administrative duties to Jason Petosa. From *Forbes*, I brought in recently retired marketing manager Bill Klein as a two-month consultant. His sole role was to work with Petosa and tell me whether Petosa had what it took to run the publishing company. Decision: yes. The board accepted my recommendation.

Thorman could be at peace. No one would steal the money.

The *NCR* masthead was almost filled, but the newspaper needed an on-target satirist.

One cannot advertise for such.

In 1978, I'd received a telephone call or a letter, I can't recall which, from a Michael Farrell in Los Angeles (not the *M*A*S*H* actor; that's another *NCR* story). He offered to write for *NCR*. We talked more—we mutually enjoyed the banter. I sent him a book to review. The review came back terse, tight and entertaining. During the next eighteen months, we frequently chatted, and I assigned him to a few articles. In 1979, Kenneth Guentert, editor of the Opinion and Feature Section, sometimes referred to as the Magazine Section, signaled he wanted to leave. I spent more time on the phone with Farrell. The moment we placed the ad for Guentert's successor, I asked Farrell to apply. *NCR* had its Jonathan Swift.

Next, *NCR* needed a new editor.

The position was widely advertised. The board reported that two good possibilities were chosen—a West Coast newspaper editor and an East Coast national daily editor. The board asked each candidate to provide an analysis of the newspaper.

The East Coast journalist, an editor at the *Washington Star*, regarded 1979 as "*NCR*'s finest hour. Your coverage of the year of three popes; your analysis of Pope John Paul's visit; your reprinting of the Pauline Fathers scandal; your timely coverage of Fathers Küng, Schillebeeckx, Pohier, Curran, Rahner and Metz; your controversial 'Saturday Night at the Seminary'; and many other stories provided insight and an opportunity for thoughtful discussion and useful controversy." He called the lead reporters, writers and columnists

> solid and prolific. From the beginning, however, *NCR* has faced the credibility charge, an inherent problem for your kind of publication. For example, the October 19 papal trip analysis—I have heard several comments about not being able to find anything good said about the pope . . . journalistically *NCR* must be a forum for many viewpoints.
>
> You asked for an analysis of *NCR*'s role in church and society. [It] is to present these issues, these controversies and trends to its readers. To interpret, to explain, to analyze them. To provide a forum for discussion. To lead. To sort things out, to make sense of confusing developments, to help Catholics cope. To ask openly the questions we wonder about privately.

There was more: about journalism, about prayer, spirituality, meditation and closeness with God.

But the point is, he got the job. The newspaper's circulation had been moving up, from 31,000 in 1974 when I was appointed to 36,000-plus the month I was leaving. That trajectory continued, nudging almost 50,000 under Tom Fox before starting an inexorable decline as the readership aged, people left the church and online reading became the mode du jour.

Fox had outlined to the board his editorship for the next seventeen years.

The masthead was filled: publisher; four editors; three full-time bureaus (Rome, Washington and the West Coast); one staff writer; a special reports writer; correspondents in Latin America, Central America, Europe, the American South and the American Southwest; and a labor correspondent. Six regular columnists and Jean Blake, assistant to the president.

It was time to go.

I was happy to do so—provided I could keep the *NCR* connection. It was the prophetic witnesses whose lives *NCR* followed and the people whose lives those prophetic witnesses devoted their lives to who kept me on track to becoming a Christian.

Why else stay connected? *NCR* was still the best game in town for a Catholic journalist. Everything is seen through the Gospel-justice prism.

My alternatives were several. But I was hooked to *NCR*, and England beckoned.

We bought a 1950 Grumman-bodied Taystee Bread truck with 300,000 miles on the engine. The Shalom Community, which included Tom Fox and his family, helped us pack up. Anything we couldn't pack, we sold. (My son Mike had to sell his huge collection of X-Men and Spider-Man comic books, for which he has never really forgiven me, though he's sweet about it.) Then off we drove to Calumet Harbor, Michigan, to deliver the truck and contents to the shipping company— to be collected later at the Liverpool docks.

And away we flew.

I became *NCR*'s diplomatic correspondent. Time to look at governments from the top down.

"Diplomatic correspondent?" My brother Roy roared with laughter.

"Diplomatic?" he quipped. "You're not even bloody tactful!"

8

1980: TOM FOX

Tom Fox's five years in Vietnam during the Vietnam War left deep scars.

"For years, I felt alienated from our country and its symbols," he said.

> Our children knew that when we attended a sports game or something, I would not stand for the national anthem. I just couldn't. I associated the American flag with the flags I saw painted beneath the wings of the jets that were bombing so many Vietnamese right there in the area in which I was working. But fate plays tricks. My daughter, Catherine, became a better and better and faster swimmer. Eventually she made the U.S. national team, and she was swimming in red, white and blue uniforms that had the effect of turning her into a U.S. flag! Slowly, I acceded to reality. My daughter and her representation of the United States in the Olympics played a strong part in bringing me back a kind of national pride I had lost for many, many years.

He joined *NCR* "still strongly critical of many U.S. policies." One antidote? "I return to Vietnam anytime I can. My wife and I have arranged to take groups back to Vietnam (some 150 people so far), building better ties and understanding between people and nations."

If he was under no illusions about U.S. involvement, he's under none concerning the current Vietnam, either.

"The people of Vietnam today have many problems. Their government is corrupt and they know it. It is not communism; it is crony capitalism. But at least the Vietnamese run their own nation, which is unfortunately being sucked into the whole Western materialistic agenda."

Fox didn't have to be in Vietnam. He had volunteered as a civilian to work with war-displaced refugees. U.S. officials and military officers slept in compounds surrounded by walls and wire and protected by guards. Fox lived with a Filipino volunteer in Tuy Hoa, a provincial coastal town in central Vietnam. It was attacked by the Viet Cong and North Vietnamese army several times during those years.

> War was raging around us, especially at night, and it was impossible to measure how safe we were. Some of the scariest nights of my life were those when the Viet Cong tried to take the city. One night, a mortar shell came through the roof and exploded. My leg got hit. I was a 22-year-old in the middle of nowhere.

> *March 1, 1968*:
> Dear Mr. Hoyt:
> As has been the case since I arrived in this country there are many uncertainties that might make it difficult for me to reply to your letter as you might like. Let me make a try at it however . . . I cannot get a deferment for writing—even from Vietnam. My organization [Fox was a noncombatant with International Voluntary Services (IVS), assisting refugees] will notify my draft board I am no longing working for IVS. Within a month I will probably be (gulp!) drafted. Sometime this week I am filing for CO [conscientious objector] papers. I will object to this war on Christian principles and I do not expect my appeal to go through. Thus, during the coming weeks I will be engaging in some very delicate affairs which eventually could mean as a much as a five-year prison sentence—as I will not enter the Armed Services. It may be necessary to return to the United States on a very short notice. As I will fight my draft in the courts I cannot afford to be delinquent . . . With this in mind I ask you for accreditation for a period between one and three months.

March 3, 1968:

Dear Mr. Hoyt:

. . . I was thinking of trying to get an interview with General Vinh Loc, the II Corps Commander who was just released from his post. He has long been unpopular in American circles here . . . he might be upset enough about his release to talk.

March 7, 1968:

Dear Mr. Hoyt:

. . . The Viet Cong attacked Tuy Hoa yesterday. From what I hear there was a great deal of destruction. I might try . . .

Hoyt's 1968–1971 correspondence with Fox is equaling compelling as the two worked out what was possible: Fox saying he could live on $7 a day including expenses; Hoyt gaining him accreditation and trying to arrange health insurance ("and a little life insurance if you can afford it"). Hoyt turned Fox's stilted prose into sharp news reports as the twenty-seven year old served a long-distance reporter's apprenticeship. Hoyt's final letter to him in Vietnam begins,

April 23, 1971:

Dear Tom:

Sorry not to have acknowledged your "bloodbath" story sooner. I have a good excuse this time. I was in jail in Washington for a week after it arrived. [Hoyt and other peace protesters were arrested in Lafayette Park, opposite the White House while expressing their opposition to the war.]

In 2013, Fox said he'd just finished reading *Kill Anything That Moves*.

It was a frightful exercise. Until 1968, almost all the reporting in Vietnam was centered on the military, the fights here and there. We were the first national newspaper to regularly write about the impact the war was having on the Vietnamese people. Only after Tet and the balloon popped did reporters begin to think about the way the war was affecting the people. By then, *NCR* was two years ahead of the game! Between 1965 and 1968, most papers would not print articles that seriously questioned the direction of the war. *NCR* was an exception. I know this because I also filed for Dispatch News Service, and we could only get into four or five other papers in the U.S.

Fox's family is Asian American. Fox himself is American Asian. The twin poles of Tom Fox's life are Asia (particularly the Mekong Delta countryside birthplace of his wife, Kim Hoa) and the Milwaukee Catholic world of his family and Marquette University High School (graduated 1962). He turned twenty-one the year the Second Vatican Council ended.

Vietnam and Catholic Milwaukee are also the poles of his spiritual life. The Foxes' rear garden in Roeland Park, Kansas, is a Christian-Buddhist center for reflection, its plantings a mix of both worlds. Its Mary grottos, Buddha and Quan Am statues and stonework and gardens provide a haven for mind and body. Introspective, sometimes intense, outwardly calm, Fox needs those gardens, nurtured by his wife.

Thomas Charles Fox was born in Milwaukee, the third of six children. At Marquette University High School, he played halfback on the football team and pitched and played center field on the baseball team. He might have had a career in either sport. He was an All-State and All-American football player who had scholarship offers from more than twenty schools, including Stanford University, Dartmouth College, the Naval Academy and the University of Notre Dame.

In baseball, his senior-year team won the state championship. Two major-league teams tried to woo him into their minor-league systems. He took the football scholarship, he said, because it would get him into a good college. (In the *NCR* newsroom, his famed pitching arm was the occasional butt of jokes.)

Fox's father, Clement, was a neuroanatomist at Marquette University medical school and later headed the Anatomy Department at Wayne State University in Detroit. He was a bright scientist and a *Commonweal*-reading Catholic, a man of strong opinions. Tom grew up in a home where it was common to have visiting scientists, including a Nobel Prize winner, at the dinner table, discussing cellular relationships in the cerebellum. Tom describes his father as "pretty eccentric—someone who, with the admonition 'If you lose your faith, you never had one to begin with,' encouraged his children to go to the best colleges they could, Catholic or not. My mother, Alice, was Polish and pious, the heart and soul of the family. We had a strong, well-knit Catholic identity."

Older brother Jim, an anthropologist who lives and teaches in Canberra, Australia, and travels to the outer islands of Indonesia for continued scholarship, went to Harvard and was a Rhodes scholar. "I was coming up in my brother's shadow as an athlete and trying to find my own identity," Fox said. The other siblings are Betty, Mary, Bob and Ginny, who has special needs and lives in a Minnesota group home. Fox decided on Stanford in part because of the climate and setting, but also because Stanford at the time seemed to balance sports with academic excellence. Indeed, it encouraged its freshman football players to apply for academic scholarships.

At Stanford, he found himself drawn to the thinking of the dean of freshmen, Dwight Clark, a Quaker and a pacifist. "At that time, I was a Catholic who believed, I thought, in just war." But he was soon learning more about nonviolence and he started reading Thomas Merton. It was a time when a young Joan Baez would show up in the dorm to sing folk songs. She eventually married David Harris, an anti–Vietnam War activist and Fox's classmate and friend.

The summer after his freshman year, Fox was one of twenty students Clark invited to visit Asia as volunteers. It was the inaugural group of an organization, now fifty years old, called Volunteers in Asia, or VIA. Fox approached the Stanford football coach to ask if he could go. The coach said no, that he'd come back too out of shape to play football. The sophomore-to-be decided for Asia, ending his football career. Before summer ended, however, he received an academic scholarship.

The nineteen-year-old visited several Japanese cities, toured Buddhist temples and spent time in Hiroshima. He went to Taiwan and then Hong Kong, where he worked in Kowloon, teaching English to young children, the sons and daughters of recent Chinese refugees from the mainland. He also laid cement for a tuberculosis sanatorium. "That was very, very physical work," he said. "That trip was probably the bug that started to get me interested in Asia."

Back at school, he concentrated on his coursework, including history and the classics. He was also active in Stanford's Newman Club, the gathering place for young Catholics. He was club president his senior year, growing more aware of and "more outraged by the events of the times." In the break between sophomore and junior years, he wanted to go with a Stanford group to Selma, Alabama, to register voters.

"My parents were just frightened and dead set against me going into the South," he said, "and because they knew I was planning a junior year in France, they proposed my going to Quebec to study French as an alternative."

He agreed.

Fox was in France at the Stanford-in-France campus when he recalls reading in *Le Monde* that U.S. airplanes had bombed Haiphong in l'Indochine. "I was just appalled. But first I had to figure out exactly where 'l'Indochine' was, to begin with." When Fox was back in the United States in 1964–1965, the University of California, Berkeley and Stanford, was the focus of the earliest Vietnam "teach-ins" and antiwar protests, and Fox was becoming increasingly more involved with them.

Throughout these years, he'd assumed he'd be a high school or community college history teacher. Then, in his senior year, the Peace Corps accepted him to teach English in Thailand, and International Volunteer Services, an organization started by the traditional peace churches, accepted him to work with war refugees in Vietnam.

"Even before our graduation ceremony, I was off to Vietnam," he recalled. Upon learning that Fox was headed to Vietnam, Michael Novak, then a Stanford theology professor, suggested he contact *NCR* editor Hoyt. Hoyt asked Fox to be the paper's Vietnam correspondent.

International Volunteer Services flew Fox and other volunteers to Saigon for a month of intensive Vietnamese language training in Saigon, then Fox was sent to Tuy Hoa in central Vietnam, a coastal provincial capital, where large camps of displaced Vietnamese, sometimes up to forty thousand, were trying to make it through the war.

"They were peasant farmers living in corrugated huts on sand along the coast because their villages had been destroyed and no one would or could take them in. Farmers living on sand," he said. "They weren't allowed to enter the town. It was mainly older women and children. The men were mostly away, fighting for one side or the other. In theory, they were supposed to get aid from the government for six months and be resettled. But they seldom received any aid." Many of the young women eventually migrated to the edges of the nearby U.S. Air Force base, selling themselves to support their families.

Fox said he rounded up rolls of cloth and once scrounged eight sewing machines so the girls could learn to sew and avoid falling into prostitution. At one point, he found conical-hat makers who could teach the young girls how to make the traditional Vietnamese straw hats so they would have something to sell, some means to earn money. At the same time, working with a Korean medical team, he walked through nearby villages trying to identify children who needed cleft lip operations.

"In America, we're hidden from life, hidden from birth, hidden from death," he said. "In Vietnam, everything was immediate and real. So clear. So in your face. Ugly death up close. I was at the hospital helping with births. Burying children. Begging for food. Trying to do something to help the people. There was so much disease and crowding. They looked to me as if I had power, and I had so very little to give. In the end, I was just a witness."

He began writing to the U.S. Senate Refugee Committee to counter the official line that the Vietnam War was going well. At that time, the American media was saying, "Yeah, pacification is working." Fox was writing in *NCR* that it wasn't.

"Ted Kennedy headed the Senate subcommittee on refugee affairs and came to Vietnam for an inspection tour. He asked if he could have dinner with me. I flew down to Saigon, I think just before the Tet offensive."

Two years later, in 1968, when Fox returned to America for a graduate degree in Southeast Asian studies at Yale, he was still eligible for the draft. He was called in by his draft board, and he told them he was opposed to the war and would refuse to serve. The draft board's standard line with objectors, he said, was "a) you don't understand the situation, b) you're a coward and afraid to go, and c) you're avoiding service to your country." Said Fox, "I knew more about the situation than they did, and I told them I was willing to go back to Vietnam, just not in uniform." He got the deferment.

Back in the United States, he accompanied religious and congressional delegations to Vietnam. During one, he met Jesuit Fr. Robert Drinan, soon to be elected to Congress. The two became fast friends. At one point, Fox made arrangements for Drinan to celebrate Mass at a side altar in the cathedral in Saigon, where Fox served as his altar server. On another delegation, he met Sam Brown, who had helped organize the October 1969 nationwide antiwar moratorium vigils that drew hundreds of thousands of demonstrators to Washington, DC, where they called for an end to the war. In Saigon the next year, Brown asked Fox if he could arrange a meeting with a Vietnamese family.

Fox did, and in the process met Kim Hoa, a social worker who was then working for the Committee of Responsibility, which transported seriously war-injured Vietnamese children to the United States for treatment unobtainable in Vietnam.

"She was beautiful, a social worker educated by French nuns, and knew the language of the Second Vatican Council. It was pretty amazing." Tom and Hoa were married in January 1971.

Later that year, fashion and portrait photographer Richard Avedon traveled to Vietnam and selected Fox and his wife as portrait subjects among a wider group of Vietnamese and Americans in Vietnam at the time. The Fox pad became a must-stop spot in Saigon for visitors from overseas. Tom recalls one evening explaining to his new wife who William Buckley was before the guest arrived.

Tom and Hoa couldn't travel together or even go out together much because many Vietnamese, particularly the youth, had a fixed and negative idea about Vietnamese women who went with Americans. That notion had been shaped by liaisons between the bar girls and American soldiers in the country. Fox was now surviving as a Saigon-based journalist—a correspondent for *NCR* and a stringer for *TIME* magazine and the *New York Times*.

"Those two [publications] liked me because I could speak Vietnamese and they didn't have to rely on interpreters," he said. "And I was cheap. They paid me $200 a month, if they paid me. Both *TIME* and the *Times* liked the idea that I would jump onto a plane at short notice and fly into a war zone. I was young and foolish, you might say."

Stan Cloud, *TIME*'s Saigon bureau chief, said Fox

> was the best hire I ever made. His ability to empathize with Vietnamese of all kinds and classes, his dedication, his tirelessness, and, above all, his moral sensibility. I used to call him "Jiminy Cricket" because he was always there, sitting on our shoulders, whispering in our ears, "Don't get carried away with the so-called big picture. People are out there dying and being maimed. Don't forget them."

Cloud and Fox journeyed through Vietnam doing interviews, hitching airplane rides and renting Honda motor scooters, staying in fleabag hotels, eating local foods. There was a saying in Vietnam attributed to both the *New York Times* Vietnam correspondent Gloria Emerson and to Cloud: "When you travel with Fox, it's always third-class."

Craig Whitney, later a *New York Times* assistant managing editor, then a *Times* Saigon bureau reporter and later chief, remembers Tom in his sandals, carrying his black Buddha bag,

> earnest and idealistic, with a religious sensibility but not being forward about it, an open, winning smile, a somewhat naive or innocent sense of humor. He could get tearfully enraged about the atrocities the Thieu government was visiting daily on the Vietnamese people. He and Hoa were a lovely couple; I thought that after Saigon, he might go to university back in the Midwest and teach Vietnamese and sociology. But it turned out journalism was what he was really passionate about.

The Foxes were not planning to leave, but a dangerous situation grew more dangerous. Hoa was pregnant. One evening when Tom was away, a close Vietnamese friend, a progressive Catholic, part of a Viet Cong cluster, went to see Hoa.

"He told her that the communist group he belonged to planned to either kidnap or kill me because for some reason they believed I was CIA," Fox said. "I'd never had any connection with government; my reporting was most often viewed as antiwar. My stories had the same theme: Students, people, all Vietnamese were getting screwed."

Hoa asked the young man to return when Tom came back. He did. Fox asked the Vietnamese to tell the group that if they would give him two weeks, he and Hoa would leave the country. "I was targeted. You can't say, 'Where do I hide?' I was just too vulnerable. It was time to leave."

The bargain was sealed. They flew to the United States in December 1972 during the U.S. Christmas bombing of Hanoi. They went to his parents' home. "I was unemployed, no job prospects, a pregnant wife, no money and in Detroit."

He went to see the editor of the *Detroit Free Press* with his clips. Bill Mitchell, then a *Free Press* general assignment reporter, later an *NCR* board member, remembers managing editor Neal Shine walking Fox around the newsroom to introduce him. Mitchell while at Notre Dame had been an *NCR* stringer and was familiar with the "Thomas C. Fox" byline from Vietnam. Fox was assigned to city hall. He covered the neighborhoods, the county courts, the jails, the state prison and the homeless. Mitchell was named city hall bureau chief, and they worked together in the eleventh-floor bureau of the then City-County Building across the corridor from the offices of Coleman Young, Detroit's first black mayor.

"I learned a lot from Tom in terms of source development," Mitchell said. "He got to know all the judges, called them regularly, worked it well. He was also something of a force in the newsroom, in the way that he has been at ease at *NCR* challenging the hierarchy. There was some foreshadowing of that the day when he walked into office of [*Detroit Free Press*] editor Kurt Luedtke at the far end of the newsroom."

"Luedtke, who later went to Hollywood—he wrote *Absence of Malice* and *Out of Africa*—was a classic hard-bitten newspaper editor," Mitchell said. "Chain-smoker, talked out of the side of his mouth, hard-edged. Fox walked in and asked Luedtke, who had his feet on his desk and a cigarette hanging from his lips, for a bicycle rack near the loading dock. He then demanded a nonsmoking section in the newsroom. That demand was about twenty-five years before its time. I think he got the bike rack."

Fox was at the *Free Press* for five years until *TIME* magazine's Cloud, by then an editor at the *Washington Star*, encouraged Fox to move to Washington and take a *Star* editor's job. A year and a half later, Fox was lured to *NCR* as editor.

The headlines on the *NCR* front page took on a fresh tone: "Minorities, women gain liberation leadership"; "Conservative Christians spread influence, attract attention"; "Jesuit superior Arrupe takes first steps to resign"; "U.S. Vietnamese face identity questions"; "Reagan links to Paraguay worry rights advocates"; "*NCR* writer detained six days in Bolivia"; "Suit may force nuclear weapon sites disclosure."

Tom Fox, the new *NCR* editor, was in town.

In the fifteen years since the council ended, the familiar sociopolitical world markers and Catholic markers had shifted. A neo-fundamentalist quartet rose before the world in a remarkably short period. In October 1978, John Paul II was its first member to appear. Four months later, in February 1979, the Ayatollah Ruhollah Khomeini helicoptered onto the scene. He was closely followed in May 1979 when British conservatives elected Margaret Thatcher prime minister. Then came Ronald Reagan, elected November 1980. Reagan was the politico-ideological fundamentalist; Thatcher, the economic fundamentalist (in writer Michael Lewis's words, "Get rid of the dole for the poor and replace it with a far more generous, and far more subtle, dole for the rich"); then Khomeini, the Islamic fundamentalist. Reagan inaugurated the American Right's "war against the poor" and launched a crusade against other people pressing for democracy. The ayatollah, fresh from the overthrow of the shah of Iran and the American hostage crisis, awoke Islamic populations' expectations with his demonstration that the "Great Satan" was not invincible. Thatcher's save-the-rich-and-eliminate-government policies were laissez-faire's reawakened "greed is good" and trickle-down national economics. Reagan (backed or pushed by the "neo-cons" Peter Steinfels had alerted us to) approved of, and employed, Thatcher's fiery style, not least her scorched-earth approach to unions. Reagan immediately fired the nation's unionized air-traffic controllers. In bloody and soon to be bloodier Central and South America, Reagan and the military-industrial complex that helped elect him, without guidance from anywhere except perhaps Reagan's own and John Wayne's old movie scripts, began battling those who battled for rights and freedoms.

Inside the church, John Paul was of the same fundamentalist ilk. The pope had stepped easily to the front, and the Catholic Right he now proceeded to galvanize fell in lockstep behind him. It later tried to surround him and did a credible job. The right had no problem with John Paul's determination to undo Vatican II and refashion the church after his personal Polish model. Where the pope was totally out of step with the other three fundamentalists was his compassion for the poor, for the worker and for women. Outside the church, he was a compassionate giant; inside, he was a dictatorial monarch whose compassion never extended to American Catholic nuns or American Catholic women, generally grouped together in Vatican-speak as "feminists."

Fox was born in a Catholic time when a letter from a local bishop to his flock was treated as revealed wisdom, a papal edict cloaked in the divine. He was *NCR* editor at a time when the foundational credibility, utility and influence of the papacy was sinking like Venice. The Vatican and the senior hierarchy sank into a spongy morass of internal ineffectiveness and external irrelevance. (Pope Francis, determined—though not necessarily destined—to stabilize the church's foundation at a different level, still has that same Wojtyla-Ratzinger senior-and-lesser hierarchy to contend with.)

Early in his editorship, the Fox assessments of the autocratic papacy and a Vatican principally, but not exclusively, understood as the Congregation for the Doctrine of the Faith under Cardinal Joseph Ratzinger, were lament-tinged. Initially, Wojtyla had successfully transitioned from archbishop and cardinal to pope and monarch. But *NCR* is rooted in the lives and work of the church's prophetic witnesses. Fox was up against the stone wall of the Wojtyla-Ratzinger clampdown. Fox—though he'd blanch at the suggestion—became a mini-Isaiah. To quote Sr. Wendy Beckett, "A prophet is not one who sees the future. He is rather the one who explains the significance of the present. Did it have to be like this?"

Fox's wilderness editorial voice continued to ring out. The newspaper stepped up its coverage, commentary and editorials in defense of those Vatican-II-inspired witnesses being most injured by the anti-council reactionaries. It was no longer "Did it have to be like this?"; it was digging in more firmly to report, "This is what it is like."

9

AN ERA OF VIOLENCE

Pacifist Tom Fox was ushered into the editor's chair in 1980 during a rising tide of violence. That tide was surging during the first half of the year as Fox and I worked through the transition to Fox assuming the editorship.

It started early: an *NCR* February 22, 1980, photograph. A gently smiling Archbishop Oscar Romero with a shyly smiling Salvadoran woman holding a naked child to her shoulder, a second child nearby. The warning, however, was in the headline above June Carolyn Erlick's article: "El Salvador: Last chance for peace." On the second page was "Romero 'most vulnerable of all.'"

A month later, on March 24, after Romero was assassinated while saying Mass in a hospital chapel: "Millions mourn slain Romero." Then, Erlick set the sorrowful, respectful funeral scene in San Salvador.

> The city was spookily calm . . . the elegant mall . . . the downtown slum dwellers' market. Despite an eight-day mourning period and a proposed four-day national strike, calm reigned. The only visible difference was in the long lines of people for blocks around the Metropolitan cathedral . . . I moved closer to the casket to take pictures. Romero's coffee-colored hands clutched the rosary. His face peaceful without a hint of his violent death . . . I climbed onto an adjacent pew to photograph the casket from a better angle.

Reflective, informative, Erlick wrote on, an elegiac accounting of El Salvador's situation and Oscar Romero's place in it. Then the first shots rang out. Suddenly, everything was transformed as her article told of the "massacre in the cathedral."

Ten months later, the hunt for Romero's killers barely underway, four American churchwomen were slaughtered: Maryknoll Srs. Ita Ford and Maura Clarke, Ursuline Sr. Dorothy Kazel, and lay missioner Jean Marie Donovan were brutally murdered in El Salvador on December 2 on a road outside San Salvador. Five months beyond that, in May 1981, Pope John Paul II was shot by Mehmet Ali Agca, who had escaped prison after murdering a left-wing journalist.

Six months later, six Jesuit academics, their housekeeper and her daughter were brutally slain. The butchered bodies of Ignacio Ellacuria, Joaquin Lopez y Lopez, Amando Lopez, Ignacio Martin-Baro, Segundo Montes, Juan Ramon Moreno and the Salvadoran women were discovered in the San Salvador university residence.

There was an Orwellian gloom to the times. The Cold War nuclear threat began to create serious, understandable and quite realistic worldwide alarm; a potential nuclear Armageddon became a possibility, and the *Bulletin of Atomic Scientists'* nuclear clock showed four minutes to Doomsday. Five years later, Doomsday was still four minutes away as *NCR* covered the first summit between Regan and Mikhail Gorbachev in November 1985 in Geneva: "Geneva neatly packaged, but package almost empty." In effect, the threat did not lessen, but Reagan and Gorbachev discovered they could talk to one another. That same month, five years into Fox's editorship, the Vatican was holding its own double summit, a meeting of the College of Cardinals and a Synod of Bishops, all rolled into one. John Paul, according to Peter Hebblethwaite, was "battening down the hatches."

Which is an excellent lead into what else Fox would be facing given the Reagan-backed Salvadoran violence and darkening world situation. Given the world situation, other 1980 and 1981 headlines pale almost to irrelevancy: "Pope asks 'self mastery' in marital sex"; "Opus Dei seeks higher status"; "Surgeon told he can't be priest and doctor."

Then the news noose began to tighten once more: "U.S. must recognize past injustices toward Iran" was a significant recounting of how the Western powers tend to bring their international problems down on their own heads along with the ruination of their "enemy" nations. "Slaughter in the Philippines" chronicled the Ferdinand Marcos dictatorship; "Bolivia becoming like Uganda" momentarily hid the larger newsroom story that *NCR* writer Mary Helen Spooner had been arrested and held by the Bolivian government for six days.

I had earlier encouraged Penny Lernoux to focus on U.S. corporate activities in Latin America (both Lernoux and I were former financial writers). Now those series were in full spate, and corporate types and economic trickle-downers fought back through readers' letters. But the series continued, headlined "Yankee go home" and "When banks go broke." (All this augured the twenty-first-century U.S. banking chaos and corporate meltdown three decades later—though viewed in the 1980s through a Latin American prism.)

NCR gave one reader, Douglas McGunagle, half a page to give the "other side." One comment was "In my opinion [Lernoux's articles] are frequently unfair, uncharitable and economically simplistic." McGunagle's arguments throughout were not without merit, but he missed the Lernoux point. He and the views of the many he represented looked at everything from the top down, from their profit and business strategy points of view; *NCR* understood those complexities but looked up from the havoc and the chaos the profit-grabbing business tactics produced—profiteering accomplished often enough with tacit or overt U.S. government backing.

Economic politics? *NCR* board member Msgr. John Egan charged that an Illinois congressman had tried to pressure Egan to end his support of a national "Stop Big Oil" demonstration.

In Washington, DC, Reagan had the most Catholic cabinet ever. Intern J. L. "Jerry" Sullivan, a Marquette junior, was sent to interview the cabinet members on how their faith might influence their work. It went cordially enough until Sullivan asked about *Humanae Vitae*. Cabinet secretaries were not amused.

The normal flow of in-house headlines punctuated the year: "U.S. Vietnamese face identity questions"; "Vatican wants 'universal' priests for global church" (this was the Vatican's opening shot in parachuting African and Indian priests into the West); "Belfast plagued by civil war"; "Texas, New York, Hispanics key voters."

Across Fox's first years through 1985, these seemingly stock-in-trade stories served their purpose. They kept a national audience informed and provided groups of readers with accounts from elsewhere that they might benefit from or needed to know. One example is that what affects black or Hispanic Americans in one area of the country could have direct relevance to people in the same situation in a difference state.

Of the nuclear threat, predictable reactions to new developments did not diminish the accumulating anxiety: "U.S. Catholic war resistance growth 'historic,' building on Catholic Worker image"; "Arms race 'final folly' for former U.S. ambassador to the Soviet Union George Kennan"; "Catholics needed to support conscience-driven war resisters"; "Catholic resisters face draft-evasion charges"; "Charities leaders: Military spending primary obstacle to assisting poor." Archbishop Raymond Hunthausen wrote a reflection that "our nuclear war preparations are the global crucifixion of Jesus," followed by Charles Kinzie on the "nuclear testing" of the church:

> Much more rapidly than many people thought possible, the Catholic Church in the United States is crossing the boundary into the most severe and decisive period in its history. In fact, if we do not read correctly the signs of the times, this will be the last historical epoch of the church: we have entered the end time, the era of crucial judgment. Like the Catholic church in Germany a half century ago, we have entered an era of historical testing.

Historical because that testing would produce, in what must figure as the U.S. bishops' twentieth-century finest hour, their 1983 pastoral letter, "The Challenge of Peace." They battled the Reagan administration and naysayers in their ranks and in their pews every step of the way. (The church-in-Rome would soon strip the bishops' conferences of any semblance of independence. Too conciliar and threatening to Rome, that independence.)

Anti-nuclear pressure built. The classic case study of Catholic response was in the small Texas diocese of Amarillo, which possessed the nation's largest nuclear weapons assembly plant, Pantex, the region's primary employer. A new peace bishop was in the making, Leroy Mattheisen.

Fox's editorial explained:

> Few who speak about the Texas panhandle describe it in other than conservative terms. It is not a place from which one would expect to shake the nation's embrace of nuclear arms. It is an unlikely spot to put a new momentum in the church's peace initiatives. Yet this is

happening in Amarillo, Texas, where Bishop Leroy Mattheisen and a group of Catholics are standing up to considerable community pressure to live out their convictions.

One can easily imagine the loneliness they feel. But they are not alone and should be told as much. Mattheisen explained . . . "Essentially it comes down to one's conscience being the final arbiter of one's decisions . . . my counsel is that they need to seek new jobs or something that they could do which would contribute to life rather than seek to destroy it."

To aid workers taking that route—the local Amarillo community services agency refused to assist—the Oblates of Mary Immaculate (Central Province) in St. Paul, Minnesota, gave Mattheisen $10,000. United Way of Amarillo withdrew its funding of Catholic Family Service, a loss of $61,000, because of the agency's refusal to "publicly defer counseling of Pantex workers."

Three decades later, Westerners may look on these events and consign the entire nuclear anxiety of the age to an unnecessary public hysteria, given there was no nuclear war. But as John Paul II in Hiroshima called for a "conscious choice to survive," Cardinal John Krol loaned his publicity machinery to protest the arms race. Pacifists were arrested during demonstrations and so were *NCR* reporters covering the events. Pantex's protesting Catholic workers stated their case as "nuclear deterrence's morality" became a "central issue for bishops." Modern readers should take note. They should reflect on their anxieties following 9/11 and today's constant threat of terrorism and the growing threat of nuclear terrorism. What they'll begin to wish for is some united church vision for today and bishops bold enough to argue with a nation about what to do next. That's what Fox's editorials contended.

As bad as things were, Harvey Cox, roaming *The Secular City*, could close out Fox's first five years measuring out a little hope. He wrote in *NCR*, "Our millennium-long habit of thinking of Christianity as being somehow centered in Europe with branch offices around the world is dying . . . I think the Vatican is caught off balance by a massive resurgence of energy from directions where it hadn't been anticipated, and where, they fear, it cannot easily be controlled."

The Vatican would soon be caught up in something it—finally—could not control: the sexual abuse crisis.

Time to take a brief look at Fox as editorial writer.

On Bernard Lonergan

The death of theologian Bernard Lonergan turns us toward some of the lessons of his life. Here was a quiet, shy man whose shadow has already fallen into the next century—a man who was content to be a teacher of teachers rather than a prophet constantly in the public eye.

In an age that seems to race from one instant "solution" to the next, Lonergan took his time, hung back, and asked the questions, learned everything he could about the issue before he moved. He once told an interviewer that "activists don't have much in the way of solutions. Their point is to act now, think later. That can be extremely destructive; it probably will be."

There is a certain steadfastness of hope in Lonergan's approach. Christian hope . . . He was able to simply do his work, as thoroughly and rigorously as possible, confident, it seems, that the seed he sowed would one day germinate and root. The ironic result is that he has ended up not behind the times, but ahead of them.

On Apartheid

South Africa, after years of relative obscurity, has finally become newsworthy in the United States.

Oddly, this has come about more through coincidence than planning: an articulate South African, Anglican Bishop Desmond Tutu, won the Nobel Peace Prize while on sabbatical in this country. Simultaneously, blacks' internal resistance grew in South Africa unlike anything in two decades.

Washington, where the Reagan Administration has shown unusual cynicism in dealing with South Africa, became the target of national and international criticism. At issue has been Reagan's policy of 'constructive engagement' which, despite the administration protests to the contrary, has been viewed as diminished U.S. resolve to work for racial justice in South Africa. The policy has allowed U.S. South Africa investors to continue their pursuits despite apartheid policies roundly condemned by world communities.

The Reagan administration is not the first to wish people would not notice the policies of the nation it was cozying up to—but it has been the most callous.

On Race

Even within the Reagan administration it was an extraordinary thing to hear: Secretary of State George Shultz, called upon to give the U.S. position on South Africa's unprecedented repression against its black population, said:

"The alternative to constructive engagement is to say 'a plague on both your houses,' and to walk away from the problem." The secretary said he would not do this.

But what is constructive engagement? It is the policy of talking to the white South African government to build its confidence in the United States as an honest broker. Now. In the face of South African police and army brutality, that policy is under fire in the United States. The administration tells us that U.S.–South African relations are under review, but the policy of constructive engagement is not.

Shultz reviews the alternative to talking to whites as talking to nobody. Talking to blacks, the second of Shultz's two houses, is not considered an option. Why? Why are blacks in South Africa so invisible from Washington?

On Nicaragua

Nicaraguan Foreign Minister Father Miguel D'Escoto [Brockmann]'s fast, which he describes as a nonviolent action to counter U.S. moves against his country, is Christian witness with a twist. How many government ministers can you think of who would use a religious fast as an element of foreign policy? Yet [Brockmann], a Maryknoll priest, is among those the Reagan administration brands as terrorists, tyrants and thugs.

On Abortion

Don't sign the [Catholics for a Free Choice] abortion ad. An advertisement gathering U.S. Catholic signatures and set to appear in the *New York Times* later this year claims its solidarity with those whose right to free speech is under attack. The ad does nothing of the sort. What the ad will do—all as a pretense to free speech and pluralism—is cause more conflict and further inhibit meaningful dialogue.

The advertisement being proposed is a deceitful, dishonest and divisive effort by a small single-issue group that may have started from a position of honest concern but seems to have degenerated into demagoguery. Thinking and caring Catholics should steer clear.

Fox couldn't steer clear of one 1985 front-page story that nearly ended his career as *NCR*'s editor. It was the watershed June 7, 1985, issue when the newspaper tore open the rectory curtains to reveal the nationwide, hidden, festering clerical sexual abuse of children.

No bishop uttered a single word of explanation or protest to *NCR* despite three pages of *NCR* reporting that began with these words:

> In cases throughout the nation, the Catholic church is facing scandals and being forced to pay millions of dollars in claims to families whose sons have been molested by Catholic priests.
>
> These are serious and damaging matters that have victimized the young and innocent and fueled old suspicions against the Catholic church and a celibate clergy. But a related and broader scandal seemingly rests with the local bishops and a national episcopal leadership that, as yet, has no set policy on how to respond to these cases.

It is not necessary to air again the details about the cases themselves (though Jason Berry's reporting on the Lafayette, Louisiana, diocese case remains a textbook example of investigative journalism at its most thorough). Nor is it necessary to discuss at length the cover-ups by bishops or popes—the church-in-Rome's self-protective culture has been revealed to all. What is worth mentioning again is that for seventeen years following *NCR*'s front-page disclosures, the National Conference of Catholic Bishops corporately and its members individually permitted the abuse to continue as in diocese after diocese, bishops shifted their pedophile priests around from parish to parish to prey again on the young.

Not until the *Boston Globe* in 2002 began reporting on the cover-up under Cardinal Bernard Law did the story truly begin to hit the nation at large and the U.S. bishops collectively. Today, in the thirty years since *NCR*'s initial account, not a single bishop has gone to prison. A couple of minions were offered up for furthering the sins of omission of their superiors.

Yet it is reasonable to assume every archbishop of a major diocese knew of cases among his own priests. The lowest estimate of the male pedophile presence in society is 2 percent. Between 1965 and 2005, the largest U.S. metropolitan archdioceses never had fewer than one thousand priests and sometimes had closer to two thousand. Pedophilia wasn't new, and it wasn't news inside the Catholic institutional structure. It was a many-centuried, well-kept secret.

Certainly, many readers seemed surprised.

> I was quite taken aback by the content and especially by the tone of your editorial comments and of Arthur Jones's and Jason Berry's articles on pedophile priests. The articles were luridly overdone. It should be clear by now that some priests are psychologically developed, some priests are developing, and some are underdeveloped. The underdeveloped ones, if arrested psychosexual development is the issue, need compassion and counseling. To suggest that the priest with this problem is insane or that the struggle over celibacy is the issue, or that homosexuality is the main factor is missing the entire point of the psychodynamics of sexual addiction. A close reading of Patrick Carne's excellent and ground-breaking book, "The Sexual Addiction," might help you, Jones and Berry, defuse the apocalyptic tone of these overstated articles. Many priests who are caught in this sexual web are innately good people and excellent ministers, like so many others in other professions. M. D. C., Chicago.

> You are to be commended for your courage in your editorial, "Pedophilia problems need tackling," and congratulated on your wisdom/prudence. . . . What Jones reported, and what your editorial confirmed, is that Catholic priests and Catholic young males merely mirror our American society—no better, no worse. This is not to rationalize, excuse, justify—simply to state a fact you, I and millions of Catholic males knew about and experienced since the first days we rang the bells for consecration, through seminary, and as active laymen in our parishes. It is not strictly "news," just better diagnosis, to admit our spiritual AIDS inside our cassocks, and blue jeans.

> Neither you nor Jones labels all priests as pedophiles, nor all seminarians as accommodating, nor all sacramentally active Catholics as incestful. Yet, these phenomena are so common as to be accepted "with the territory." I am a "recovering" sexaholic, and Jones has merely scratched the surface of what *really* exists in our seminaries, parishes (priests, brothers and laymen alike). It is hard to admit there are so many millions of us—but there are. . . . May I ask as a favor . . . you also publish an article, as counterbalance, on the "success" stories you know of: wherein priests who took advantage of young boys, and/or young boys who were "victims," both eventually overcame,

recovered and were successes in managing their lives. Name With-held.

Our bishops who are quick to speak out against any consensual sexual activity not blessed by the church—homosexual relationships, divorce and remarriage, artificial contraception, lesbian nuns—are shamefully and embarrassedly silent on the sexual abuse of children by their priests.

NCR is to be commended for breaking silence on pederasty in the church. Hopefully, your article will prompt ecclesiastical authorities to develop programs of help for these men and their victims. R. G.

A fourth writer said,

We all have our horror stories to tell of dirt shoved under the carpet by those in charge. The point to be faced is how to improve the situation so that the number of victims might be lessened and hopefully become non-existent. Is it not time to sit down with the devastating fallout and discern through prayer and loving interaction, a remedy? . . . A church infiltrated with narcissism depends on the suppression of women for its very existence. A church that flaunts feminized males to the exclusion of their true manliness precludes their individuation and the wholeness of the body they serve. A church steeped in self-righteousness only echoes [Andre] Gide's "there are none so blind as they who will not see," and it serves no one. S. M. B.

The denunciations of *NCR* continued apace. (These came as no surprise. The easily offended always surface early—no matter the topic. *NCR* was denounced when, in a Christmas issue, the paper ran a photograph of a woman with a baby at her bared breast as a representation of Mary and Jesus. Equally predictably, other readers called the prudes ridiculous.)

I think it's disgraceful for you, as a Catholic newspaper, to publish news items about our Catholic priests. You know as well as I do these few are sick men and do not deserve this publicity. This is totally uncalled for and undeserved. Your obligation is to build up the church—not tear it down. J. H.

So much for concern about the victims.

These few excerpts from the first letters, precursors to many hundreds over the years, covered everything from suggesting financial sanctions against *NCR* to insider accounts from brothers and priests as to how corrupted the internal workings of the church were.

> What stands out clearly is the stupidity demonstrated by persons in positions of authority. Instead of dealing with the case with direct honesty, trust, charity and the use of professional competence, many authorities, Nixon-style, opt for a cover-up. They give an order in "holy obedience" for a transfer to different location. In "ostrich style" they pretend they have solved the problem. This method of handling the problem is the initial cause of all the harm and scandal that evolves. J. W.

> The shocking revelations in Jones' investigative article on priest child abuse is not that there are priest pedophiles—such persons can be found in all professions. The real horror comes from the realization that the pastors, fellow priests, personnel directors and bishops engaged in a "conspiracy" of silence and denial. After spending 17 years in a Catholic brotherhood I witnessed the most tragic form of denial around the problem of alcoholism [including] an alcoholic brother who was also a pedophile . . . sexually molest[ing] two-year-olds and other boys. When I and another brother told this to the superior, the offending brother was called in for a fraternal reprimand but remained in the position where he could continue to prey on the boys . . . To my knowledge he never received treatment for the disease of alcoholism or his pathological pedophilia.
>
> The irony and hypocrisy of the situation was to dawn on me years later when I was forced out of the order because I voluntarily admitted my own homosexuality and was involved in gay ministry. If I had chosen to engage in the characteristic denial so prevalent in the authority structures of the church, I might still be a member. J. A. I.

> The major underlying difficulty, to which your editorial only alludes, is the church's failure to take seriously the findings of contemporary sex research and to develop a moral teaching that respects that impressive body of information. We can no longer imitate the ostrich in dealing with what researchers are telling us about the nature and various meanings of sexual identity and genital behavior.

Perhaps it will take the impetus of such notoriety and millions of
dollars in settlements with victims to convince church leadership to
establish educational programs in schools, parishes and seminaries to
effectively equip all ages for developing a healthy process of sexual
self-discovery. T. N. T.

It has taken "notoriety and millions of dollars in settlements" to
convince the church leadership they have a serious problem on their
hands. Whether that leadership developed "a healthy process of sexual
self-discovery" remains an open question.

The cover-up by the bishops met the church's description of a true
scandal—the sin "that cries out to heaven for justice" and causes people
to lose their faith.

At the next *NCR* board meeting, Jesuit Fr. Joseph Fichter wanted
Tom Fox ousted as editor. Fichter made a motion to that effect. It did
not get a second. He resigned.

Years later, Fox said,

> I always admired Father Fichter. He was a scholar and strong *NCR*
> supporter over the years. But he was as hardheaded as I was and we
> basically disagreed on the importance of the pedophilia story. He
> thought we were exaggerating. He wanted us to stop writing about it.
> That led to the impasse and his motion of nonsupport.
>
> Years later, we met in New Orleans and dined together. By this
> time, he had softened a bit. Time had passed; the deepest of wounds
> had healed. I left the meeting feeling we still had differences, but
> had put them aside and gone on.

NCR's editorials, articles and investigation continued. The ecclesiastical authorities did not develop public programs to help identify the
priests and their victims. Not for seventeen years. Many bishops ran for
deeper cover, continued to move around their abusing priests or, at a
bare minimum, sent some for treatment. The victims were handled as
before: with little, if any, help until the moment the lawsuit loomed.
Lack of alacrity was transformed into fervid jitters when, in 2002, the
Boston Globe exposed in great detail the cover-up in that archdiocese.
The target was the man who allowed or orchestrated the cover-up,
Cardinal Bernard Law.

Only then did the bishops as a group form a national review board
made of laypeople. When the board started to do its job, the bishops

panicked and began to rein it in. Eventually, they succeeded. (Some local dioceses established their own committees.)

Rome did nothing, in contrast to the Vatican's lively action when a bishop was too pastoral, too willing to listen to the people, too outspoken on peace, poverty and sexual issues. The church-in-Rome did not chastise bishops who oversaw and shielded the immoral and criminal activities of the priests or remove those bishops from office. The Vatican's customary silence was its way of saying no problem existed. Or at least, it was suggested through the cracks in the wall the Vatican had built around itself on the topic that if there was a problem, it was "an American problem."

10

"THE BIG CHILL"—JOHN PAUL II

October 1987 offered a fine contrast in Catholic agendas. In Rome, the month-long synod of the laity was underway. Women were briefly on the agenda. Simultaneously, in Cincinnati, three thousand Roman Catholic women and dozens of Anglican, Protestant and Jewish women from across the United States and more than twenty countries "did the discussing." Susan Hansen reported, "In contrast to the Vatican gathering, talk centered not on new, expanded women's ministries within the church but on reclaiming the best of Roman Catholicism Vatican II tradition, forging links with women of other faiths and nations and building a new social order and a new, all-inclusive locally based spirituality movement."

At the synod, all was less than well. The malaise was summed up in the closing headline "'Unloved' synod dies, 'unmourned' with few assets: Bishops called hard put to find positive comments." A brief dip into the month-long synod on the laity is useful because it reveals the extent of both John Paul's intervention in everything in the church debate and the reestablishment of the Curia's primacy over the world's bishops.

The world laity, looking on, witnessed nothing revealing or even promising underway. By October 13, not even the synod halfway mark, 201 interventions to the direct debates were summed up in a working paper. The dozen questions the small-group synod gatherees dealt with were not divulged. Peter Hebblethwaite divulged them.

What immediately strikes the reader is the questions' superficiality and generality. Not "what is keeping the youth away from the faith of their forbears," but the tortured, curialese that began like a statement from Mao Zedong's People's Committee: "Following the example of Pope John Paul II, the fathers insisted on the importance of youth for the future of the church and the world." Such insight. Then a question that could be answered by reading the U.S. news headlines since John Paul's ascendancy: "Why are there so few Christians active in politics?"

The "women" question went nowhere.

Hebblethwaite laid out the reality.

Had the month-long synod ended quietly two-thirds of the way through the deliberations, and had the reports from the synod's twelve discussion groups been made public, he wrote, the church would have been edified, the world enlightened and the Holy Father well served. This did not happen. Instead, the synod reports were "processed" by synod organizers who twisted their contents as they boiled them down into propositions to be submitted to the pope. Eventually, fifty-four propositions were submitted, but they no longer reflected the direction and thrust of most of the synod's thinking on key lay matters, as a study of the secret language groups reports, obtained by *NCR*, reveals.

Hebblethwaite contrasted the bishops' reports with the Curia's final version.

Bishops—On women's roles, the almost universal consensus was that all nonordained ministries be open to them.

Curia—reported there was limited support for expanded women's roles.

Bishops—On lay ministries, there was support with some cautions for their expansion.

Curia—said there was no position take on lay ministries.

Bishops—On lay movements (Opus Dei, Communion and Liberation, and such) there was some striking opposition, especially from Third World bishops who feared they would cause loss of local control. (Earlier, in a nice dig, New York Cardinal John O'Connor guaranteed the fundamentalist youth movement *Communione e Liberazione* "the support of a great American diocese if they set up shop in the black ghettoes of Harlem.")

Curia—stated there was considerable support for lay movements.

Continued Hebblethwaite, "The reports—hasty but not superficial—were then subjected to homogenization, adulteration, censorship and emasculation, which led to the final fiasco. Some synod fathers concluded they had been 'robbed' of their synod."

Fox's *NCR* editorial went directly to who had really been robbed: "At what point did the fruits of 'our' work no longer belong to us, the world laity? The final process of the synod reaffirmed the clericalism it was meant to disavow."

Hebblethwaite wrote that women's issues had been pushed to the back burner. In Rome, perhaps, but not in the United States. The bishops' "pastoral draft on women's concerns charts an 'all but ordination' course." Susan Hansen reported it called for "a radical conversion of heart and mind," vowed to forge a new equal partnership and invited women's participation in decision-making. Recommendations included encouraging theological preparation of women to preach the Gospel.

The church-in-Rome's attitude toward women and women religious occupied much of *NCR*'s attention for Fox's final seven years as editor. The 1980s had closed out in October with the loss of a woman who was a close friend to many of us and a beacon to the world: Penny Lernoux. From Sao Paulo, Brazil, the Franciscan Cardinal Paulo Evaristo Arns wrote at length what so many wanted to say. His second paragraph summed up her work life: "She loved us as a sister, as a mother, as a wife would have—and used her knowledge and tremendous dedication to help the poor and unjustly treated."

Fox, writing how the doctors who'd diagnosed the rapidly spreading cancer had told Lernoux to relax, said, "Penny relax? She was a driven woman who worked at a whirlwind pace. The poverty is now; parents are feeding their children now. People were being imprisoned now for speaking the truth. She lived and wrote with an unrelenting sense of urgency. She was all energy, and had a piercing intellect."

The beleaguered U.S. bishops might be confessing "sexism in the church" in the first draft of their pastoral letter on women, but that wasn't sufficient for the women's hard-hitting critiques at the Leadership Conference for Women Religious assembly. Nor for the writers in *NCR*: "A subtle sexism flaws the letter," said Margaret Susan Thompson of Syracuse University. "Good, but it only patches potholes," said Mary Collins of the Catholic University of America. Conservative commentator Helen Hull Hitchcock called the pastoral "essentially incoherent.

This may reflect the bishops' apparent ambiguity about the impossible task of addressing feminist demands."

The bishops tried anew. Then, led by a coalition of progressive bishops, the conference voted and the proposed letter was abandoned. As that was happening, reader M. W. S. Royce of Rockville, Maryland, wrote, "The bishops have been asleep for years, they awaken in 1990, issue a document that might have had some interest in 1972, but today is little more than an irrelevant anachronism." The bishops cared enough to name Dolores Leckey as executive director of the U.S. bishops' conference's Secretariat for Family, Laity, Women and Youth to head an expanded secretariat to serve "the NCCB Committee on Laity, Family Life and Women."

Undeterred and not surprisingly, women and women religious continued their work. Sister of Notre Dame Sr. Mary Evelyn Jegen wrote an *NCR* article suggesting that annually "an international committee award a prize to that nation which had excelled in providing hospitality internationally." Fox brought Benedictine Sr. Joan Chittister on as a *NCR* columnist, and she also served as a board member, reminding her sisters, "We will have to risk something. And we will have to be prepared to do it alone. And in ordinary time." (She was talking about world peace, but the exhortation applied elsewhere too.) Karen Kennelly edited *American Catholic Women: A Historical Exploration.*

From Baltimore to Liberia, women religious lived dangerously, just as they had in El Salvador. Sr. MaryAnn Glinka, the Baltimore Franciscans superior, was found dead in the Baltimore convent, hands and feet bound, strangled and sexually assaulted after she apparently interrupted a burglary in progress. The suspect arrested two days later had a previous record that included manslaughter and had been hired to do some painting at the convent. In Liberia, nine nuns were slain, including five American Sister Adorers of the Blood of Christ from Illinois: Barbara Ann Nuttra, Mary Joel Kolmer, Shirley Kolmer (cousin of Mary Joel Kolmer), Kathleen Maguire and Agnes Mueller. Three or four Liberian aspirants were missing, possibly abducted.

In June 1992, the U.S. bishops issued "When I Call for Help: A Pastoral Response to Domestic Violence against Women." U.S. society at large preferred not to know. Rosemary Johnston wrote that the number of women in jail nationwide had tripled to ninety thousand, with abuse and/or addiction in the backgrounds of most. Separation from their children was very much in the foreground of their concerns.

Overall, the institutional church-in-Rome hadn't perceptibly altered its views on the status of Catholic women since a quarter-century earlier when a laywoman catechist was dismissed from the Josephinium in Columbus, Ohio, by Bishop John Carberry for disagreeing with his pastoral letter urging an end to the discussion of celibacy. Women's issues were always in the news and *NCR*. Now women were being told not to discuss women's ordination. Disinvitation was a newly revived tool against women. Popular lay speaker and writer Edwina Gateley was disinvited from three dioceses after her participation as a presider at a Call to Action conference liturgy.

Some brave bishops appeared unable to shy away from putting their heads in the mouth of the Roman lion. Saginaw, Michigan, Bishop Kenneth Untener carefully argued, in a two-thousand-word article in *Seasons*, the Saginaw diocesan quarterly, a challenge to the all-male priesthood as "a question that clearly has arguments on both sides which cannot be taken lightly."

In *Commonweal*, Bishop P. Francis Murphy of Baltimore wrote he believed women should be ordained because justice demands it. When *NCR* ran a 1994 front-page "Women ordained" headline, it quickly added, "but they're Anglicans, and the event sends a chill down the Tiber." Fox wrote of visiting his daughter, Christine, at college. Two of Christine's female college friends intended to become priests, one a Catholic, one a Baptist, "but given current conditions, both plan to become Episcopalian priests."

Columnist Tim Unsworth took himself to Catholic Theological Union in Chicago, where "tomorrow's churchwomen don't want to be trapped in an 'ecclesiastic cul-de-sac.'" Mid-1994, John Paul II, in *Ordinatio Sacerdotalis*, reserved ordination for men. Not unexpectedly, *NCR* followed all this with a major special; the front cover was a stylized illustration of a woman celebrating the Eucharist. The Call to Action national conference that year had its largest gathering in years: 1,800 attended, and Loretto Sr. Mary Luke Tobin was pictured distributing the Communion bread.

Rome was also heard from again as Cardinal Joseph Ratzinger, in an interview with *Rheinischer Merkur*, said the church must not seek short-term solutions to the question of women's role in the church and called for further study and "examination of the anthropological question 'What is woman, what is proper for her, how can she really obtain that place which is due her in church and society?'" To be fair to Ratzinger, he was not just knocking women's hopes. In an *Il Sabato* interview, "he criticized environmentalists, threw cold water on the Assisi peace meeting of the world's religions, and offered a negative evaluation of continuing dialogue with the Jews."

In criticizing the environmentalists, however, Ratzinger had gored *NCR's* new ox. As becomes apparent, the newspaper turned that around by linking ecological issues to Ratzinger's two worst nightmares: women, as in "eco-feminism," and spirituality, as in the work of cosmologist Thomas Berry. The new cosmically aware people were cleverly captured in *NCR* by writer Tim McCarthy's picturesque "like sleepwalkers come suddenly awake, dazed, disoriented, because the nature of what we thought of as reality has changed."

Editor Fox's fascination with Berry was one with another change to *NCR*—or if not change, an expansion of *NCR's* mission. *NCR* was no longer only the defender of prophetic witnesses, the reporter and commentator, the analyst and forum for debate. Additionally, it was *NCR* the educator. Fox as a young man had thought he'd be a high school or college teacher before journalism's siren call snared him. The newspaper had long presented in-depth specials and series, and perhaps accompanying bibliographies. Under Fox, the additional elements were practical catalogs of where instruction and guidebooks that dealt with the matters at hand—from peace studies to Christian ecology—were available.

Rosemary Radford Ruether wrote that "basically what feminists seek in claiming the immanence of God is an understanding of the divine as holistic, a God who is not seen as mind against body, spirit against matter, but who is the source of all life and reality in its fullness."

Benedictine Sr. Ruth Fox's investigation into the omission of key women of the scriptures from the lectionary was an eye-opener. In one instance, her comparison of the Bible's Book of Proverbs that praised the worthy wife with the lectionary version revealed passages omitted from the lectionary that praised the woman's initiative, business acumen, dignity and wisdom. In the Luke 2:22–40 presentation at the temple, the family is met by Simeon and the prophet Anna. The lectionary told Simeon's story, but Anna's was "optional and may be omitted."

Ruth Fox, a member of the Benedictine Sacred Heart Monastery in Richardton, North Dakota, was president of the St. Gertrude federation of monasteries. In her search for Miriam, her article revealed the lectionary omits the passage where Miriam "is called a prophet and led a song of thanksgiving (actually a liturgy in these pre-priest days) after crossing the sea." However, the lectionary does reveal Miriam's sin and punishment with leprosy. Other women, including Ruth, fare no better.

For the first half of the 1990s, there was a continuing internal *NCR* discussion regarding what Tom Fox called "the continued lonely walk on pedophilia. We kept promising to put aside coverage for six months, always to recognize we could not." Basically, reporters didn't want to handle it but felt duty-bound to do so, none more so than the dogged investigator Jason Berry. The paper kept up regular coverage, if not in every issue. (In the early 2000s, *NCR* would pick up the story again and stay with it, anchored by reporting from Los Angeles, where Cardinal Roger Mahony was withholding key documents regarding abusive priests.)

The numbers of abuse cases proliferated. The more shocking event was the false accusation leveled in 1993 against Chicago Cardinal Joseph Bernardin. In a photograph that showed Bernardin backed into a corner by the press and cameras at the bishops' meeting, the cardinal did not yield. He declared, "I have never abused anyone," and gave an address that tried to "balance denials with sensitivity." His accuser was Steven Cook. The charges were based on evidence generated under hypnosis that lawyers said did not meet the minimum standards of generally accepted court standards. By February, Cook said he could no longer "in good conscience" continue to pursue what *NCR*'s Tom Roberts called "the hastily drawn case."

As more accounts appeared, the damaging abuse cases—as at the Santa Barbara Boys' Choir, connected to the Franciscan St. Anthony Seminary high school—revealed sordid tales of duplicity. Said one boys'-choir parent, "The friar implicated used to visit our home often and we often asked his advice about raising our sons. He told us he had studied child psychology but in truth he was a history major." Said another parent, "Our history as a Catholic family has changed forever." The most horrifying article in *NCR*'s files was and remains the case of an altar boy who was abused by the pastor for several years. When that pastor was transferred, he handed over the altar boy to further abuse to the incoming pastor and his associate, as if the child were depersonalized offal.

In late 1994, just five years after Penny Lernoux's death, *NCR* stalwart Peter Hebblethwaite died. He was sixty-four. There were two pages of appreciations, including excerpts of some of his keenest observations and incisive asides. He was the journalist-theologian-analyst. Unique and remarkable. His books, particularly his *The Year of Three Books* and biographies of John XXIII and Paul VI, remain the starting points for many that have followed from others.

NCR's range never faltered. In a three-part series, theologian Bernard Cooke analyzed the pope in modern times. "The real issue is monarchical power, whether the monarchy in question be worldly or spiritual." As always, the political scene gave clues to the future. Newt Gingrich had given the country a Contract with America. In a 1995 cartoon, cartoonist Tony Auth showed how the Republicans executed their contract to the National Rifle Association as they repealed the assault weapons ban. In another Auth cartoon that same year, a cemetery scene showed the GOP burying health care reform.

The "Church is alive with the sound of liturgical music," said one front page; Dorothy Day became a Paulist Fathers biopic; Guatemala was reeling from violence; and Ernesto Cardenal explained why the dream died in Nicaragua: "We need new paradigms, new global solutions. We must seek a new, more civilized political and economic system." The actuality was summed up in a different *NCR* front-page headline: "Has the greed of the rich eaten away democracy in America?"

Bishop Tom Gumbleton took over one front page with "He's not disordered, he's my brother: A bishop risks some straight talk about gays." Gumbleton was, in effect, answering his eighty-seven-year-old mother's question about whether her gay son Dan would go to hell. Tom, who rarely wore a miter but pinned a pink ribbon on his the next time he did, assured her Dan was as loved by God as God loved all her other children.

Henri Nouwen died, and an *NCR* November 1996 headline asked, "Candidate for sainthood?" In that same issue, gutsy Jersey City Sr. Kristin Funari told of being general contractor when her Sisters of St. Joseph of Peace transformed their foundation. She was overseeing its multimillion-dollar conversion into an alternative high school and transitional housing for homeless and battered women and a nurturing center for their children. The mob wanted its cut. Funari threatened a public hunger strike. The mob backed off. A week later, there was a special pullout section when Bernardin died. The tributes explored the seamless garment that was his life.

Fox tackled "the John Paul II/Ratzinger focus on pelvic issues" in his 1996 book *Sexuality and Catholicism*. The final issue of 1996 announced the retirement of *NCR* publisher Bill McSweeney, with Fox assuming the editor and publisher role. Michael Farrell was named executive editor, and John L. Allen Jr. moved up to Opinion editor.

That issue's front page featured Sri Lankan Oblate Fr. Tissa Balasuriya facing excommunication. Balasuriya fought Rome to a standstill and remained a priest and practicing theologian as a mainstay of Asian liberation theology.

11

1997: MICHAEL J. FARRELL

The back section of the newspaper has been known by different names at different times: Trends and Topics, Opinion, currently Opinion and Arts. Essentially, it is the magazine section, as distinct from the news section. For seventeen years under Michael Farrell it roamed far, wide and handsome—and deep. He was not a newsroom editor, the shirt-sleeved editor demanding their all from the reporting staff. He was multitalented, a fine writer and skilled commentator on the arts, with more than a touch of the artist himself.

In the newsroom, Farrell was much as he was on paper—a wit whose mood took him from the droll to the facetious, the dour to the audacious. The entertainer with a cutting edge close at hand.

As I've described him elsewhere, Farrell was *NCR*'s Jonathan Swift: a satirist and a wit in the best eighteenth-century sense. Certainly he was the best satirist ever to grace *NCR*'s pages, a journal that needs satire to handle the lunacy with which it frequently has to deal. Theologian Jesuit Fr. Bernard Lonergan, for example, saw satire and humor "as having a profound significance in the daily politics of the examined life, for both are tacit allies of the desire to know."

Farrell and I met on the telephone, so to speak. We'd chat and I'd ask him to do occasional columns and reports. We got to know one another. We spoke the same patois and relied on similar frames of reference.

We came from opposite sides of the same small pond: the Irish Sea. There were commonalities of reference and place. Of *NCR*'s editors,

Farrell and I were the only immigrants; transplants with feet in two countries and a detached view of both the new place and our old places.

Before he joined *NCR*, Farrell, a former priest, was selling furniture in Los Angeles, but not much of it and not at all enthusiastically. He had a master's in theology from the Catholic University of Leuven, in Louvain, Belgium, and a doctorate in philosophy from the Dominican Pontifical Institute in River Forest, Illinois. He also had an MFA from the University of Southern California. He was the ideal magazine editor. (In the newsroom, my relationship with him was an easy-going "Mikey-Dikey and Arty-McFarty" that remained cordial for the next seventeen years. Farrell and Fox enjoyed a similarly close and easy friendship.)

With a satirist one has to be acutely attuned not only to what is being said or written, but how. Deadpan confuses people. Satiric writing is deadpan. To quote Swift before Farrell, "Last week I saw a woman flayed, and you will hardly believe how much it altered her person for the worse." Some people, hearing that, or reading it, take a while before they realize what was said, and realizing it, can be uncertain where to go with it. To quote Farrell after Swift: "The word patriotism has grown frayed around the edges, but everyone knows it means kicking communist ass and being rugged and self-reliant and even rich."

Plucking one-liners and phrases from Farrell is an entertainment in itself. Reagan "having the mendacity to tell the truth." Curial offices "smell of intolerance." "Jesus was a fundamentalist's nightmare." Longer snippets carry the same punch: "Liberals are better at name-calling; conservatives excel at condescension." "The gospel of prosperity believes romance is for losers. It envisages a capitalist God and a supply-side providence." "It's interesting how laissez-faire holy writ is about money and how earnest it is about other matters, in particular the well-loved sins of the flesh. When it comes to sex you don't hear the magisterium talking metaphor." "The amorphous, intractable curia, while it may slumber for a while, has a life and momentum all its own, a pallid, tired old patient on some secret life-support system to which no pope can find a plug to pull."

But one-liners and snippets distort appreciation of the breadth and bite of the overall satire. There was far more to Farrell than playing the Irish entertainer. Key words are stretched almost to snapping point. The clear-eyed view is exaggerated, but it never blinks. Though an edge of bitterness lurked behind some topics—corporate capitalists among them—he neither rises to virulence nor descends to acrimony.

There was little in the Ireland of Farrell's 1940s–1950s boyhood to endear one to capitalism. The experience of his aunt in New York simply confirmed the antipathy. She'd worked all her life for a New York brokerage firm. Overnight it closed its doors and threw its employees out on the street, pensions gone. But in New York newspapers, the principal partner could still be seen photographed with his racehorses.

Farrell himself was ambivalent almost to the point of hostility about possessions and devoted more than one column to that problem and to acquisition for its own sake. One Sunday the priest's homily was about it being easier for a camel to pass through the eye of a needle, and it downplayed the commanding point. Farrell's headline was "How to be filthy rich without going crazy." In that column we read,

> I'd sweat if I were rich. I'd buy me a camel and the biggest needle available and I'd do some test runs. I'd get very fussy about the meaning of "rich." I'd dabble in semantics and chase down dictionaries. I have books that say, "80 per cent of the gross world product is consumed by the richest 20 percent of the population." I'd worry about being in that 20 percent. . . . I'd stay away from where the poor are. If I don't see their faces, it will be easier to believe the man with the homily.
>
> I read in another book (but these figures are in plenty of books) that there are 30,000 homeless on the streets of New York. If they have no homes, they probably don't have much food either. They have no TV set, much less a second TV set; no car, much less a second car.
>
> If I lived in New York and made $50,000 a year they'd make me uncomfortable. I couldn't possibly buy them a home (with that money I couldn't buy myself a home). Maybe I should give them my second TV. But what could they do, being homeless, with a TV set?
>
> I could buy them food with my kind of money. But how do I give them food? They don't live in my part of town. . . .
>
> But God forbid, if I were making really big money, the kind that's harder to count because it sways daily on the Dow Jones, stocks and property, but millions, man. I know it's millions—if I were that rich (now I can't avoid the R word), I'd really be in trouble.

I'd hire experts to see if American ingenuity couldn't find a way, whatever the cost, of getting that camel through the eye of even one needle.

And I'd go to Mass only where the preacher, a kind man who knows we all have enough troubles already, says Jesus didn't really mean it.

Farrell's news-page reporting was occasional, but well-selected. He was incensed when a foundation aimed at helping Latin America's poor was manipulated to create a game reserve in Texas for big-game hunters. His ire almost showed through the spaces between the lines.

He used words and phrases with a velvet-gloved flair. When he visited the National Nuclear Museum in Albuquerque, New Mexico, he watched the movie *Ten Seconds that Shook the World*. He wrote, "Finally the big bang. We do not, of course, see it as the people of Hiroshima or Nagasaki saw it. In fact, they are never mentioned, except the grateful acknowledgement that their leaders surrendered."

Farrell did not receive a free pass when he angered the readers. It was his turn to be savaged when he defended Andres Serrano's 1987 *Piss Christ* as art. He had the background from which to make such judgments.

In the early 1990s, the front page featured a drawing of a laughing Jesus, with the headline "Does this jolly Jesus know something we don't?" Wrote Farrell,

God, it is said, made us in his own likeness, and we have returned the compliment. Over and over we make the Son of God a sign of the times. In the early years he was Jesus the Good Shepherd. For a while he was Jesus *Pantokrator*, the almighty ruler. On and off he has been the Suffering Servant, the Lamb and other manifestations of how we felt.

And now, late in the second millennium, can you believe—Jesus the Laughing Lad?

The illustrations included a stern, even fierce fourteenth-century icon, *The Savior of the Fiery Eye*. There too was "The Laughing Christ" by Willis S. Wheatley, and the "Smiling Christ" by John Steel. Yet in a newspaper there's no pleasing all the readers all the time. Wrote Robert Albrecht of Winooski, Vermont, "The article on Jolly Jesus exceeded the usual banality of this paper. It was repellant."

Farrell the theologian was rarely openly seen on the page. But when the front page and an inside page had swirling Gustave Doré etchings of swooping, devilish design, one knew it was Farrell. Under the heading "The hell, you say," he wrote an extensive essay sparked by Jerry L. Walls's *Hell: The Logic of Damnation*. Here's the gist of Farrell setting the scene:

> It is amazing that such a distasteful prospect should prove so popular for so long. Yet, since the dawn of history, hell has pervaded not only the Judeo-Christian tradition but most others—an ultimate bottom line to brandish in the face of the iniquitous everywhere.
>
> Then, in the last century or so, as reason gave belief a run for its money, the hot grip of hell has loosened. "Hell is neither so certain nor so hot as it used to be," said philosopher Bertrand Russell in 1927 . . . on the other hand—and in theology there is always another hand—there are the words of Jesus, repeated and categorical and hammered home, not only to the effect there is a hell, but that it is a fiery and totally miserable place, and eternal, too.
>
> Thus reason and faith thrust and parry over the abyss, the two horns of life's biggest dilemma. The true believer needs no proof; for the true unbeliever, there's not enough evidence.

And with that Farrell introduces Walls's *Hell* and is off on another thousand words.

Of course, with Farrell, there was as likely to be a garbage truck on the cover as Gustave Doré. There it was in October 1993, under the headline "Garbage truck, how great thou art." The inside article was on Mierle Laderman Ukeles's *The Social Mirror*, a garbage truck covered with mirrors so that reflected onlookers would be reminded of their role in creating trash.

In January 1997, after seventeen years with *NCR*, Michael Farrell was named executive editor.

As such, a few months later, he met with the board. He was being proposed as editor by Fox.

> [Board chairman John] Caron: What are the things you would like to see the *NCR* do as a result of your influence?
>
> Farrell: . . . By temperament I guess I am inclined towards analyses, essay, feature, regurgitating what is going on rather than reporting it. Now I know I'm a minority in that regard. The reality is that

the back of the book is really supplementary to what is going on. I can't fight with that.

But, yeah, I'll be I hope not too cerebral about it, but I guess I will be a little bit in that direction of analysis more than reporting.

Caron: Although you said that Tom [Fox] writes for the solution. How does that conflict with analysis and solution?

Farrell: Well, I don't know. There's a lot of reporting to be done. It's where we started, the beginning and end of who we are. I am not going to change that and that is why Tom Roberts [managing editor] will be very important in the operation. I am aware of that. Again, to make it a news weekly and to reflect on it and so on, but I am aware that the reporting up front is what is the engine that runs the newspaper.

Caron: You said your style is: life is hopeless. I noticed that in your style. I refer to it as the "ain't it awful" kind of journalism. But it leaves me dangling. I like the solution. I like to see something or at least I like to see some kind of action, even small, that can be done.

Farrell: Well, to a high degree I was being facetious in making this distinction between Tom [Fox] and myself. . . .

Sr. Mary Roger: How are you with other staff people?

Farrell: In fairness, you better ask them. Please do, but I do think we get along. If we're not getting along, they haven't told me.

Caron: You mentioned that you sorely missed Peter Hebblethwaite and Penny Lernoux. Are those areas where the paper needs strengthening a bit?

Farrell: I guess this pause as the pope [John Paul II] kind of winds down, works in our favor while they have nobody quite in place. But yes, when the new pope takes over it is to be assumed there will be a lot of—whatever this pope does—there will have been an awful lot of interest. It may turn out to be badly placed and therefore we won't need anybody to cover Catholic. I think that's extremely unlikely.

As Farrell assumed the editorship in July 1997, he was true to his words. There was a strong emphasis on analysis, much of it quite excellent. He continued his potpourri column, Sic, that had succeeded his Swiftian column. Los Angeles–based Leslie Wirpsa was the ever-dependable South and Central America reporter who succeeded Lernoux. Wirpsa also regularly turned her hand to national reporting. From Washington, DC, there was the political news. In a publication such as NCR, though, it is a newspaper's constant enterprise reporting across the issues of the news beat that provides most of the factual material worthy of analysis.

Post-Hebblethwaite, *NCR* had already been without a Rome correspondent for three years and would be without one for a further three.

As editor, Farrell had a magazine editor's touch for engaging the reader in new ways: "Vote for best book" and "Your 20 greatest Catholics" (John XXIII by a landslide). Poetry was indeed a welcome addition to the magazine. Farrell opened "Inside *NCR*" with

> "I want to stand on that rock which tells no lies," writes Desmond Egan in a poem. Only a poet would have such gall, an echo even of Jesus himself—upon this rock I will build. And true enough, the poetic and the holy have been first cousins since the druids and shamans, since Solomon and all that wild-eyed breed . . .
>
> I myself don't know what a poem is. But this did not stop me from publishing other people's poetry in my callow youth. No doubt I stumbled betimes, but I got lucky betimes, too, because Desmond Egan tells me now that I was the first to publish his poems.

And off went Farrell to discuss the movie *Desmond Egan: Through the Eyes of a Poet*.

Farrell had usefully created *NCR*'s page 2 "Inside *NCR*" box. In July 1999 he announced, under the headline "*NCR* art adventure—Search for a contemporary Jesus," a worldwide

> visual art competition to find an image of Jesus for the new millennium. When Y2K is raised in conversation most people seem to think of computer glitches or parties. There is little or no mention of what the millennium is fundamentally about—the arrival, 2,000 years ago, of Jesus Christ among us. It's extraordinary what impact Christ's life had. He founded a church and it's extraordinary what impact that church, in turn, had. . . . But we have lost touch with this Jesus, a down-to-earth person who at the same time incarnated divinity and pointed to a transcendent world.

For the competition, the newspaper would accept slides only, at least initially, or artwork in any medium. The first prize was $2,000, with three additional prizes of $200. The news spread—at first just to Canada, in the Toronto *Globe and Mail*. Then Carmelite Sr. Wendy Beckett agreed to be the ultimate judge after three well-known artists had first culled the submissions. With a *USA Today* story mentioning the popular television art commentator Beckett, interest mushroomed. Farrell was there on the *Today Show* with Matt Lauer, and the interview demands expanded exponentially.

The winner was announced on December 24, 1999. She was Janet McKenzie, of Island Pond, Vermont, with her "Jesus of the People." Beckett wrote of her entry, "This is a haunting image of a peasant Jesus—dark, thick-lipped, looking out on us with ineffable dignity, with sadness but with confidence."

Farrell said there may be more to this dark, indigenous Jesus than meets the eye. "When the church was overwhelmingly a Western institution, we in the West made Jesus in our likeness. But now at last Christianity has spread to the ends of the earth as the founder once prayed it would." The artist McKenzie wanted her young mixed-race nephew to be able to recognize himself in her work. She used a female figure, an African American woman, she said—the resulting image masculine but a man whose features reflect feminine elements.

For Farrell this was a high point that led to a particularly low point a few months later. The beginning of his end as *NCR*'s editor began with a letter from publisher Tom Fox in May 2000.

> Dear Michael:
>
> I have told you on more than one occasion you have brought the paper to a new level, to a new credibility. I believe this. I commend you for it. The most prominent advances you have made, in my opinion, are: 1. You have done a better job than I did in separating news and opinion. 2. You have brought to the paper a greater variety of subjects (including poetry), and approached these with ease and clarity. 3. You have successfully navigated the editorials through a complex, Cold War-period. 4. You have established a new and energetic interaction with the readers in the Inside *NCR* box.
>
> Added to that you have brought greater national and international attention to the paper through the Jesus 2000 contest to cap *NCR*'s twentieth century. You and Jesus 2000 will be wedded in the annals of *NCR*. You spoke of pain. Within this pain, however, you have the satisfaction for the whole Jesus 2000 effort.
>
> My pain, I've concluded, after examining and self-examining for some weeks, is in acknowledging that the source of the strain is growing out of my recognition, and possibly yours too—that we are entering a transition period for the paper . . . and it is my sense that

in the years you will remain at *NCR* your greatest contributions are likely to come from exploring ideas and concentrating on your writing . . . the titles of Senior Essayist, Arts and Literature Editor, Editor Emeritus come to mind. . . .

I think it is time that *NCR* takes another step forward and that I appoint Tom Roberts to be the next editor. . . . You have given Tom a large responsibility for the news component of each week's paper—you have used his talents well—but he currently lacks the authority to place story decisions into a long-term strategy.

Farrell, in October 2000, wrote to the *NCR* board a ten-page, 3,500-word letter. When this book was in embryo, I wrote to Farrell and invited him to write whatever he wished about his dismissal and it would run as part of his profile. He did not respond. It would be unfair in the circumstances to reply to all the many points he made in a ten-page letter. He left feeling betrayed. He and his wife returned to Ireland; Farrell was devastated as he closed the *NCR* door behind him.

Excerpts from Farrell's letter:

I was, as you know, recently dismissed as editor of the *National Catholic Reporter*. The board, presumably, was given reasons for my removal serious enough that you endorsed the decision. For my part, I swear before God I do not know why I was fired. So conscience prompts me to send you this memo.

NCR was and is a puny messenger in this culture, modestly produced with limited resources. . . . I believed and still believe that such a newspaper and message as this could confound the world in some way I don't even understand. If not now, later. Like a message in a bottle, I used to say—someday it would come ashore and the people would be ready for it. I worked hard for 20 years to play my part in this big little crusade. It gradually became my life, that which, in the end, would define me. For better or for worse it would be my legacy.

May 15 Tom Fox dismissed me as editor. For me this was as unexpected as if the moon fell from the sky. Five days earlier, for example, Fox asked me if, in another couple of years, when John Allen might be returning from Rome, I might want to taper off my career by being European correspondent. Such talk did little to prepare me for what was to come.

It's a truism that those in power get to write the record for posterity. That would mean, in this instance, that my history would be whatever you heard at the June board meeting—let's say it out-right—Fox's spin on what kind of person and writer and editor I was and how I became a problem, all his doubt nuanced by what a talent-ed fellow and fine human being I was, if only if only.

. . . For several years before [publisher] Bill McSweeney retired, Tom Fox became heir apparent . . . and for most of our tenure I was his closest confidant, or so he indicated. . . . Fox took pains to point out that his being publisher would be good for the paper, to protect editorial integrity against outsiders. But Fox would remain editor as well as publisher; rather than hand over the editor's job to someone else. . . . But since he needed someone to do the actual work in the newsroom I became executive editor.

Soon, however, Fox found he had no time for being editor. I said I would accept the responsibility so long as he gave me the matching authority. . . . Fox possessed an inordinate sense of proprietorship over the vision, running and destiny of the paper, never ceded edito-rial control. This created a bone of contention that, I suspect, some-how led to my firing. . . . During the past few years the only area in which there was a policy a disagreement between Fox and myself was the Web. He seemed to want to put the entire paper on the Web each week, and later he seemed to want to augment that by daily updates. (I say "seemed" because in all the years he never spelled out orally or in writing any specifics whatsoever about this electronic dream.)

I said repeatedly I would be willing to go as electronic as he wished if someone offered a plan that did not give away what our entire company was working hard to sell. Then Sr. Rita [Larivee] contrived an electronic version for subscribers. This seemed an ideal solution, and would greatly help overseas readers. . . .

Then odd things began to happen. Fox took decisions out of my hands that would ordinarily have been mine to make or participate in. This was untypical of him. He pressured me about matters about which there was no urgency, and which were, in any case, within my purview. For example, how to proceed if the pope should die.

Much of what I'd learned about being editor of NCR I had learned from Fox over 17 years. The cornerstone of that legacy was editorial independence. Keep outside sources of pressure and con-tamination, including the publisher, at bay for the sake of the paper. . . .

One Monday (in February, I think) the conversation led to his complaining about a lack of correspondents. Ironically, if correspondents were a problem that would be the domain of Tom Roberts [then managing editor] but I took the hit and assured him we would work to get more.

The plot thickened a few days later when I received an e-mail letter from Arthur Jones in Washington. This letter was, in its key concepts, an uncanny repetition of Fox's outburst about lack of stringers, etc. Fox, I now realized, was listening to a different drummer.

The Jones letter was not so much communication as campaign. Basically it claimed *NCR* was at its worst ever. What I found odd was Jones's sending copies of this letter to Tom Roberts and Tom Fox. I would never have gone to publisher McSweeney to rat about then-editor Fox for whom I worked and to whom I felt it my duty to be loyal. . . .

The Jones letter is a series of gratuitous allegations so sweeping it would be pointless to address them. . . . Am I over-reacting to a harmless memo? The Jones letter would be of no consequence had I not, some weeks later, been fired as editor of *NCR* for the same alleged but insubstantial reasons as the Jones letter offers. . . .

I make bold to mention a few ideas I had for the paper, clawing for an opportunity to justify myself and to plead that I, too, was not without vision.

There was "Jesus 2000."

The poetry page of NCR is a big success. Such features were not intended to replace old-fashioned reporting but to complement it. If the paper is not more entertaining, not in the tabloid but in the reader-friendly sense, it will be difficult to attract new readers who may not share the 1960s commitment to what is becoming a boring repetition of peace, justice and church reform.

A humor page is no longer new, but readers repeatedly confirmed that Sic brought freshness to a paper that badly needed a light touch.

A history project. In the May 19 issue I prepared the ground for an ongoing project that would ask all Christians: who are we? . . . NCR should confront the search for whatever other transcendent story would give individual Americans a sense of significance in this pivotal time.

The Liberal Project. Nothing less than a think-tank. Copies are available. This could have brought NCR more attention than the Jesus 2000 event, and grounded the company for the new millennium. . . .

> At the same time, I make bold to suggest, the news coverage was as good as any time in the past 25 years, even better. My policy was to let the news team do its job.

It was a fine vision, for a magazine. But hands-off is not editorial leadership. Simply said, as editor, neither Hoyt nor Farrell had a news reporter's experience or newsroom instincts. The difference was Hoyt allowed his news staff to guide him. Consequently, Hoyt was deeply involved in shaping—and sharing in—the news coverage and its direction, and supplying the funds and bold backing to do the enterprising story and the deep digs into troubling topics.

Under Farrell, the news team felt constrained. That was why I wrote—as the longest-serving and most experienced member of the news team. I required no collusion with or support from anyone— including Fox, to whom I'd talked practically every day for the previous twenty years—to tell any editor what I thought, Farrell included. That is how I unhesitatingly operate.

I had differences with Farrell; Fox had difficulties.

My May 19 letter to Farrell from Washington reads:

> Dear Michael,
> Tom Fox called me earlier and told me of yesterday's meeting. It must be hard. I'm sorry you're hurting.
> And Tom Roberts just called and said you are staying on. I'm delighted. I hope we can continue to work together as the occasion demands.
> Yours
> Arthur

The next I heard was that the arrangement had fallen apart.

Should the readers have been told more about Farrell's firing? Possibly, though it's difficult to know precisely what without opening the pages to a "he said" versus "he said." There was the usual severance package with the customary agreement not to say anything. But telling the readers in greater depth about the news versus magazine balance essential to a reporter's *Reporter* would possibly have cleared the air a little. Or not.

Farrell was correct when he told the board in his letter, "It's a truism that those in power get to write the record for posterity." He was also correct when, as executive editor, he told the board, "By temperament I guess I am inclined towards analyses, essay, feature, regurgitating what is going on rather than reporting it."

He was initially invited to remain, and he declined. Like Lernoux and Hebblethwaite, Farrell was a jewel lost from *NCR*'s editorial tiara.

He was an excellent back-of-the-book editor. He wrote political satire of the highest order. His 1998 novel *Papabile: The Man Who Would Be Pope*, was favorably reviewed. In Ireland, in 2009, Farrell's book of short stories, *Life in the Universe*, was greeted with high acclaim by the leading Irish newspapers and journals.

In Kansas City, Farrell's was a departure that left everyone uncomfortable and many grieving. Fox had invited him to remain. He could have, should have, stayed. He'd still be writing for us all.

Established in 1964, the National Catholic Reporter began as a newspaper and is now a print and web news source that stands as one of the few independent journalistic outlets for Catholics and others who struggle with the complex moral and societal issues of the day. NCR is headquartered in Kansas City, Missouri. All photos courtesy of the National Catholic Reporter unless otherwise noted.

"Founding Fathers," original editorial staff with publisher Donald J. Thorman (December 1965–November 1977). Foreground: (L) Robert Hoyt, editor, and (R) Donald J. Thorman, publisher. Background, left to right: Tom Blackburn, assistant editor; Jim Andrews, managing editor; Art Winter, associate editor; Bob Olmstead, news editor. (Source unknown.)

Original National Catholic Reporter crew with founding publisher Michael Greene, circa 1965

Michael J. Greene, founding publisher October 1964–November 1965

Donald J. Thorman, publisher December 1965–November 1977

Arthur Jones, publisher 1977–1979

Jason Petosa, publisher July 1979–July 1985

William L. McSweeney, Jr., publisher January 1985–December 1996

Michael Farrell, trends and review editor 1980–1996, editor 1996–2001

Thomas Fox, publisher August 1985–December 1985, January 1997–November 2004, January 2011–December 2013. Courtesy of Fox family

Sr. Rita Larivee, SSA, publisher December 2004–September 2008

Tom Roberts, editor/editor at large January 1995–present

Joseph Feuerherd, publisher October 2008–May 2011. Courtesy of Rich Reinhard

Dennis Coday, editor January 2012–present

Caitlin Hendel, publisher January 2014–present

Toni-Ann Ortiz, layout editor/art director, October 1987–present

12

2000: TOM ROBERTS

It was spring of 1970. The phone rang. Twenty-one-year-old Tom Roberts answered it.

He was the contact. He had a job, therefore a phone. The gruff New York voice rasped, "I've been hearing from these folks all week long. No reason to waste time on an audition—you better be good." The caller was a famous, semi-retired creative artists' manager.

Roberts was the contact for the Valley Company, a quartet that started as a trio with two friends in the choir of all-male Allentown College of St. Francis de Sales (later De Sales University) in Pennsylvania. It became a quartet with the addition of a young woman, a high school senior with, said Roberts, "a really husky alto. Untrained, but a big, big voice. That was it." They were the Valley Company: Roberts, Ursula, another Tom, and Daniel.

Over the next couple of years, they went from covering folk songs of the era to developing some of their own material and built up their skills with constant rehearsals. They'd go anywhere for gigs, especially college and coffee house appearances. They did New York a couple of times. The big break came—though they didn't know it at first—when their "finders," the curator of the Museum of the City of New York and his longtime partner, who escaped to Pennsylvania on weekends, heard them rehearsing. That led to an invitation to perform alongside the hors d'oeuvres at a Rogers and Hammerstein gala at the museum.

The hitch was that they wanted us to do a few Hammerstein tunes, way outside our comfort zone. But Dan Wyatt, who was the real musician of the group (and went on to a master's in sacred music and a career in church music), sat down at the piano and worked out some arrangements. I think we worked up four or five familiar show tunes for four voices and two guitars in a couple of weeks. The night of the performance, we apparently did well enough beside the cheese and wine table that they inserted us into the show. We stood there and sang songs in the spotlight. The event went really well.

What they didn't know was that their two finders had prearranged a gathering at a Fifth Avenue penthouse where, if things went well enough by the hors d'oeuvres table, they would perform their normal material. And if that went well enough, they'd find themselves on a career path. "We quite frankly were in way over our imaginations. I'll tell how crazy it was, they asked us to give Myrna Loy a ride to the party."

"The dinner party was a crowd of old Broadway types and managers. We didn't know who they were. They really grilled us, asked us to do a set of our own stuff. There was a dinner. After that we were asked to leave." They had just been vetted by talent scouts, and the group had been impressed.

Then came that telephone call.

The gruff voice arranged auditions with booking and record companies. A couple of trips to New York followed. The Valley Company made a "demo tape" at Decca.

On their final trip to New York, they went to Columbia Records where they spent an hour auditioning for and being interviewed by the legendary John Hammond. He ended by talking about getting more material and maybe setting up a session with a music producer.

"We were ready to go," said Roberts. "And almost that quickly—when it was getting really serious—it just all fell apart. For all kinds of reasons."

His fallback position was the journalism career that had already begun in 1968 in Pennsylvania at the Pottstown *Mercury*. It was continuing at the *Bethlehem Globe-Times*. Post–Valley Company, he turned really serious about the journalism work, which coincided with a rediscovery of his Catholic faith and a sober assessment of the social scene that went a bit deeper and was more critical than folk tunes.

One experience returned his attention to the work of the religious left. Forty-plus years later, Roberts explained.

I've been a liberal all my life. But I was really having trouble with that broad late-1960s, early 1970s liberal coalition. Yes, it was the coalition we were part of, the coalition whose issues we wrote songs about. But a turning moment came when I went to Washington, I think in 1970, for a huge rally, an antiwar rally, on the Mall. Huge. While I certainly agreed with the sentiment of the gathering, what I saw and heard all day really caused me to stop and think about how much I wanted to be part of it—whether I wanted to go deeper into this movement. I didn't like the demagoguery, the lack of nuance, the mob mentality, the way people analyzed the situation.

I'd been to other rallies, religiously based, rallies outside prisons, protesting on behalf of those being held. Those, I felt at the time— and do now—those held so much more promise. Really, I came away from Washington terribly disillusioned. I remember saying to myself, "I don't like this demagoguery. I don't like what this thoughtless mob is." It really made me uneasy.

His dilemma wasn't uncommon. It was the paradox of wanting, through the music of the times, the Valley Company's music, to be involved—but not in "mass marketing" for the far end of the leftist scale. Even so, Roberts acknowledges that such protests "are one of the engines that move social change."

Thomas William Roberts is a warmhearted, open-faced, open-minded Pennsylvania Italian with white hair. The family name, when his paternal grandfather left Italy for America, was Rabattini. It wasn't changed at Ellis Island.

"My grandfather didn't come through New York," Roberts said.

For some reason he landed in Boston, worked the railroads to Pennsylvania. He lived for a while in Philadelphia and it was while in Philadelphia that he went through the citizenship process. It is 1903, and somewhere in the process, someone misheard. In Italian, the "Rab" in Rabattini is pronounced "Rob." The clerk said, "You're Roberts." And that was that. Anglicized in an instant and apparently too unsure of things to argue. Part of the price of entry.

All four grandparents came from Italy. Robert's mother's maiden name was Palladino.

In gritty Pottstown, Pennsylvania (heavy industry—Bethlehem Steel, Firestone Tire and Rubber, and the like), Roberts, his brother and two sisters were raised in an extended Italian family. The family included fifteen aunts and uncles, dozens of first cousins, as well as scores of other relatives and close family friends in the outer rings of the local Italian universe.

It was family 24/7. Many of his mother's in-town family lived within several blocks of one another. His father's side lived mostly along a single road that approached the home farmstead about two miles from the town.

In 1968, at age nineteen, Roberts had quit Allentown College of St. Francis De Sales for a reporter's job at the Pottstown *Mercury*, his hometown paper. That was why *he* had the telephone. He had taken the job that summer after he quit school to make enough money to go to the Philadelphia Folk Festival: "Pete Seeger, Odetta, Tom Rush, Oscar Brand, Dave Van Ronk, and on and on."

When he applied to the *Mercury*, he'd figured he could get a job as copy boy, not really knowing what a copy boy did. "Writing had always been my ace in the hole. I would always rather write a 40-page paper than take a test," he said. "I loved researching and writing and always did well with it."

"I can recall almost precisely the step in front of the building where the thought occurred—I wonder if copy boys get to write?" The man interviewing him heard his question and told Roberts that with his background he didn't want to be a copy boy, but a reporter. Two days later the editor, Robert Boyle, "a zany character, called me to come in for an interview. Boyle was a legendary eccentric." Roberts was handed an Associated Press writing test. Boyle said he'd be back in a half hour. "I apparently imitated newspaper writing style well enough," Roberts said. Boyle "returned, ripped the copy paper out of the typewriter, looked it over, and said: 'I don't know why I would hire you. You look about 12. But I'll give you a 30-day tryout.'"

That was the start of it. "At the *Mercury* I didn't get paid much, but I got paid. And I didn't get a grade at the end of the week. I was having so much fun doing the music, delightful, but the journalism had a home-feel to it."

When the promising music career disintegrated before it began, Roberts's next newspaper job, which he described as "the most important to my extended career," was at the now-defunct *Bethlehem Globe-Times*. The editor was the nationally known and highly admired Pulitzer

Prize–winner John Strohmeyer. If Boyle was a good introduction to the basics of newspaper journalism, Strohmeyer was a master class.

"Strohmeyer," said Roberts, "was a giant. On his return from [Naval service in World War II] he graduated top of his Columbia Journalism School class. Immediately after graduation, he won a Pulitzer traveling fellowship to teach about U.S. journalism in Eastern Europe. He later won a Nieman Fellowship at Harvard and finally won a Pulitzer Prize for editorial writing at the *Globe-Times*."

"With that background," said Roberts,

> Strohmeyer attracted a high level of talent (yours truly excepted) to Bethlehem, Pennsylvania. I found him by accident and as an act of desperation—I really needed a good job. People who went through the *GT* wound up at the *New York Times*, *Newsday*, *Sports Illustrated*, *Wall Street Journal*, *Washington Post*, *Los Angeles Times*, as well as a lot of second-tier places. That's in the era before the great downsizing of the print press in America.
>
> Toward the middle of my 12 years there, I was given increasing freedom to pursue stories beyond the borders of Bethlehem. In the late '70s, I spent several days in the bowels of the Pentagon (before electronic databases) researching military spending in the two counties where the paper circulated. I then took the numbers and the list of manufacturers and spoke to the clergy, Catholic and Protestant, who represented the considerable number of mainline denominations that had passed statements condemning nuclear weapons and modern warfare.

In 1981, with a journalist from another newspaper, he was in Central America: "Ten days in Guatemala at the height of that country's civil war, plus a few more in Honduras." It appeared as a series in the Christmas special edition because Bethlehem, Pennsylvania, was blessed with a Christmas name. To take advantage of the fact, the *Globe-Times* always produced a special Christmas edition ordered by people far beyond the *GT*'s normal geographical boundaries. Consequently, Roberts's Central America account went to thousands outside the paper's circulation area.

In the years immediately following the Second Vatican Council (Roberts was a high school junior the year it ended), "I had become increasingly enamored of the broad religion story," Roberts said.

The Catholic air was so full of new energy and promise, the edges of the community teeming with exploration. The church had become engaged in the big issues of the day—Vietnam War, militarism, poverty, civil rights—not primarily through its hierarchical level but through its priests, nuns and ordinary laypeople. Ecumenism was blossoming and a great deal of enthusiasm, thought and activity was issuing from sanctuaries, church basements, seminaries and religious orders.

The downside to it all was a growing resentment by those who felt their church had been unceremoniously yanked from them. In hindsight, it is easy to see that the council's thought was badly and unevenly conveyed. Catechesis suffered.

"Music went from badly performed traditional hymns to even worse performances of poorly composed and theologically inept modern 'folk' tunes." He said the balance "tipped badly in many places from an overemphasis on transcendence to an overemphasis on imminence. God as buddy, Jesus as rainbows and butterflies."

As Roberts summarized the years ahead, he said,

Those left seething at what they perceived as loss soon turned their energies to the politics of the matter and, with the cooperation of the John Paul II papacy, gained a strong footing on the path that turned back toward a pre-conciliar era. The tensions set up by those groups marching in different directions would seed much of the Catholic narrative for the coming decades.

The narrative grabbed my attention and I began to turn from a career in investigative and political journalism to religion writing. In 1981, shortly after Tom Fox became editor of *NCR*, I answered an ad for a job with the paper in Washington. Fox responded with a personal note that I've kept. He loved [my] clips and the resume but said *NCR* just couldn't support a family in DC. In lieu of a full-time job, he wanted to stay in touch and have me do writing from the East Coast. I agreed and went to work for *NCR* as a stringer while still working fulltime for the *GT*.

As a *GT* investigative reporter in the mid-1970s, Roberts dug into the disappearance of water from local wells. It was a story that involved deep explorations into local geology and the complexities of water law.

A local zinc mining company, a subsidiary of the multinational Gulf & Western Industries, was cutting into major aquifers. Legal discovery during an entire year of investigative stories surfaced early engineering documents that stated that over time the mining operation would affect the water supply in an ever-widening circumference. Gulf & Western went from absolute denial of any culpability, Roberts said, to an admission and a promise of restoration of the supply, and the beginnings of discussion of the company's contribution to a public water-supply system.

"The series won two major national awards of $1,000 each," said Roberts, "and they provided us (Sally and me and, at the time, three kids) the down payment on our first house. James, the youngest, didn't show up until we moved to Freehold, New Jersey, from which I commuted to a job at Religion News Service (RNS) in New York."

For *NCR*, Roberts was covering labor news. He wrote, too, about Philadelphia's Cardinal John Krol when Krol agreed to go public with an endorsement of the nuclear weapons opponents in the era of the nuclear freeze movement.

When Scranton, Pennsylvania, Bishop John O'Connor was named archbishop of New York, Roberts traveled to Scranton to interview him for *NCR*. It was Roberts's work for *NCR* and his writing on religion for the *Globe-Times* that brought him to the attention of the folks running RNS.

The news service wanted Roberts as news editor. "They opened the books and told me the deal: The service had almost gone out of business. The *United Methodist Reporter*, headquartered in Dallas, agreed to take on the service." For a three-year period the *United Methodist Reporter* would underwrite the service, in diminishing amounts. If, in that time, RNS "had managed to raise the bar journalistically while also bringing it into the black, the service would continue. If we failed, it likely would be shut down. It was the closest I'd ever get to fashioning something from the ground up."

"My boss, Judy Weidman, was primarily involved in bringing in money and new technology. I had a day of introduction under the editor I was replacing and off we went." Within the first few weeks, he called such RNS principal clients as *Time, Newsweek*, the *New York Times, Washington Post, Chicago Tribune* and the *Los Angeles Times*. As a result, he convinced his boss and the staff that the service sent out

far too much material that was of little, if any, value. We cut the size
of the service (in the pre-digital era it was mailed) by half, and I got
rid of most of our "stringers," who were sending in mail sacks full of
useless copy. I made new arrangements with established writers and
benefited from skilled in-house experts on the Protestant, Jewish and
evangelical communities. One of the bright lights was Bill Bole in
Washington, who wrote knowledgably and engagingly of the intersection of religion, politics and contemporary culture. Darrell Turner
was an encyclopedia of information on Protestant evangelicals, Jews
and cults. Jean Caffey Lyles was an expert on mainline Protestant-
ism. That was the core of the staff in New York, joined eventually by
Gus Spohn, who later became a publicist for Yale University's Divinity School, and by Pam Schaeffer, who took over as news editor.

With help from the Lilly Endowment, RNS established an intern-
ship program, produced a groundbreaking study on the readership of
religion news, and published an RNS 50th anniversary history. "By the
three-year mark," Roberts said, "we had done enough journalistically
and economically to stay in business. By the sixth or seventh year, we
caught the attention of the *New York Times* News Service. It looked
over our shoulders for about six months and finally decided to syndicate
us." Syndication expanded the reach of RNS exponentially to dozens
more newspapers and some electronic. From 1984 to the end of 1992,
Roberts was eight years the RNS news editor then editor at large for the
final two. His full-time employment with *NCR* began on January 1,
1994.

On January 2, Roberts headed out Interstate 70 West for Kansas
City, Missouri. Through snowstorms in Ohio and Indiana, on to the
rolling hills of Eastern Missouri until, finally, the Bellerive Apartments
across the street from *NCR*'s aging Armour Boulevard mansion. "My
commute," he said, "went from a minimum of four and a half hours a
day to about two minutes. The sense of liberation I felt in that simple
fact was emblematic of much more.

"*NCR* was like a sweet homecoming, an arrival at a destination for
which, wittingly or not, I had been preparing for a long time. I came on
as news editor and later was named managing editor and then editor in
2000, following Michael."

The 1990s closed with European bishops worried about the rapidly
expanding Muslim presence in Western Europe. In Europe, said *NCR*,

reporting the European bishops' concerns, the revenues of oil-exporting Muslim countries were not being used to create work in "poor North African or Middle Eastern countries, but to build mosques and cultural centers in Christian countries with Islamic immigration, including Rome." (No one anticipated that Islam was also on the U.S. religious-cultural horizon. Yet *NCR* would spend many special sections introducing Islam in its many aspects to the readers.)

As the millennium was about to turn, explaining the Catholic church's leaders to the readers remained as problematic as ever. In America, Chicago's Cardinal Francis George was castigating liberal Catholicism as "exhausted, parasitical" and "unable to pass on the faith." He then switched his attention no less unfavorably to Loretto Sr. Jeannine Gramick and her promotion of ministry to gays and lesbians.

The year closed out, too, with Philip Berrigan writing from jail in Towson, Maryland, waiting to be sentenced: "The 20th century has been dubbed 'the bloodiest of centuries,' with more than 200 million dead from war. How many more are crippled physically, psychologically, spiritually by war? Four hundred million? . . . If we executed the Lord of Life in the green wood, what will we do in the dry wood?"

Early in the New Year, Berrigan and three others would be sentenced to various prison terms for battering military hardware.

The Jesus 2000 exhibit, Michael Farrell's creation, debuted in New York. Its catalog (mailed free to all *NCR* subscribers) went through another press run. And the New Year kicked off with a Farrellian front page, a bottle tossed in the sea carrying the readers' messages into the New Year.

In the opinion pages, Pamela Schaeffer wrote on human beings as active participants with God as just stewards of creation, and bioethical challenges came to the fore as fears of human cloning and designer babies became part of the popular parlance. In the news, a Gallup Poll–*NCR* survey by William D'Antonio told us who we were and what we thought. Fifty-six percent of respondents felt one could be a good Catholic without donating time or money to help the poor and without having their marriage approved by the Catholic church (60 percent and 68 percent). The majority believed they should have a role in selecting their parish priest (73 percent) and in deciding whether women should be ordained (63 percent). The sacraments were regarded as the most important aspect of church practice.

The front page ahead of Good Friday 2000 was a startlingly fine painting, the anguished, brooding *Tenebrae* by Melissa Weinman. Anguish was present, too, on another *NCR* front page, a headline warning, "Nuclear power play: Public sidestepped as government extends lives of aging reactors."

At this point, Michael Farrell left and Tom Roberts was named editor. Years later, Roberts said, "In hindsight my career as editor was sandwiched between two moments of internal crisis, the leaving of Michael Farrell and the expensive and unsuccessful magazine experiment by publisher Sr. Rita Larivee."

Roberts appointed Pamela Schaeffer managing editor and John Allen as *NCR*'s Rome correspondent. The paper had been without a full-time presence in Rome for more than fifteen years and, since Peter Hebblethwaite's 1994 death, without a Vatican correspondent for six years.

The newsroom malaise caused by Farrell's departure Roberts addressed by organizing a staff retreat in rural Missouri. It was half therapy session—talk it all out—and half editorial meeting: What topics had the paper neglected to cover? What's on the horizon? With the news team reoriented, *NCR* got back to work.

John Allen, born the year the council ended, was a child of Vatican II in his education. The Catholicism he witnessed as he came of age was factionalized. It was contentious—outside its immediate Catholic-parish, Catholic-school center—and sometimes within it. The pope of his time was John Paul II. Said Allen, "I didn't grow up in a stuffy, all-controlling pre-Vatican II church, so I don't have the same 'reform DNA' as the previous generation of *NCR* folks."

Apart from freelancing several pieces to *NCR*, Allen had had no practical journalism experience when Roberts, as managing editor, hired him. He was teaching journalism at a Catholic high school.

The weekly news flow continued.

True to form: a lay Catholic can be president of the United States, and Catholics can be presidents of the world's largest corporations and universities, but they can't advise and serve the Catholic bishops in a top post. To Rome, the hint of a skirt in the old boys' club was sufficient for the church-in-Rome to turn down the U.S. bishops' proposal that Mercy Sr. Sharon Euart, the bishops' conference associate general secretary, apply for the top post.

Allen, by this time in Rome, wrote of other tone-deafness examples. One was John Paul II's decision to beatify Pius IX (Pio Nono of infallibility fame). Pio Nono was, like Ratzinger, a liberal turned conservative. But Pius IX was unique. In 1858, a six-year-old Jewish boy, Edgaro Mortara, was ordered removed from his Jewish home because a caregiver reportedly had secretly baptized him. The pope adopted the boy. Mortara eventually became a Catholic priest.

Meanwhile, Ratzinger's "Don't call us 'sister church'" managed to rub salt in the Catholic-Orthodox wounds as ecumenical and interfaith relationships smarted from the Congregation for the Doctrine of the Faith's *Dominus Iesus* statement that said followers of other religions are "gravely deficient" in comparison to Catholicism. This followed the Asian synod of bishops meeting. It brought the report and retort from Oblate Fr. Tissa Balasuriya who said that in Sri Lanka the reaction was "we are not interested in a dialogue that has the ulterior motive of conversion to Catholicism."

Dominus Iesus gave *NCR*'s *Celebration* editor Pat Marrin the theme for one of his most pointed—and smile inducing—cover illustrations. The pope is seated in a towering gothic wooden throne before a table set for eight, with no one else present. The headline: "Interfaith monologue." Reader Nancy Sullivan Murray of Syracuse, New York, responded to the same theme. She acknowledged the Asian synod as one motivating force behind Ratzinger's edict and added to it "the interreligious gathering in South Africa last year. It must have been threatening to those who cling to exclusivity to hear or read about leaders from a multitude of faith traditions accepting each other as equals on the journey toward wisdom." Mike Walsh of Yorba Linda, California, apologized "to all my Christian and non-Christian friends for the comments made by a very un-Christian and misguided individual [Ratzinger]."

In the wheels-of-justice-not-grinding-quickly-enough department:

—The Legionaries of Christ took over an Atlanta Catholic school, firing the staff. Parents pulled out their children as Legionaries' founder Fr. Marcial Maciel continued to escape censure for his sexual predations. He did not escape Jason Berry's dogged reporting.

—Three bishops not scrupulous about the company they kept pulled out of the Food for the Poor board after the charity founder and organization faced an FBI investigation.

—Twenty years after the four U.S. churchwomen were slain, two Salvadoran ex-generals faced trial for responsibility for the deaths.

In the irony department, Pax Christi cofounder Eileen Egan, long associated with peace and justice issues, died at eighty-eight just as John Paul II honored the military as "a force for peace" and pacifists in Italy held their own unofficial "Jubilee of Conscientious Objectors." On an allied topic, St. Joseph Sr. Helen Prejean linked war and capital punishment to a common source. U.S. cities from Charlotte, North Carolina, to Philadelphia, from San Francisco to Baltimore were calling for a death penalty moratorium. *NCR* praised this editorially as a "good first step."

Sr. Theresa Kane was still waiting for Pope John Paul II to take the next step after her 1979 personal plea to him for equal roles for women in the church. Nonetheless, she said, she felt John Paul did "want to do something for women." She spoke also to the "divisiveness" in the U.S. church and described the anti–Second Vatican Council movement operating from a "quiescent, conservative" backdrop.

A new thorn pushed into the church-in-Rome's consciousness, which resulted in more than the anticipated ouch, was what editor Roberts called

> alternative forms of family. Family is no longer the exclusive domain of heterosexual couples and their children. More and more, single parents, divorced and remarried couples, and combined families are making claims on the language and culture of the family. Gay and lesbian couples, too, are openly professing their love and extending that love to the children they are adopting.
>
> . . . We are well beyond the point of debate over whether such alternative unions, "de facto" unions in Vatican parlance, and nontraditional family groups should happen. They have become a part of life and will increasingly play a role in church and society.

Paul Wilkes reported in with an extensive survey of "great parishes" around the country. They come, he wrote, in all sizes and locations, and accommodate a wide range of views. One wasn't a parish Roberts mentioned: The East Coast parish where the young priest told the congregation on Christmas Day 2000, "If you did not attend yesterday (which, remember, was a Sunday) you may not go to communion." "Great parishioners" probably ignored him.

Overseas, courage was on display in Myanmar (formerly Burma), where protesters pushed for democracy. And four years after the horror, tears still flowed in Rwanda. As Rwandans hunted down the Tutsi minority, Archbishop Christophe Munzihirwa of the Congo issued "a broadcast for help to anyone who was listening." No one responded. In a chilling account, Munzihirwa told *NCR*'s Allen, "There are things that can be seen only with eyes that have cried."

On the poverty front, truth spoke to power in a Teresa Malcolm story when a twelve-year-old seventh-grader asked a Missouri state senator, "Have you actually *met* a poor person?" And at a level below poverty, *NCR* reported the global slave trade was prospering. It showed a map of the trade routes, then followed the links to a cover story revealing the potent exploitation that often exists behind the "Made in U.S.A." labels.

NCR's Malcolm was also scaring the life out of herself. She read the *Left Behind* series:

> A Protestant friend told me about her memories of childhood nightmares about the "Rapture" . . . Christ would snatch away to heaven all the true Christians leaving behind the unfortunates . . . under the reign of the Antichrist. . . . I heard her tale just as I was diving feet-first into the end of the world in its most prominent pop culture form: the *Left Behind* novels by Tim LaHaye and Jerry B. Jenkins. What I found therein—melodramatic end-of-the-world horrors heightened by a vindictive vision of faith—gave me nightmares too, and at the age of 33.

In the same wry tone, Colman McCarthy noted that George W. Bush was quoting "pacifist-anarchist-Karl Marx sympathizer Dorothy Day" at Notre Dame's commencement. McCarthy thought the president might want to invite to the White House some followers of the Catholic Worker cofounder. But McCarthy didn't bet his bicycle it would happen.

The faith community, twenty centuries late but better late than never, was said to be "the new frontline for aiding abused women." An *NCR* story quoted the woman who obtained a restraining order and a divorce. Her ex-husband didn't pay his child support. She said she went to her priest, who told her, "Let us pray." Later, she said, she learned the priest and her ex-husband were golfing buddies; her husband, by then a bigwig in the church, made calls to threaten her and ripped the front door of her house off its hinges at Christmas. It wasn't directly related, but a reader a couple of issues later asked, "Why must Mrs. Bush, her daughters, indeed any woman, cover her body with a black dress and wear a mantilla on her head in order to have an audience with the pope?"

In a tale of Vatican intrigue anyone with a sense of humor could love, an African Catholic archbishop, Emmanuel Milingo of Zambia, married a Korean acupuncturist in a ceremony the Rev. Sun Myung Moon conducted. The Vatican then facilitated the unwedding and Milingo's return to the church.

Moon's liturgy obviously couldn't meet Catholic standards, but liturgical renewal was under attack anyway. Ratzinger censured a liturgy specialist, Fr. Reinhard Messner at Austria's University of Innsbruck. For good measure, Chicago's Cardinal George fired liturgical publisher Gabe Huck from the archdiocese's Liturgy Training Publications.

Then the world seriously changed. Certainly for Americans.

It was September 11, 2001.

13

AMERICA INVADED: SEPTEMBER 11, 2001

"It was just minutes before the start of our daily morning meeting," editor Tom Roberts wrote, "when someone called from the outside and told us to check CNN. A plane had just hit the World Trade Center. By the time we got to the TV, the second plane had hit."

He responded first as a father with a daughter in Manhattan: Was Rebecca safe? She was. Then as editor, he presented the staff with two options: go with something perfunctory and publish the issue going to bed thirty-six hours later, or scrap the issue and go for broke. "Go for broke" was the unanimous response. As the staff plunged in, Roberts worked the phones, calling all *NCR*'s correspondents.

The front page carried only a photograph of that nightmare New York scene, and the opening lines of *Celebration* editor Pat Marrin's reflections, the remainder of which accompanied the inside pictures.

> We are pulled forward into a future we do not want
> Come sooner than we feared
> Like terror at the thought of judgment
> We are not prepared for this
> The scale of this
> The loss of it
> The threat delivered like a blow
> To the fact of who we are.

Many pages of photographs later Marrin concluded,

> These images describe the urgency, the surprising
> Inevitability of his promised presence in our hour of need:

"Like a thief in the night" . . .
But also this parable:
"Like a woman in labor"
Whose time of anguish gives birth to new life
The long sorrow that yields to new worlds
Resurgent hope that what we—one generation—
Could only conceive but could not do
Others will do, must do.
A birth of new hope
Not in the possibility of peace
But its necessity—our end or our beginning.
The sowing we will reap.

Roberts, presciently, wrote what many of *NCR*'s readers and most of its writers feared: "We will be asked to make judgments about justice and retribution, about proportionality and vengeance." Rich Heffern pointed to "the bitter irony . . . September 11 was the day set aside this year to mark the International Day of Peace."

From New York, Patricia Lefevere wrote, "While thousands went to church, many others simply dropped to their knees on the sidewalks of New York, watching in disbelief as workers jumped from the fiery heat of the melting twin towers of the World Trade Building . . . on the day many already called '9/11.'" There was a photograph of Washington, DC, Cardinal Theodore McCarrick donating blood; many bishops were quoted by *NCR*, but the key reporting was in the U.S. Muslim community.

Salam Al-Marayati, national director of the Muslim Public Affairs Council in Washington, said, "This goes beyond any religious legitimacy or justification. This is an act committed by a criminal and nothing any decent human being could reconcile with any religion."

Meanwhile, Muslim groups across America were reporting acts of vandalism and threats of retaliation. Radio Afghanistan in Encino, California, removed its sign from its building. It continued on air, said senior correspondent and former Agence France-Presse Soviet-Afghan war correspondent P. Shahnavaz Khan. Khan said the radio's talk-show callers ranged from "pro-Taliban, to pro-Northern Alliance, to people who oppose both."

Detroit Auxiliary Bishop Tom Gumbleton understood. He said that U.S. foreign, political and economic policy had "built up this anger," that Pope John Paul II understands full well "the tragedy of these times" and had challenged President George W. Bush, at Castel Gandolfo, July 23, 2001, to deal with that tragedy. "But," said Gumbleton, "all the U.S. media reported from that meeting was stem cell, stem cell, stem cell."

Jesuit Fr. Robert Drinan had his finger on the American pulse. Under the headline "Time to reassess nation's attitudes: revenge, retaliation not the way to build goodwill for America," he warned, "Widespread anger and frustration can prompt politicians to cater to the deep feelings of many who want 'the world's one superpower' to display its might and assert its hegemony. Not many public leaders will be calling for restraint. But religious leaders must remind all of us that the desire for revenge can hardly ever justify the use of massive violence."

Press day done, Roberts asked the staff what the next three cover stories should be. The answer: "Who hates us and why?" "Is war the only answer?" and "What is patriotism?"

Bush's private wonderings were revealed in public at an October 11 news conference, when he posed the question aloud to himself "How do I respond when I see that in some Islamic countries there is vitriolic hatred for America? I'll tell you how I respond: I'm amazed. I'm amazed that there's such misunderstanding of what our country is about that people would hate us. I am—like most Americans, I just can't believe it because I know how good we are."

Had Bush read *NCR* in 1998 when he was cranking up his presidential campaign, he would have learned why "they" hate us. In an October 2, 1998, Viewpoint titled "Truth is, we're terrorized because we're hated," Robert Bowman wrote, "If deceptions about terrorism go unchallenged, then the threat will continue until it destroys us. . . . In country after country, our country has thwarted democracy, stifled freedom and trampled human rights." (With many thanks to William J. Nottingham of Indianapolis who, on December 28, 2001, reminded the readers and *NCR*'s editors what Bowman had presciently written.)

A week after the 9/11 issue, the front page asked, "Who hates us, and why?" John Allen interviewed Mideast expert R. Scott Appleby at Notre Dame's Kroc Institute for International Peace Studies. Appleby spoke for many when he described three elements to the answer: "resentment of the U.S. presence in the Middle East; perception that the United States is hypocritical—that its actions belie its professed beliefs; contempt among conservative Muslims for Western culture."

NCR readers' letters echoed and probed. Jesuit Fr. Danny Tesvich of Grand Coteau, Louisiana, was unimpressed by all this and countered, regarding *NCR*'s editorial stance, "You simplistically portrayed America's choice as being either to respond out of hate and recklessness or respond with self-blame for past sins and no military response at all. Any view of responsible, measured self-defense in response to this attack was ignored."

Wrote Cyrus Johnston of Montgomery, Alabama,

> It is clear the United States is hated and despised by many people around the world. Would it hurt us to take time to reflect on the roots of this hatred, to discern if there may be something in our national behavior that is capable of provoking such fanatical hatred? Or are these people to be written off as simply diabolical, choosing to do evil for the pure joy of inflicting suffering on people, without hope of any other benefit? . . . The God I believe in would be no more capable of condoning the kind of retaliation being contemplated by the powers that be in this nation than He could have condoned the acts that provoke it.

Kathy and Paul Ruez of Vista, California, said, "We are faced with deciding how we are going to react to this recent tragedy since war can legalize the act of killing another being, but it cannot make it moral, unless of course you subscribe to the extreme fanaticisms of the attackers." In a sentence that has true resonance more than a decade later as one ponders in horror the carnage in Iraq and Afghanistan, the Ruezes continued, "Often the majority of the people killed in retaliations are not responsible for the conflict. Like our victims, many are innocent men, women and children. In order not to lower ourselves to the level of the attackers, we need to use reason and logic. Communication and principled consideration must be our constant companions."

Paul Whitely Sr. of Louisville, Kentucky, wrote, "We must be careful not to get caught up in the cycle of violence that Israel and the Palestinians have been engaged in for years. To this day, an 'eye for an eye' mentality has produced no winners, only losers."

Dianne Cotton of Houston challenged all Americans when she wrote, "It is hypocritical to ask for healing when we, as a nation, do not seem willing to do our part to allow healing to occur. We do not trust peace. We are so afraid that pursuing peace can only be accomplished with additional suffering, that we will not take the chance. We choose the sufferings of war over the sufferings of peace."

If Bush could make it worse, he did. On September 16, 2001, he used the word "crusade." The word shot around the Islamic world. And shocked it. He said, "This crusade, this war on terrorism, is going to take a long time." As the Muslim uproar swelled, Bush quickly apologized.

The damage was done. To Muslims, the crusades were a "holy war"; if that's what the West wanted, that's what the West would get. In these "nerve-jangling times," to use Roberts's phrase, *NCR*, with scholar experts, dug deeply into the crusades from the Muslim point of view to explain.

The administration not-so-secretly wanted someone to strike out at. Iraq looked good; Afghanistan looked better. Constitutional lawyer Drinan wrote that as Congress approved "hastily concocted measures," it took advantage of "a period of almost open hysteria." Cheney and Bush were doing no less; in October, Bush ordered the immediate invasion of Afghanistan. Less than two years later, he would order Iraq invaded.

In shell-shocked and bleeding Afghanistan, there was a brief respite for healing moments. Claire Schaeffer-Duffy reported back on the meeting and mutual consoling of Americans and Afghans who respectively had lost relatives to terror in 9/11 and U.S. bombs on Afghanistan.

Schaeffer-Duffy had returned and was now in America's high schools and colleges, reporting on the ROTC system: "Feeding the military machine: Armed forces a growing presence in nation's classrooms." There was also an advertisement in *NCR* encouraging serving soldiers to lay down their arms.

The hawks came out to protest.

"As a veteran with 26 years active and reserve duty, I was appalled at the naiveté of the articles," wrote Barbara Knight, U.S. Navy (retired), from Sandwich, Massachusetts. Wrote Jean Short of Surprise, Arizona, "I believe it is reprehensible to print and distribute such vitriolic, unpatriotic misinformation directed toward influencing service personnel. Haven't we had enough scandal in this church? . . . It is sadly fascinating to witness the self-interest and lack of integrity in the writers of this crassly uninformed and irresponsible diatribe."

Peter M. Kopkowski of San Diego took the opposite view: "Our current rash of excessive patriotism has blinded us to the values to which we are really called by God, in favor of those that are convenient, useful and expedient."

Before the Iraq invasion, the Bush administration dispatched Michael Novak to Rome in a bid to persuade the Vatican of the morality of a possible "preventive war" in Iraq. Cardinal Walter Kasper, president of the Pontifical Council for Promoting Christian Unity, predicted the mission would fail. "I do not see how the requirements for a just war can be met at this time."

Joe Feuerherd wrote, "The moral justification for military action against Iraq requires the reconciliation of a twenty-first-century military doctrine with teachings first developed by a fourth-century African bishop." Bush released a thirty-five-page unapologetic document for first strike against perceived enemies. *NCR* editorially commented, "President George W. Bush is about to embark on a war of unintended consequences."

Columnist Jesuit Father Raymond Schroth wrote, "We went to war because we wanted someone to beat up. The country, as Bush reads it, was hankering for some kind of victory."

As the inevitable followed the predictable, it was revealed in an *NCR* headline that the United States was "under fire for treatment of detainees: Critics abroad cite inhumane conditions, ambiguous legal status of prisoners." This, then the torture; the unconscionable death toll of civilians and soldiers, a killing fields for which no one has been tried.

The "why" has never been answered for the families, homes and hospitals of the cruelly maimed, the courageous, determined victims known as "heroes." The national shame is hidden behind the glowing stories of amputees with tremendous guts.

That the U.S. national media did not call the administration out on its weapons of mass destruction madness, neither probing nor critiquing, but using its laptops as accompanying war timpani, signaled a low point in journalistic duty.

Such was the situation for Roberts's first four years of editorship.

In 2004, former President Ronald Reagan died. When *NCR* refused to share the glorifying and hadn't a tear to wipe away, readers in their letters appreciated the honesty.

Briggs and Stratton had sued *NCR* for $30 million over an article on the corporation moving its production from Milwaukee to Mexico. The suit dragged on. *NCR* was well-represented by a top New York libel

lawyer, Tennyson Schad. The pretrial document collection and deposi-
tions carried on for years until it finally got to a judge's desk and at that
point, it was thrown out. After Schad's death, his colleague, David
Korzenik, continued in his stead.

Roberts explained how the editors work with their lawyers. "I spent
a lot of time with David on the phone vetting Jason [Berry's] digs into
the Legion [of Christ], Vatican corruption—the money being thrown
about in the Curia and the papal palace—and stories on the [Legion
founder Marcial] Maciel children [who accused their father of sexual
abuse] began to surface." Feuerherd's probing investigations also were
vetted by Korzenik.

—The collapse of the Pope John Paul II Cultural Center and revelations that Cardinal Adam Maida of Detroit sent the center $40 million
from a diocese headquartered in one of the poorest cities in the country.

—The Raffaello Follieri/Cardinal Angelo Sodano capers. Follieri,
who dated movie star Anne Hathaway, was Sodano's nephew. The
nephew borrowed money, ostensibly to buy up old churches and flip
them as commercial properties. Follieri went to jail.

—A profile of Deal Hudson, the Catholic presence in the Bush
White House, turned into revelations of Hudson sexually abusing one of
his Fordham University students. Hudson left the White House and
Crisis magazine.

Two wars, terrorism and Islam remained fixed in *NCR*'s collective
mind. But while the newspaper never relaxed its full quota of terror
news, it now softened its attention to deal with the widest range of
Catholic-Christian inquiry and reflection. Its special issues surveyed the
frontiers.

—Ministries: "The lay apostolate in a clerical church."

—Ethics: "Crossing a moral threshold: Do any benefits justify human cloning?"

—Racism: "Does America need a 12-step program to break the racism habit?"

—Overconsumption: "Food fight: The ethics of eating too much."

—Bioscience: "Stem cell dilemma."

There was an extensive guide to assessing Mel Gibson's blood-
drenched movie *The Passion of Christ*. (Is it anti-Semitic?) The movie

was quickly dubbed "the gospel according to Mel." The readers were quick to join in.

Dawn T. Nelson of Pass Christian, Mississippi, ruled on Tom Beaudoin's *The Passion of Christ* article: "Excuse my language, but what a bunch of crap." Nick Sternberg of Ferndale, Michigan, dubbed it "just about the best article I have read on the issue. Concise and unashamed. Mel Gibson, however, should be ashamed . . . a film about Jesus that is little more than a cheap horror flick."

NCR was quickly adapting and re-adapting itself to the benefits and challenges new technologies were offering. At this same time, there was an extensive essay by Richard Thieme that provided one of the best insights into the dark side of the technologically adept decade that was changing Americans' perception—along with how they lived and worked. Thieme's "Sliding into the crazy place: The whirling images of the digital age put our sanity at risk" was a giant step into uncharted territory.

NCR did not overlook peace-related specials, from 2002's "Paths to Peace" to 2004's "Fundamentalism: A modern rage against secular modernity—Who Islamists are and what they want"; then "Islam vs. McWorld." These wide and deep inquiries punctuated the decade-long Afghan-Iraq coverage.

On the Catholic front, 2000–2004, a new and cohesive priest-laity group, the Voice of the Faithful, arose from Boston's discontents. In January 2002, after months of investigative research, the *Boston Globe* revealed Cardinal Bernard Law had knowingly transferred a sexually abusive priest to another parish. Voice of the Faithful coalesced in response to Law's cover-up. John Paul II transferred Law to Rome, with a comfy monthly income plus a Vatican apartment.

Law's path to a lifelong sinecure gained its greatest momentum when fifty-eight Boston archdiocesan pastors called for his resignation: "The priests and people of Boston have lost confidence in you as their spiritual leader." *NCR* reader James Ullman of San Marcos, California, neatly noted that Hans Küng, in his 1979 book *The Christian Challenge*, wrote, "One member of the parish who goes to the parish priest does not count, five can be troublesome, fifty can change the situation. One parish priest does not count in the diocese, five are given attention, fifty are invincible."

He was right. That's why Rome pulled Law behind the Vatican walls, out of prosecutorial harm's way.

Editorially, *NCR*, in congratulating the Boston priests and lauding Voice of the Faithful, also praised the thirty priests in Rapid City, South Dakota, who agreed to donate 5 percent of their monthly income to help pay for counseling for abusive priests and their victims.

NCR's front-page headline on the Voice of the Faithful echoed its cry: "Keep the faith, change the church."

Simultaneously, Feuerherd was writing of Boston's archbishop-elect, Sean O'Malley: "Another Fixer-upper for O'Malley." The Franciscan bishop had already resuscitated the Palm Beach, Florida, diocese where two bishops in a row (J. Keith Symons and Anthony O'Connell) had resigned in the face of molestation charges. O'Malley had the grace to admit that Law's elevation to Vatican status—seen by people as "a reward . . . some sort of prestigious, powerful post"—was "poorly timed."

Whatever the U.S. bishops as a group may try to achieve, individually, some of their actions astonish. The case of "Mansion Murphy" is not atypical. As Boston vicar general, Auxiliary Bishop William Murphy was tarred with the Law sexual-abuse cover-up brush for transferring one accused priest and establishing a job bank for others. As newly appointed bishop of Rockville Center, New York, Murphy decided on a $5 million spending spree on "my" cathedral and his upscale lodgings. He dislodged the six Dominican sisters living on the third floor of their convent. Some $800,000 later, he had what he described as the privacy suitable to his office. The $120,000 he spent on three oriental rugs and a dining room table just about matched the diocese's $140,000 deficit.

The breakaway Spiritus Christi church in Rochester, New York, welcomed newly ordained Mary Ramerman as a celebrant. Ramerman and Fr. Jim Callan were key figures in Rochester's Corpus Christi Catholic community, a community that many members re-formed in 1998 as Spiritus Christi to provide the possibility of full liturgical roles for women.

Elsewhere, in response to the priest shortage, there was an increase in the number of lay preachers. The Dominican Word of God Institute in Washington, DC, was a center for the revival.

Despite bits of reluctant lip service to freedom of speech for Catholics, there was always someone firing a Catholic diocesan newspaper editor or getting rid of a priest with an opinion and the courage to express it. Then there was Nebraska. Archbishop Elden Curtiss rebuked by mail two Catholics who'd criticized in the *Omaha World-Herald* Curtiss's reassignment of a priest accused of viewing Internet child pornography. Curtiss complained the two Catholics were "a disgrace to the church" and should have dialogued with him first. The letter-writers probably knew in advance how far a dialogue would get them.

It didn't just happen in America. In Poland, the bishops ordered that priests would need their permission before giving comments to the media. Polish Jesuit Fr. Stanislaw Musial, a leading commentator and essayist, said he would "never agree" to having his media statements checked in advance.

Those U.S. bishops keen to stifle discussion, let alone dissent, took to banning speakers from diocesan property. Theologian Anthony Padovano, due to talk on hope for the future church in a Detroit parish, was blocked. The ban came from Cardinal Maida. Padovano simply shifted the talk off church property. Local Voice of the Faithful groups did the same when faced with bans in Newark, New Jersey (by Archbishop John J. Myers) and elsewhere.

Chicago's Cardinal Francis George, who ousted liturgist and director Gabe Huck from the archdiocese's Liturgy Training Publications firm, must have been gratified when the bishop conference's director of its Secretariat for the Liturgy, Msgr. James Moroney, urged removal of all Huck's writings from approved lists. George at the time was a member of the conference's administrative committee.

Where the bishops were mostly starkly exposed was in their dealings with the initially enthusiastically welcomed thirteen-member National Review Board. After the Boston-Law exposé and the growing national uproar from Catholics regarding clerical sexual abuse, the U.S. bishops—who'd known about the abuse for decades—met in Dallas in June 2002. The result was the "Charter for the Protection of Children and Young People." Seriously meant, the "Dallas Charter" was not always seriously followed, as future reporting and scandals revealed. Also established in 2002 was the National Review Board.

The board, chaired by former Oklahoma Governor Frank Keating, had been holding meetings around the country. Many bishops were growing increasingly uncomfortable, none more so than Los Angeles Cardinal Roger Mahony. That came after Keating bluntly told the *Los*

Angeles Times that for the bishops "to act like *La Cosa Nostra* and hide and suppress, I think is very unhealthy . . . eventually it will all come out." Eventually it did. Even in Mahony's LA.

Mahony wanted Keating ousted as chairman. Yet no cardinal was closer to acting the protective godfather (with attentive *consiglieri*) than Mahony. Later, as the spotlight of scandal moved westward, Mahony for years more sat on twelve thousand incriminating sexual abuse–related church documents until finally forced by the courts to reveal them.

Keating, standing by his remarks, had quit the board. His successor was Illinois Judge Anne Burke, no less forceful than Keating. The bishops were soon nervously muttering about the board straying beyond its mandate. Worse, the board was unaware that the bishops were considering shelving or delaying some of the board's key recommendations. "In short," said Burke, "we were manipulated. Nothing—I will say this again," she told a Loyola Chicago audience, "nothing could have adequately prepared one for the encounter with the politics of the institutional church. I have been around Chicago politics for a very long time [her husband, Edward, was a Chicago alderman for thirty-six years] but the machinations encountered in the ecclesiastical version during this period of fear, perplexity and suspicion were at times medieval, certainly Byzantine."

The bishops changed the players. That changed the play. (Mahony's successor in Los Angeles would publicly criticize him for his handling of the archdiocesan abuse scandal.)

Of course, it wasn't solely Mahony. In "Inside *NCR*," editor Roberts wrote,

> The members of the board, high-profile and faithful Catholics, have reached the top of their respective disciplines and professions in the real world, where a certain give and take—call it cooperation, compromise, communication, trust—is essential. In New York they ran into one of those members of the Catholic hierarchy who seems to move in another world.
>
> Cardinal Edward Egan has shown himself, in legal transcripts taken in his previous diocese of Bridgeport, Conn., and in more recent comments about the sex abuse crisis, disdainful of legal and other processes that dare to call into question his handling of things.

The Vatican apologized for "cultural cruelties to the people of Ocea-nia and Asia for the sexual cruelty of priests toward nuns." The pope expressed regrets. Yet under the headline "Bad confession," reader Michael Welch of La Crosse, Wisconsin, wrote,

> Are Vatican "apologetics" merely a device designed so that popes are permitted to ignore any injustice of the church in their own times, just to leave it to a future pope to make the apologies for them? Frankly, I think of this arrangement as "a bad confession," for one of the prerequisites of confessing a sin, I understand, is the resolve not to continue committing it. Whatever "resolve" the pope may have had, it appears that the Vatican curia readily abandons it for the cold but comforting secrets they have often resorted to in order to choose power in this world over life in the next. They are cold men, it seems, with colder hearts, and loyalty is their god, not the truth.

There wasn't much loyalty to the troops when two military chaplains expressed support for victims in the sex abuse crisis. Dominican Father Thomas P. Doyle, an Air Force chaplain and colonel, and Msgr. Eugene Gomulka, a Navy captain, lost their "ecclesiastical endorsement" from Archbishop for Military Services Edwin F. O'Brien. There was not, of course, any due process.

Celibacy, never popular, took many a toll, including the surprising one NCR's delightful Tim Unsworth reported back from a cruise. The ship had no Catholic chaplain. Shipboard scuttlebutt, Unsworth reported, was that the cruise lines "now preferred to have married men."

The celibacy crisis damage was best explained in NCR by an anony-mous priest who wrote of "just the bare facts that led me to offend."

"I was a 'lifer,'" he wrote. "I entered minor seminary in the early 1960s at age fourteen and went straight on to college seminary, theolo-gy and holy orders. . . . The only women were the nuns in the kitchen." Seminary rules dictated no dating or the frequent company of girls, even on summer vacation. Because the teenage lifer found himself fur-tively glancing at other boys in the dorm as they undressed, he thought he was gay and became "the perfect, asexual seminarian who was never troubled by fantasies or masturbation." And on the letter went until his account was unfolded. There was much in it that every priest could probably recognize and sympathize with, without condoning the eventual outcome—the priest's sexual encounter with a young adult parishioner.

Reader Mark Shirilau of Irvine, California, wrote, "In all the discussion of this subject it is so rare to hear a balanced attitude that has any perspective other than narrow-minded, hate-filled judgment. . . . Your choice to go out on a limb and publish this beautiful article by a caring, real-world servant of God, even under his unfortunate but obvious need for anonymity, makes *NCR* shine out as perhaps a solitary beacon of truth and justice as this tragedy unfolds."

From Rome in 2002, John Allen reported that for the first time since the crisis began, Pope John Paul II and senior aides had spoken about the abuse crisis—while insisting that most priests are innocent and "suggesting that American outrage may be exaggerated."

Rome's premier example of twisted sexual logic, however, came with the beatification of an Italian husband and wife whose prime claim to sanctity appeared to be that for twenty-six years they had renounced sex and moved into separate beds. *NCR*'s readers responded with the requisite disbelief, wit, amusement and anger at the crude depiction—and honoring—of what the papacy and church-in-Rome thought conjugal sex amounted to.

As over the next few years the news flowed on, too often sexual abuse dominated the headlines. As accounts of incidents in the United States continued to surface, and reports of sexual abuse proliferated around the world, there was little option but to report them.

In 2004—as *NCR* marked its 40th anniversary, there was a party; there was also a departure—Tom Fox announced he was retiring as publisher effective January 1, 2005. He had served *NCR* for a quarter-century. (If he could live without *NCR*, *NCR* in the future obviously couldn't live without him. He was invited back to serve once more as editor, and stayed to serve twice more as publisher.)

In 2005, he was succeeded as publisher by his deputy publisher, St. Anne Sr. Rita Larivee.

14

2005: A WOMAN AT THE TOP

NCR's new publisher, St. Anne Sr. Rita Larivee, later its second editor in chief, had joined *NCR* six years earlier as its director of operations. She'd arrived with a roster of unusual credentials: She was a doctoral candidate in moral theology and Christian ethics at the University of Chicago, had a master of theological studies from Weston Jesuit School of Theology, had done doctoral studies in mathematics and computer education at Boston University, and had gained a master's in mathematics, physics and education from Rhode Island College. She had also served as president of her order's Anna Maria College in Paxton, Massachusetts.

The slaughter in Iraq and the war in Afghanistan plunged America's flawed policies deeper into a bubbling cauldron of resentment and hatred as thousands of U.S. soldiers died and tens of thousands were badly maimed, physically and/or psychologically. The United States' own moral core was in danger of a meltdown. The front page told what the readers knew: "Fifty years of teaching torture leads to the abuse at Abu Ghraib." For *NCR*, the CIA torture-manual story was an old one; only the consequences—for the new colonizing version of the American empire in the Middle East and Afghanistan—were new. The torture both paralleled and exceeded the Bush-Cheney Patriot Act domestic threat to American civil liberties. Domestic colonialism, profit-seekers grabbing what they could while they could, led the hands-on approach to deregulating anything that would impede more money for the wealthy.

Tom Roberts had much to editorialize on.

Enough.

Little else is left to say to an administration that:

—Led a country to war on false premises;

—Continues to link the war against terrorism with the war in Iraq when the two had no relationship at the outset;

—Dismisses the Geneva Convention and holds prisoners incognito for years, without charges or access to legal representation;

—Places detainees on planes bound for foreign countries known for torture and abuse of prisoners;

—Maintains secret CIA prisons on foreign soil;

—Subverts laws guarding civil liberties of U.S. citizens, including searches of personal records and infiltration of religious and peace groups by the FBI;

—Defers to a vice president who argues for legal exceptions so that U.S. personnel can engage in torture;

—And has, at various times, created mechanisms to plant false news reports domestically and overseas and most recently paid to have stories planted in the Iraqi press.

Where are we headed?

The nation, carried by a wave of jingoism, ill-served by a mainstream media that generally accepted the Bush-Cheney White House hype, fanned by the "moral values" platform of cultural conservatives—including many Catholics—headed into a second term with George W. Bush. The man was sworn in to wreak a further four years of havoc. The script was crafted more in energy megacorporations and military-industrial corporate boardrooms than the White House, more in downtown clubs, Wall Street and all-pals-together bird hunts than in Congress. (Iraq-and-Afghan-invasion-urging warrior Dick Cheney, who had managed consecutive student deferments to avoid service during the Vietnam War, could still shoot birds—and pepper his friend's face with buckshot while trying to do so.) The country was a colony again, and the in-charge domestic colonists were gathering up remaining natural resources and pickings from the government purse.

NCR was watching, commenting on, reporting on the consequences of an invigorated Bush-Cheney renewing the crusade to hand over as much of the country's money to the care of the corporate and financial world as possible. The classic example had been the insurance companies' heyday and pharmaceutical companies' bonanza under the Bushboondoggled drug prescription plan, which granted grazing rights on ailing people's wallets.

Federal lands and waters were thrown open to exploitation, regulations were slashed, or a hands-off approach ordered, even for food inspection. Starting with Reagan and under Bush-Cheney, the American constitutional way of life was thrown open wide to allow Wall Street and the executive suite to run the government. The actuality of it would show up in the economic tables: the 1 percent's new golden age.

NCR was keeping its eye on the rest of the world as best a small newspaper could: Barbara Fraser and Paul Jeffrey in El Salvador; Neve Gordon writing on militarism versus messianism in Ariel Sharon's plan to exit Gaza; and the plight of Cambodia. A photo essay of Catholics in rural China from the camera of Yang Yankang took the readers into the lives of Catholics in Shaanxi Province where, despite the Cultural Revolution, farm families had clung to their faith since the seventeenth century.

On the theology front, there was the 2005 front-page story "Theological disputes," which considered Vatican procedures and the case of Fr. Roger Haight. The Congregation for the Doctrine of the Faith was not letting up on its "Whac-a-Theologian" game. There was a highly relevant front page on Christians at risk. It gave insight into the worsening conditions facing Christians in the Middle East. A decade later, the greater worries have been borne out—the bigotry is intolerable, and daily living conditions, from Syria to Egypt, dangerous.

At home, Bush's "ownership society" program masked the economic truth: Bush's deregulation society would soon result in millions of Americans losing their homes because Wall Street's largest and worst were let loose to quench their greed. Richard Thieme, in February 2005, returned to the consequences of the rapidly developing digital world with another landmark article: "The face we see in the digital mirror: How technology is changing religion."

Meanwhile more protests in Boston—by now, a common dateline on issues as thorny as Cardinal Bernard Law and abuse, and parish closings. Boston articles, however, always contained an element of the ordinary lay Catholic fighting back. This was true for parish closings where parishioners occupied their churches, and true in the case of women survivors of sexual abuse by priests. They were protesting. Not about their own grievances, but with the sort of twist Boston datelines invariably offered. Women survivors of sexual abuse, such as Kathleen Dwyer and Ann Hagan Webb, picketed the chancery to charge Vatican officials with scapegoating gay men and dodging responsibility for the abuse.

As the year sped by, television audiences were caught up in the panoply, pomp and prayer of the death and funeral of one bishop of Rome, John Paul II, and a conclave and more processions and pomp to usher in his successor bishop, Cardinal Joseph Ratzinger as Benedict XVI. *NCR*'s special supplement on the papacy of John Paul II is bedrock material for any future biographer. (There is, though, the saying "No one is deader than a dead pope.")

Of the new pope, Benedict XVI, it could be said that at the Congregation for the Doctrine of the Faith, Ratzinger hadn't quite scored 100 on Matthew Fox's "Ratzinger tally" of investigated, criticized or silenced theologians and others. Ex-Dominican Fox named the ninety-three notches on Ratzinger's crozier.

In November 2005, *NCR* editorialized,

> The U.S. bishops, once collectively a voice to be reckoned with in the corridors of U.S. power and in the ornate halls of the Vatican, are withdrawing from the national stage and from any meaningful engagement with Rome.
>
> Bishops once bristled at the prospect of becoming, in their words, branch managers or errand boys. They are now only too willing to take orders and leave the questions to others. . . . We are watching the disintegration of a once great national church, the largest denomination in the United States, into regional groupings bent on avoiding the spotlight and big issues.
>
> Perhaps what we're seeing is inevitable, given the massive internal problems facing the church, chief among them the ongoing sexual abuse crisis. Internally, the bishops have been battered by their own mishandling of the crisis, a problem about which they speak with little honesty or authority.

In 2006, Dawn Gibeau, *NCR*'s first female managing editor, died. She joined *NCR* in 1972, was promoted to managing editor in 1975, and retired in 1995 after a twenty-three-year *NCR* career. She was in large measure responsible for the continuation of *NCR*'s "down" style: Everyone referred to by last name after first mention; "church" without a capital *C*—except in the appropriate "St. Philomena's Church" usage. In *NCR*, "God" is fortunate to get away with a capital *G*.

Gibeau was also the second editor of *NCR*'s *Praying* magazine, founded by former *NCR* managing editor Art Winter. She was industrious, dogged, occasionally stubborn, and she played a mean piano.

NCR still ran poetry. In 2005, the readers responded, riveted, to Amy Ilva Tatem's "The Power of One" as she confronted the carnage of war.

> "Thirty have been killed
> in an attack
> on their convoy . . . "
> Wait!
> Thirty? Thirty what?
> Thirty (men).
> Now, hold that thought
> before reading on.
> What is thirty (men)
> divisible by?
> Try one.
> One (man).
> Now, hold that thought
> before reading on.
> One man killed.
> Who is his mother?
> Who is his father?
> his sisters?
> his brothers?
> One man killed.
> Does he have a name?
> a face?
> Is he tall or short?
> a little heavy in the middle?
> olive skin?
> white skin?
> black skin?
> My son
> or yours?
> The boy down the street?
> What city?
> What state?

Thirty killed
in an attack
on their convoy.
That is:
thirty ones
thirty men
beloved of God.

The message behind poem was captured in another fashion, in an August 12, 2005, editorial as a supportive reminder of the issues raised:

In one of her last public appearances before she fell ill for several years, Dorothy Day stood, with trepidation, before an audience at the 1976 Eucharistic Congress in Philadelphia. The date was Aug. 6, the Feast of the Transfiguration and the 31st anniversary of the dropping of the atomic bomb on Hiroshima.

The late Eileen Egan, an ardent peace activist and longtime associate of Day, set the scene in her book, *Peace Be With You: Justified Warfare or the Way of Nonviolence.*

Nearby, at another event on the Eucharistic Congress schedule, church officials were conducting a Mass for the military. "That morning, as Dorothy Day, Mother Teresa and I made our way together . . . Dorothy confided to me that she dreaded the talk" because she felt she had to raise the issue of the Mass for the military and the fact that the day marked the anniversary of the bombing of Hiroshima. The Hiroshima anniversary was nowhere mentioned in the Eucharistic Congress literature.

"It is almost easier to stand before a judge and go to jail than to come before you," Day told the gathering, confessing that she had taken the unusual step, because of her fear, of writing out her remarks.

"Our Creator," Day continued, "gave us life, and the Eucharist to sustain our life. But we have given the world instruments of death of inconceivable magnitude."

Day suggested that the Mass for the military, "and all the Masses today" be regarded as "an act of penance, begging God to forgive us."

An ovation broke out, Egan reports, and lasted several minutes after Day finished the speech, an ovation joined by "Mother Teresa and all on the platform."

Patrick O'Neill reported on Fr. Bob Cushing of Savannah, Georgia, who created a storm of controversy over Hiroshima. Cushing made a reconciliation pilgrimage to Japan. He delivered an apology to the Japanese for the U.S. atomic bombing of Hiroshima and Nagasaki. Many St. Teresa of Avila parishioners had helped make a thousand paper peace cranes "as an act of prayerful solidarity with the people of Hiroshima." Cushing presented them to Nagasaki Archbishop Joseph Mitsuaki Takami.

Cushing said, "People came up to me in tears, embracing me, crying. I was just stunned. I was totally knocked off my feet." Naturally, there were repercussions. Not all the parishioners agreed, and a rift developed. However, one parish couple, the Wildes, told Bishop J. Kevin Boland that while they did not support Cushing's "political position," they supported him and admired him and asked Boland to help heal the parish rift.

There was a burr under the Catholic right's saddle: Pope Benedict. *NCR* editorialized,

> That Pope Benedict XVI is a European is hardly news. [However,] in his Easter "urbi et orbi" address, Benedict declared, "Nothing positive comes from Iraq, torn apart by continual slaughter as the civil population flees." To most American Catholics, and certainly to most Europeans, the pope's words reflect the terrible reality that is post-invasion Iraq under occupation. He simply spoke the truth.
>
> To the neocons, Benedict's sentiments were, at best, an overstatement; at worst, the Vatican equivalent of the "cut-and-run" calumny leveled at domestic opponents of the United States' Iraqi misadventure.
>
> The pope, imply his new critics, could learn something from the steadfastness of President Bush.
>
> What they think, of course, is significant because they had great access to the highest levels of authority during the previous papacy and because they have had a role, disproportionate we would say, in shaping the Catholic conversation in the United States.

January 2007, and pacifist Bishop Tom Gumbleton had to move out of his St. Leo Parish. He faced mandatory retirement as a Detroit auxiliary. This was the year, too, Gumbleton revealed that he, as a young seminarian, had been sexually abused by a seminary priest.

When in 2005 Hurricane Katrina struck, native son Jason Berry, well-known to *NCR* readers, had to move to the home of relatives in Covington, Louisiana, to ride out the storm. Berry wrote, "Hemingway called courage 'grace under pressure.' I have seen that grace in great display these terrifying days, grace entwined with another kind of valor: the realization that in order to be brave, you must first be afraid."

No one was more afraid, though with no visible display of courage apparently, than President Bush. When informed what had happened, he hadn't a clue as to what to do next.

New Orleans poverty was legendary. Joe Feuerherd took a broader look at the national problem in a lengthy article, "War on Poverty: New consensus promotes work and 'safety net' to help nation's poor." Promoted somewhat fruitlessly, of course, for as Feuerherd also realistically remarked, "President Bush has talked more about poverty and its ill effects than any president since Lyndon Johnson (whether he's done much to address the problem is another topic)."

On the theological front, the Catholic Theological Society of America honored the young Asian Gemma Tulud Cruz, a feminist theologian from the Philippines, who won the Best Essay by a New Scholar Award for "One Bread, One Body, One People: The Challenges of Migration to Theological Reflection." A January 2006 cover story, "Women priests—What it means in a church that doesn't allow them," reported on women who sought ordination by other hands. One photograph was of the Rev. Mary Ramerman celebrating the Eucharist in Toronto's Anglican Church of the Holy Trinity.

An October 2006 front page asked, "Who's out there? What life elsewhere would mean for us, for religion, and for our ideas about God." Coincidentally, there was a story in the same issue saying what wasn't out there: limbo. The church-in-Rome had finally pushed limbo into the closet of figments past. Another issue that was eye-catching and, on a day-to-day basis far more important, was an examination of revenge—and the lust for it.

The reader responses ranged from the hilarious to the profound. There was the wife who "was really put out with my then-husband sitting in the other room waiting for supper. I took this raw egg into where he was continuing to read the newspaper, and I just squeezed it hard and it went plop on the top of his head." And there was the newly moved-in woman and the dog-walker who would let his dog wander into her yard to poop. He ignored her appeal to curb his dog. She knew where he lived, collected dog poop from around and about, and dumped it on his porch. Both writers displayed a wry understanding of their actions.

On a more somber note, a World War II vet, Myron Ratkowski of Milwaukee, told of that war and offered St. Augustine's precept reworked: "I have found, in a homemade parable, that driving a car named 'Revenge' in a reckless manner is an opportunity to crash head on at the revenge-related intersection of 'Delight' and 'Small Minds.'" Angela J. Kovitch of Ohio wrote,

> We refuse to beat our swords into ploughshares because it doesn't fit our agenda of retaliation. If we seek revenge, are we able to justify, with a shrug of the shoulder, the collateral damage we ignite? Our enemies are trying to live their lives and raise their children, just as we do. They are the ones we hurt. "You shall not fear the terror of the night because I will be with you in distress." These are words to comfort the suffering. But aren't we all in pain?

Some readers were no doubt jolted by the 2007 front-page story "Consecrated virgins: Today they're firefighters, nurses, Harvard students, even feminists."

That was quickly followed by letters. In May 2007, Joseph Maciejko of Bettendorf, Iowa, asked, "Can't men be consecrated virgins too?" Next came an article, "Being single"; 51 percent of all women now lived without a spouse. The readers also loved this one. Helen T. Kock of St. Paul, Minnesota, a single adult in a senior residence, spoke of it as her "peaceful haven," her contemplative calling. Marie West of Bethesda, Maryland, closed her letter, "For me, religious life or marriage is a train to another's neighborhood. Being single is the train home." Katrina Stoeckel of St. Louis, teaching in an all-girls Catholic high school, asked her class what omitted elements in a person's life warranted their own sacrament: "I cannot say that I was surprised when more than half of the class devised a sacrament for the single life."

Reminisced Betty L. Wolfe of Colorado Springs, Colorado, "I was single once when I was young. Now after 48 years of marriage, I am single again. . . . The hardest part is when I speak. Now instead of 'we,' it's only 'me.' I live alone, sleep alone, eat alone. I plan alone. . . . But if I had a choice, I would still rather be 'we' instead of just 'me.'"

After the special appeared, St. Joseph Sr. Alice Leclair in Pembroke, Ontario, wrote, "Thank you for the articles. . . . It is so rare to even have our single friends alluded to by the institutional church or mentioned in print."

NCR's special issues continued with Lenten and Advent reflections, and books issues. Other special-issue titles sometimes waxed and waned. Most often the range included "Religious Life," "Spirituality," "Ministries," "Theology," "Peace and Justice," "Deacons" and "Family Life."

The longest-lasting of all specials was "Summer Listings." In its heyday, Summer Listings was huge, occupying more pages than the newspaper. It listed the best in seminars, programs and immersion sessions across the widest variety of topics. In the 1970s, one priest slyly dubbed it "The Priests and Nuns Datebook."

In 2007, women religious were being given "straight talk" by one of their Generation X colleagues. At the Leadership Conference of Women Religious annual meeting, Dominican Sr. Laurie Brink told 750 leaders of U.S. women religious that religious women "have lost our prophetic place on the margins . . . and fallen off the edge of the church." She discussed how congregations could regain their "relevance and authenticity," even while caring for their aging members.

On women's leadership in the early church, Joseph Dyer of Newton Highlands, Massachusetts, in July 2007 wrote he was

> distressed by the title of the article, "When Theodora was a bishop," reinforced by a front-page photo showing a portion of St. Zeno Chapel at the Roman church of Santa Prassede, with a female figure surmounted by the inscription "episcopa." In fact, the lady in question was Pope Paschal's mother and not a member of the clergy at all! On their visit to the church, your feminist scholars probably walked right by the Latin inscription that says so. This mosaic was a touching way for Paschal to memorialize his mother at her burial site, one of the jewels of Christian art.

A Robert McClory article reported on "simmering dissatisfaction with the leadership style of Bishop Edward Braxton" of Belleville, Illinois. In 2006 in New York, a Committee of Concerned Clergy for the Archdiocese of New York castigated their cardinal, Edward Egan, and called for a vote of no confidence. The committee protested Egan's "vindictive nature," "arrogant manner" and his "cruel and ruthless way" of dismissing seminary faculty. It was one with what Roberts had earlier written of Egan's "disdain."

In stark contrast, among courageous archbishops there was Zimbabwean Archbishop Pius Ncube of Bulawayo. He called for peaceful mass protests as the nation's economic and political crisis deepened. Making a public enemy of Zimbabwe's dictator, Robert Mugabe, by calling on him to "step down now" was a brave move in the African cronyist police state.

Liberation theologian Jesuit Fr. Jon Sobrino, being vetted by the Congregation for the Doctrine of the Faith, received disdainful sniffs but no outright censure. In January 2007, a well-known, sharp-faced, firm-jawed profile in courage passed from the scene. *NCR* columnist Robert Drinan, five-term Congressman, nationally known and a widely admired activist, died at age eighty-six. Drinan and Tom Fox had remained close since Vietnam when Fox had shown Drinan the realities.

Detroit's Cardinal Adam Maida—of Washington, DC, white elephant fame—orchestrated a new business deal: the diocesan seminary as a luxury hotel, golf and conference center. With a fine-wine cellar, of course. Joe Feuerherd's "Boon or boondoggle?" had fun with a 2007 story on the Inn at St. John's. The brochure gloated about the "unparalleled elegance and luxury" of the inn owned by the archdiocese and gracing the former diocesan seminary grounds. It was leased to a group of private investors "who have asked to remained anonymous" and did not want to reveal its costs. Why hide, one wonders? O the joys of being a bishop, and corporate solo.

In Minnesota, University of St. Thomas President Fr. Dennis Dease canceled a 2007 invitation to Archbishop Desmond Tutu to speak at a youth conference on peace-making. The university's Cris Toffolo, who issued the invitation, was dismissed as director of the St. Thomas Justice and Peace Studies Program. Dease contended Tutu's criticisms of Israel were hurtful to some members of the Jewish community. In the wave of criticism that washed over St. Thomas, Dease reversed himself, and reinvited Tutu. Tutu refused unless Toffolo was reinstated. Dease resisted, and Tutu declined—though he did attend the subsequent Twin Cities "Peace Jam." Toffolo left St. Thomas for Northeastern Illinois University as a professor and member of the justice studies board.

The headline over one 2007 *NCR* essay was "Stop abusing our troops: A soldier's mother speaks out against the war in Iraq." Columnist Stephen Zunes expanded on that. He posited that fighting radical Islamic movements could lead to

> an increasing number of civilian casualties. As part of an effort to fend off criticism for these casualties, Washington has embarked on a campaign to convince the public that the deaths in Afghanistan and Iraq from U.S. air strikes—as well as the high number of civilian casualties in last summer's Israeli attacks on Lebanon—are caused by the victims' fellow countrymen, not by the forces that attacked them.

Close to the heart of church matters, Mother Theodore Guerin, founder of the Sisters of Providence of St. Mary-in-the-Woods, was canonized. A front page proclaimed, "Confession: The disappearing sacrament?" Catholics trod the halls of Congress, trying to drum up more federal support for Catholic Relief Services (CRS) among House members. Congressional representatives thought CRS stood for "Congressional Research Service." People for the Ethical Treatment of Animals (PETA) targeted a South Carolina abbey's egg farm; and the Catholic University of America was urged not to kill off its prized think tank, the Life Cycle Institute. As 2007 progressed, came a John Allen account of "the feminization of the church": "The plain truth is that lay ecclesial ministry is rapidly 'feminizing' pastoral leadership in the Catholic church."

15

CHANGES AND DEPARTURES

At the May 2007, board meeting, publisher Rita Larivee recommended a shift from the existing *NCR* newspaper to a monthly newsstand-quality magazine; shifts in editorial leadership and the relationship between publisher and editor; and an investment in the company from its assets that could amount to $1 million spread over three years. The previous November, Larivee had radically, and sensibly, proposed a change to *NCR*'s publication schedule. To reduce costs, not least because of rising postal service expenses and slightly declining circulation, she recommended the newspaper go on a twenty-six-issue cycle. She'd done a superb job building up *NCR*'s online presence, and in written remarks for this book listed among her three greatest accomplishments the growth of the online daily news.

> I'm very proud of this every time I go online to ncronline.org for the latest news [Larivee gave the site its name. Previously it had been natcath.com]. I remember the first time I mentioned the word "blog" to the members of the board—the entire idea of a strong Web presence was hard to sell in the early days. And to allow the readers to give their feedback was unheard of . . . today it is an automatic assumption.

Of becoming editor in chief, Larivee said, "it was a strategic shift. Without the title, ncronline.org would never have become what it is today. The title had little to do with the day-to-day editorial work, but much to do with the editorial content of ncronline.org. Because Tom

Fox had been editor for many years, it wasn't an issue that he had served as publisher with the title editor in chief."

Larivee contended *NCR* was "too small" for the separate publisher (business side) and editor (journalism side) model. "For instance," she said,

> if an editor is too negative, it hurts the paper. Or if an editor isn't strong enough on issues of accountability [within] the church, and is afraid of the story that has to take a big risk, it hurts the quality of good journalism. But for me, having not worked in editorial, it was as if I was just the business end of things—which is very far from the truth. So, to fix this situation, the board gave me both titles.

The veteran journalist and Pulitzer Prize nominee Pamela Schaeffer, a previous *NCR* managing editor, had been brought in as the newspaper's executive editor. She'd accepted on the understanding she would be the new magazine's editor.

Larivee said later, "We were not really trying to found a magazine. We were simply responding in all ways possible to the challenges facing us for the print publication."

The May 4, 2007, board meeting pro forma financial projections provided for "transition costs for changing from a newsweekly to a magazine. [Larivee] will begin work by late summer and proceed immediately to managing the first six issues of the new magazine."

An expenditure of $455,680 was projected for the 2008 magazine transition costs. In executive session, the board approved "the management recommendation that the *National Catholic Reporter* newsweekly be transitioned to a monthly magazine with a tentative target date of June 2008 . . . and the publisher was given the title of editor in chief."

In the Inside *NCR* box, editor Roberts introduced the new editor in chief. In the same column, he wrote, "Leadership at *NCR* is becoming a joint venture and it starts now." Roberts, it was stated, after a three-month sabbatical, would be "news director" (no job details provided) and editor at large. (In private Roberts had told Larivee a magazine was not something he could, or wanted, to edit.) Larivee took over writing the Inside *NCR* column.

At the December 2008 board meeting, Larivee "explained the need to rethink the plan to move to a magazine." The magazine idea was abandoned. Schaeffer left. A total of $218,600 had been spent in the magazine attempt. Larivee was elected general superior of the Sisters of Saint Anne, and she prepared to leave. Tom Fox, back as editor pro tem when Schaeffer left, wrote of Larivee, "Her mark on the paper and the entire *NCR* operation has been considerable, from design of the print product to development of a sophisticated website. It is not a stretch to say that *NCR* might still be in the dark ages of the computer era had it not been for her deep understanding of the potential of that technology."

16

THE NEWS FLOW: 2007–2010

In the years 2007 to 2010, the news flow offered plenty of articles and insights into a church-in-Rome in stasis. That, and the gathering discontents.

Under the headline "Full participation before all else," *NCR* editorialized, "Upon learning about *Summorum Pontificum*, Pope Benedict XVI's [2007] apostolic letter allowing greater use of the Tridentine Mass, no doubt quite a few *NCR* readers reacted like Bishop Luca Brandolini, a member of the liturgical commission of the Italian bishops' conference. 'I can't fight back the tears,' he told the Rome daily *La Repubblica.*"

Benedict also changed John Paul's rules for papal elections to a two-thirds majority no matter what. (John Paul had ruled for a simple majority if no two-thirds majority was reached after twelve days or thirty ballots. Benedict was elected on the third ballot.)

In Cleveland, Anton Zgoznik, the diocesan former assistant treasurer, was on trial for allegedly accumulating $17.5 million through kickback schemes; "Left recovers its language of faith: Clinton, Obama find values outreach working"; "Charities brace for leaner economy" (Wall Street's money-grabbing was impoverishing the nation—except for the 1 percent). There was a charming peek into a song's past: a pleasant little tale as Mercy Sr. Suzanne Toolan told in 2007 how, in 1966, she'd been asked to write a song for a San Francisco archdiocesan event. She taught in a Catholic girls' high school. Deadline looming, she worked in an unoccupied room next to the infirmary. Said Toolan, "I worked on it, and I tore it up. I thought, 'This will not do.' And this little girl came out of the infirmary and said, 'That was beautiful.' I went right back and Scotch-taped it up." The schoolgirl had saved "I Am the Bread of Life."

NCR's front pages were magazine-y, with "Mystery of the mind: Consciousness"; "Weaving images in the soul: Meet Meinrad Craighead, artist who explores the feminine divine"; "Have we brought this on ourselves? A new EPA report links extreme weather with global warming"; "Think about it: Does the educational value of plasticized body exhibits trump the moral questions they raise?"; "The greening of the church"; "Meet the newest face of Catholic music" (the Matt Maher Band and others); and "Experiencing the Divine in our lives."

Inside the newspaper, Colman McCarthy's riff on the death of William F. Buckley was priceless:

> The conservative movement that Buckley pulled together lies in ruins. In place of "Firing Line," his television program that ran from 1966 to 1999 on which he debated with élan everyone on the left from Noam Chomsky to Gloria Steinem, we now have the Limbaughs, O'Reillys and assorted dyspeptic ranters. "Firing Line" would become the Firing Squad, the cheap-shot division.
> In place of Buckleyan civility, we have right-wing snarlers like Tom Delay and Dick Cheney. In place of a Buckley newspaper column that provoked thought, we have right-wing columnists . . . who specialize in bile. In place of conservatives who think, we have vulgarians like Ann Coulter who smear. Neocons have become neo-Neanderthals.

When it came to new frontiers for Catholic women, executive editor Pam Schaeffer kept tabs. Datelined St. Louis, she wrote in 2008, "Two Catholic women are being ordained by Roman Catholic Womenpriests here, prompting outrage from Catholic officials—outrage that, surprisingly, is directed less at Catholic women, or at the movement ordaining them, than toward a rabbi who agreed to host the event."

Elsie McGrath, a retired writer and editor for a Catholic publishing house, and Rose Marie Dunn Hudson, a former teacher, were to be ordained by a Dominican nun, in a synagogue.

The Catholic hierarchical ire was directed at Rabbi Susan Talve, senior rabbi at the Central Reform Congregation—the synagogue host. Ronald Modras, professor of theological studies at St. Louis University, found it fascinating and symbolic, "a remarkable demonstration of sisterhood." Catholic officials huffed it would set back Catholic-Jewish relations; Jewish officials puffed it could provoke a backlash against Jews.

A thousand women who'd been nominated for the Nobel Peace Prize (though none were awarded it) were honored in a 2008 traveling exhibit, "1,000 PeaceWomen across the Globe." A new United Nations report, "Girls Count: A Global Investment and Action Agenda," warned that ignoring girls' welfare carried a high global price. It delved into the details. In Catholic circles, lesbians had a different set of difficulties to deal with. When a Catholic man and his daughter were set to give a Minneapolis parish talk on how the family had coped with the daughter's coming out as a lesbian, St. Frances Cabrini's pastor—prodded by the archdiocese's communications director—canceled it.

In October 2008, Bill Callahan, battling Parkinson's, stepped down from the Maryland-based Quixote Center leadership. The justice-in-church-and-society center he and Dolly Pomerleau founded had led them into the thorniest issues of the time. Those issues had cost Callahan his standing as a Jesuit. Also in the courage stakes, Brazilian Bishop Luiz Cappio of Barra was awarded the Pax Christi International Peace Award. Cappio led 2005 and 2007 hunger strikes to protest a plan to divert the Sao Francisco River.

Sexual abuse by priests claimed now another bruised victim: Los Angeles Cardinal Roger Mahony. It was reported that a man who made angry statements about sexual abuse by priests had knocked down Mahony and kicked him—shortly after the archdiocese's $660 million settlement with 508 plaintiffs. A Vatican official in the Congregation for the Clergy was caught on camera propositioning a young man he assumed was gay. When the encounter was shown on Italian television, Msgr. Tommaso Stenico, quickly suspended from duties, contended he was investigating groups that were targeting the church.

NCR carried a 2008 front-page story, "After the Fall," on the Rome-dweller Cardinal Bernard Law. Reader Steven Shea of Milwaukee noted that John Allen wrote, "Catholics from cultures lacking Anglo-Saxon concepts of corporate liability, which includes Italy, sometimes struggle to understand why bishops should be held accountable for the misdeeds of their priests."

To which Shea said, "Are Vatican leaders really that delusional? Bernard Law did not lose his seat in Boston because of the misdeeds of his priests. He lost his seat because of his own misdeeds. He repeatedly covered up the crimes of his pedophile priests. He lied to the people of his archdiocese about his own work in moving those predator priests from parish to parish." Catalina Echeverri of Midland, Michigan, added, "When I saw Cardinal Law on the front page I felt nauseated, to put it nicely. How could you?"

A priest with the courage to risk an archbishop's wrath—and suspension from the priesthood—was Polish-born Fr. Marek Bozek. He was the priest who stepped in when the St. Louis parish of St. Stanislaus Kostka refused to hand control of the parish and its $9 million in assets to Archbishop Raymond Burke. Burke deprived parishioners of their priest—and therefore the sacraments at Stanislaus. He moved to laicize Bozek. The priest, who had left his Springfield–Cape Girardeau, Missouri, diocese to serve the shunned parishioners, knew the price he'd pay. He didn't aid his situation when he donned his vestments and laid his hands in blessing on two women being ordained by Roman Catholic Womenpriests. (The parish later separated from the archdiocese and became affiliated with the Episcopal church.)

Elsewhere in the world, a Korean priest, Fr. Robert An Soong-keel, told a Seoul *Gaudium et Spes* Pastoral Institute symposium that the Catholic church should embrace democracy in order to be relevant to modern society. At a time "when the whole world operates on the basis of a person's vote," the church's way of proceeding, with only bishops and priests making the decisions, had to be reconsidered.

The bishops battling the Barack Obama presidential candidacy were not without allies. Catholic convert Randall Terry and his cohorts were arrested in the parking lot of St. Thomas More Cathedral in Arlington, Virginia. They had refused to move off church property where, as part of a nine-state strategy, allies were passing out anti-Obama literature in pamphlets that lectured Catholics on their duty to vote against the candidate.

Unlike the Brazilian Cappio, the U.S. bishops weren't collecting many social-justice awards. *NCR* characterized their November 2008 meeting, which followed the election of Obama as president, as "a defeat in their three-decades-long political strategy aimed at overturning *Roe* v. *Wade*." The Catholic bishops' strategy of cozying up to Republicans and the religious right, regardless of their new friends' views and inactions across an entire spectrum of other life and justice issues, had failed.

As 2008 was turning into 2009, Maryknoll Fr. Roy Bourgeois, who spread hope around as easily as honey on hot toast, "awaited," one headline stated, "word on [his] excommunication."

Commented Joan Chittister, "The church has been excommunicating saints for centuries."

Responding to *NCR* articles, reader Pat Chervenak of Louisville, Kentucky, wrote that onetime *NCR* columnist

> Garry Wills seems to personify an increasingly large segment of the Catholic population when he counts himself among "people who are totally disaffected from the hierarchy, but who still believe and still go to church." . . . The pew cannot hold captive those who come to the table to be fed on mercy and find themselves presented week after week with the lukewarm trivia of meaningless directives on uniformity of customs, phrases and postures. At the same time, hungry to be called to the heroic demands of the Gospel, these people may be scandalized by excommunication threats against those, such as Fr. Roy Bourgeois, who are moved by the Spirit and responsive to inner imperatives to live a radical, conscience-driven life worthy of emulation, not condemnation.

Pope Benedict XVI had Legionaries of Christ serve his midnight Mass and declared he wanted 2009 to be "the year of Africa." John Allen wrote that the move wasn't exclusively humanitarian: The continent represented the church's "growth market." As with most sweeping papal announcements, there was little evidence Benedict's declaration amounted to concrete action on behalf of either the African nations or the many Catholic churches there. African Catholic actuality is as uproar-filled as rapidly developing U.S. Catholicism was in the nineteenth and twentieth centuries.

Case in point could be tiny Benin. For twenty-first-century Benin's interethnic and subethnic rivalries, the lack of liturgies in minorities' languages, conflict over the ethnicity in episcopal appointments, and the ethnicity of priests sent to serve—think nineteenth-century U.S. Polish-speaking minorities in Irish-majority dioceses.

Washington's big guns, too, turned on women religious: Two American nuns had just made the U.S. Department of Homeland Security's terrorist list. This was some escalation in dealing with domestic pacifist dissenters. Homeland Security's listing of Dominican Srs. Ardeth Platte and Carol Gilbert of Baltimore's Jonah House community "raises frightening questions for those who dissent from U.S. government policy in this national security age."

Tom Roberts described the "terrorist designation as an absurdity."

While the Vatican moved toward excommunicating Bourgeois, Benedict XVI in 2009 lifted the excommunication of four bishop followers of the late Archbishop Marcel Lefebvre. By itself, the move was offensive to everything the Vatican II church represented. In the wider context, it was a classic example of Vatican bureaucratic bungling: One bishop was a Holocaust denier. The church-in-Rome discovered that the hard way. Benedict didn't help smooth Jewish-Catholic tensions when he let it be known that during his visit to Jerusalem he would not enter the Holocaust museum.

The Vatican banned Jesuit Fr. Roger Haight from publishing on theological topics. Reader Jeanette Blonigen Clancy of Avon, Minnesota, wrote,

> Vatican watchdogs consider Haight's book *Jesus: Symbol of God* "dangerous" because, without . . . exclusive claims, Christianity is just one religion among many.
>
> Christians, let's grow up. It is both naive and implicitly insulting to insist that our way of imagining spiritual reality is the only correct one. . . . Our superior Christian attitude cannot long survive in a world that technology shrinks by the minute.

Reader Bill Giel of Clinton, New Jersey, joined in with "Fr. Haight must have known his writings would trigger a Vatican 'shoot the messenger' response. He joins company with Fr. Teilhard de Chardin and more recently with Australian Fr. Michael Morwood, author of *Tomorrow's Catholic*."

One place where Catholics had considered changing the church—and paid heavily for their audacity—was Holland. *NCR*'s Robert McClory in 2009 reported on the dramatic decline in Dutch Catholicism. Holland had long been a global centerpoint for innovation, and a bull's eye for papal and curial wrath.

In Rome, Benedict opened a fresh line of attack on the living emblems of Vatican II, the U.S. women religious. The plan to conduct a study of U.S. communities came from the Congregation for Institutes of Consecrated Life and Societies of Apostolic Life, headed by Cardinal Franc Rodé. Rodé is best known to history for his extreme dressing-up: his twenty-one-foot, red watered-silk train delicately held at the end by a young page decked in sixteenth-century velveteens and lace. Rodé in 2009 appointed Apostle of the Sacred Heart of Jesus Mother Mary Clare Millea to head the apostolic visitation that would examine U.S. religious orders. The Vatican, in its inimitable way, added insult to injury and told the U.S. bishops to pay the anticipated $1.1 million cost.

Back in the Letters pages, reader Paul J. Ackerman of Columbus, Mississippi, commented,

> So the U.S. bishops are being dunned by Cardinal Franc Rodé for $1.1 million to pay for the investigation of our nuns, an investigation not needed and not requested. Yet our "impotent potentates" will no doubt send the money of the people of God to the Vatican as requested—money not a dollar of which have they ever earned, money that should have been given out of justice to the retirement fund for these religious women who founded and staffed our Catholic schools, hospitals, orphanages. These women of God might well ask of the Vatican and the bishops, "For which of our good deeds are we now being punished?"

The aggressive move against the sisters aroused the ire of U.S. Catholics. Tom Fox wrote,

> Say it isn't fair, but when the Vatican announced Jan. 30 [2009] it had begun a study of U.S. women's religious congregations, I couldn't help but recall the utterly failed effort of the U.S. bishops in the late 1980s and early 1990s to write a pastoral on women. . . . It could be argued that talking about a study of Catholic women then, and a study of them now is like mixing apples and oranges. I can hear some people saying this time it's different because two American women religious are in charge . . . but they will then return [the report] to the man who commissioned it, Cardinal Franc Rodé.
>
> In the final analysis, it is men studying and reporting on women.

Mercy Sr. Theresa Kane at the National Coalition of American Nuns' 40th anniversary offered a stinging rebuke to the Vatican for its treatment of women in general and American women religious in particular. Calling the Vatican incapable of adult behavior, she said the church today was "experiencing a dictatorial mindset and spiritual violence." Meanwhile, *NCR* editorialized that it was the sisters who'd delivered the church that Vatican II had promised.

Equally pressing on American women religious was the need for a sustainable future, hence the question "To merge or not to merge?" Many orders were studying it; some accomplishing it.

How far had American women religious traveled since Vatican II? Indeed, how far had the rest of the laity traveled? A nun was the main character in the 2008 film *Doubt*, set in the Bronx of 1964. Movie pastor Father Brendan Flynn (Philip Seymour Hoffman) wants to bring the church closer to the people. He tells Sister Aloysius Beauvier (Meryl Streep), "We [clergy and nuns] are really just like them [the parishioners]." Beauvier strongly disagrees.

NCR contributor James Flanigan, who grew up in the Highbridge section of the Bronx of that era, took readers back in time to that Irish Bronx, a Catholic time many could recall.

> [The Irish] had come with little formal education from small farms and towns in the west of Ireland, and they were happy to have the work. They were between two worlds. Their temporal lives were hitched to the economy of the New York metropolitan area, while their emotional lives remained back in Ireland, which they always called "home."
>
> But their spiritual lives, and most important, the guidance of their children, were cared for by Sacred Heart Church, which comforted the old and taught the young.
>
> Its schools took their children, corrected the Irish brogues they brought from home, and taught them of a new country and a wider world. . . .
>
> The church protected them in practical ways also. If a young man stole a car, the police didn't book him but telephoned the pastor of Sacred Heart, then Msgr. William Humphrey, who inevitably would "know the boy's parents." Msgr. Humphrey would then ask the car's owner (probably a non-Catholic) not to press charges, assuring him the car would be restored and any damages paid. The church would pony up the money. The parents would pay it back, then the boy

would work it off. A police record was avoided, a productive life, perhaps, saved.

If the young fellow persisted in recalcitrant ways, as my friend, the rangy, wild Bobby O'Toole, did, he would be sent to Lincoln Hall, a reform school in then-rural Westchester County run by the New York archdiocese.

The church was a protector, but a distant one necessarily. Sister Aloysius [in the movie] understood that.

The unlettered parents seldom if ever spoke to priests or to the nuns and Christian Brothers who taught their children with anything other than bowed deference.

In May 2008, *NCR* lost its laughing (and revered) wordsmith Tim Unsworth. Later, when a collection of his columns was published, Tom Fox wrote, "His was a generous spirit always finding the good buried beneath the foibles, rarely judgmental, never condemning. Rather, he'd poke fun at each of us, coaxing us to enlarge our own circles."

On the justice front, Maryland Governor Martin O'Malley was urging repeal of the death penalty (Maryland achieved that four years later). The Bush-inspired Great Recession and the bankers and mortgage firms were robbing people of their homes, the downturn robbing them of their jobs. Social ministries were strained for resources. Even the Voice of the Faithful reform group reported it was critically low on funds.

Dennis Coday wrote tellingly, "When you're mentally ill, no one brings you a casserole." He reported on those who were working to change society's aversion to the mentally ill, a stigma not imposed on people with other special needs. Alice Popovici delved into the difficulties of ex-offenders' "struggle for a second chance"—as in finding work.

Americans fighting foreclosure were on the "Recovery Bus" from California to Washington to defend their homes. In 2009, Joe Feuerherd ripped away the mystery surrounding huge bills in Congress. The topic was a $787 billion economic stimulus bill, with Republicans politicizing the issue by challenging members of Congress to "read the bill." Under the headline, "Don't read that bill," Feuerherd explained that no one in Congress reads large spending bills because "the content does little to enlighten the reader about the content of the measure," while groups such as the Congressional Budget Office and the Government

Accountability Office (in this case and others) provide thorough analysis and user-friendly interpretation.

Contributor Tom Gallagher was asking, "Fired! Do church employees get unemployment benefits?" Of 45 diocesan respondents to a survey, 13 dioceses participated in state programs, 12 in state programs on a reimbursement basis, and 20 did not participate in any state unemployment program. (Not part of the survey: A few dioceses do offer severance packages.)

Few things arouse Catholic ire like threats to close their parish. In response to a Tom Roberts report, they weighed in from across the country. From Nevada, Paula Stone wrote,

> I am reminded of Los Angeles Cardinal Roger Mahony's [2000] pastoral letter, "As I Have Done for You" . . . [that] maintains lay ministry is anchored in the priesthood of the baptized and as such is not just a Band-Aid measure to shore up the priest shortage. If this is so, rather than closing parishes, there could be created new models of lay participation and governance in the saving mission of the local church itself. A giant point of emphasis is that this type of lay involvement is not the result of hierarchical delegation, but rather comes by virtue of baptism.

From Fayetteville, New York, Geri Hall said,

> We are in the throes of merging two fine progressive parishes that have been served by one pastor for five years. One is in the inner city and the other in the university area. The anguish is immense since the smaller one closed voluntarily so as not to risk the loss of presence of its inner-city sister. The cultures of each are quite different, and we are attempting to both preserve them and form something new—an interesting paradox. There was absolutely no reason for these two healthy entities to combine except for the will of the bishop, not the pastor, that there be "one priest, one church," and small and thriving communities be damned. Why don't we just plan on Mass in large stadiums and forget all the talk of the charism of various parishes? That at least would be honest, if more homogenizing for Catholic identity, as the pope apparently wishes.

From Portland, Maine, William Slavick delivered a biting response to the situation.

If, as most bishops and Rome appear to believe, community is unimportant, a solution to the present situation presents itself: Rome need only to approve televised Eucharists as meeting the Sunday obligation. The bishop's homilies at the single Sunday Mass will give him total control of diocesan communication. The priest shortage disappears, since there's a sufficient number for baptisms, marriages and funerals. Women would find ordination less attractive. Closed churches would reduce expenses radically. Drive-in or supermarket machines could collect offerings or dispense Communion. A login number would give the bishop absolute control over who gets Communion.

Ridiculous? It's the direction in which we are heading with a leadership indifferent to the community-nourished spirituality and life of the laity, blind to all save having a titular celibate male in charge of a gathering of estranged strangers.

Marie Morgan in Santa Fe, New Mexico, said, "The reality is that Rome's continuing decision to ignore our answered prayers for vocations when women and married men are ready to serve is already creating priests who are little more than frantic Eucharist dispensers. More creative forms of spiritual and pastoral leadership will inevitably continue to blossom in the void."

In May 2009, the news flow reported that seventy-four-year-old American priest Fr. Lawrence Rosebaugh, a member of the Missionary Oblates of Mary Immaculate, was shot to death during a robbery in Guatemala City. Rosebaugh lived on the street with the homeless who were his "parish community" and his ministry, in addition to his ministry to people with AIDS. He was shot in a car stopped at gunpoint. Four other Oblates were in the car during the robbery, one of whom was wounded. Rosebaugh was a dedicated pacifist—one of the "Milwaukee 14"—and during the Vietnam War assisted in the looting and burning of ten thousand Selective Service documents.

In Singapore, in a spirit of forgiveness, Archbishop Nicholas Chia lifted diocesan sanctions against Fr. Joachim Kang, convicted of embezzling $3.49 million from the Church of St. Theresa. Kang was playing the stock market on behalf of the parish, he said. He was ordered to return $1.6 million to the parish, and $1.2 million to a parishioner, Emily Chan. Kang spent four years in prison and nine months in home detention.

Sexual abuse, of course, was constantly rearing its ugly head. On that topic, Eugene Cullen Kennedy wrote the bishops were "more comfortable doing little or nothing in the face of a crisis" as they "searched for some surrogate authority to stand in for them." Enter the lawyers. Kennedy referred to the bishops' behavior as "the Great Inertia." As for the next generation of priests and, eventually, bishops, the Vatican said that seminaries should screen for aggression and gay tendencies. Screening for aloofness, narcissism, nascent authoritarianism, control freak-ness and dressing-up could be usefully added.

It was the issue that never went away. "Thousands of children abused in Irish institutions; Irish government to push religious for more abuse compensation"; "Los Angeles archdiocese sex abuse investigation now a federal case"; "Plaintiffs' advocates call for release of L.A. documents"; "Legionaries are in a mess over new Maciel revelations"; "Jesuits' Oregon province files for bankruptcy . . . facing hundreds of claims"; "Bishops were warned of abusive priest . . . as early as the mid-1950s."

A Gail Risch article reported, "Although young Catholics increasingly postpone marriage, they usually do not postpone committed relationships and sexual intimacy."

There was blindness and denial everywhere.

On condoms, reader J. M. Zatlukal of Wappingers Falls, New York, asked, "Why would the pope go to AIDS-plagued Africa to speak about the evils of condoms? Well, it's rather easy for a man in his 80s to say that condoms won't work, but try to sell abstinence to a young buck and lady in their 20s with their God-given hormones hopping."

In October 2009, editor Tom Fox could report from Thailand that the leaders of 113 congregations across Asia and Oceania meeting there had issued a statement of solidarity with their sister women religious in the United States. Those leaders also called on their own congregations to develop ministries "radical" in their outreach.

Fox put the newspaper front and center in the coverage and defense of the women religious under siege by Rome—or their local bishop. This was the latest incarnation of *NCR* defending the prophetic witnesses of the day. When theologian Mary Daly died in 2009, Fox described her as "a mother of modern feminist theology . . . one of the most influential voices of the radical feminist movement through the latter twentieth century." In his next Editor's Note, Fox drew attention to the Winter Books Section—books written by and reviewed by women—and praised a recently deceased former Leadership Conference of Women Religious executive director, Notre Dame de Namur Sr. Mary Daniel Turner. He ended by noting that Servants of Mary Sr. Joyce Rupp would begin a year of reflections on *NCR*'s website, following a year by Fr. Ed Hays.

Mary Ann Foy of Redwood City, California, asked, "Am I reading correctly? On Page 3 of your Oct. 30 [2009] issue was the story 'Delaware diocese in Chapter 11' and on Page 4 'Child abuse report out soon.' Did you say the sisters are being investigated? It's the Year of the Priest. I think it's their turn."

From Merrill, Wisconsin, Sister of Mercy of the Holy Cross Celine Goessl said, "I am amazed at the positive attitude that *NCR* continues to show despite the horrendous realities of what is happening from inside the church today. I am struggling with the answers to the apostolic questionnaire. . . . It is worth all the pain and sadness that sisters are enduring when we see so many signs of hope."

Overseas, Thai Camillian nuns were sending missionary sisters to Haiti; in the Philippines, Servant of the Divine Healer Sr. Adelia Oling was aiding thousands through her microfinance work; while at home in the United States, Redemptorist Fr. Maurice Nutt, remembering Franciscan Sr. Thea Bowman, said she was "canonized in the hearts of all who knew and loved her."

Possibly the greatest U.S. sociopolitical victory for women religious in this period was their role in the Obama health care reform passage through Congress. Public faces included the Catholic Health Association's Daughters of Charity Sr. Carol Keehan and Social Service Sr. Simone Campbell, director of NETWORK, a Catholic social-justice lobby. When Obama was signing the bill, said Campbell, the president "told me it [passed] because of us."

In November 2009, Charity Sr. Louise Akers was on the front page as she "revs up the [Call to Action] audience." The Cincinnati archdiocese had dismissed Akers after she had taught there for forty years—dismissing her for not retracting her support of women's ordination.

Fox, in a lengthy interview with Immaculate Heart of Mary Sr. Sandra Schneiders, offered,

Schneiders writes that "the very heart of ministerial religious life is its participation in the prophetic mission of Jesus." In the process, she states, "this will inevitably lead to tension between the status quo of the church as hierarchical power structure, enforcing doctrinal uniformity and moral subordination, and the church as the body of Christ in this world, caring by preference for those on the margins, whose who do not and cannot measure up, those who can only say, 'Lord, have mercy on me, a sinner,' even when they cannot promise to meet the standards."

In a 2010 talk to lay Catholics in Cape Town, South Africa, Bishop Kevin Dowling began by reading Jerry Filteau's *NCR* account of the Latin Mass celebrated in the Washington, DC, shrine of the Immaculate Conception by Bishop Edward Slattery of Tulsa, Oklahoma, another flaunter of a twenty-one-foot-long *cappa magna* "that has come to be one of the symbols of the revival of the Tridentine Mass."

Dowling, bishop of Rustenburg, South Africa, said,

> For me, such a display of what amounts to triumphalism in a church torn apart by the sexual abuse scandal is most unfortunate. What happened there bore the marks of a medieval royal court, not the humble, servant leadership modeled by Jesus. But it seems to me that this is also a symbol of what has been happening in the church especially since John Paul II became bishop of Rome and up till today—and that is "restorationism," the carefully planned dismantling of the theology, ecclesiology, pastoral vision, indeed the "opening of windows" of Vatican II—in order to restore a previous, or more controllable model of church through an increasingly centralized power structure, a structure that now controls everything in the life of the church through a network of Vatican congregations led by cardinals who ensure strict compliance with what is deemed *by them* to be "orthodox." Those who do not comply face censure and punishment. . . .
>
> I think that today we have a leadership in the church which actually undermines the very notion of subsidiarity . . . [collegiality] is virtually non-existent . . . the mystique which has in increasing measure surrounded the person of the pope in the last 30 years, such that any hint of critique or questioning of his policies, his way of thinking, his exercise of authority, etc. is equated with disloyalty . . . the appointing of "safe," unquestionably orthodox and even very conservative bishops . . . what is perceived to be "liberal" is both suspect and

not orthodox, therefore to be rejected as a danger to the faith of the people.

Is there a way forward? . . . I do not have the answer, except that somewhere we must find an attitude of respect and reverence for difference and diversity as we search for a *living* unity . . . At the heart of this is the question of conscience. As Catholics, we need to be trusted enough to make informed decisions about our life, our witness, our expressions of faith, spirituality, prayer, and involvement in the world—on the basis of a developed conscience.

The bishop concluded with an excerpt from the early writings of Joseph Ratzinger when he was a Vatican II *peritus* (*Commentary on the Documents of Vatican II*): "Over the pope as an expression of the binding claim of ecclesiastical authority, there stands one's own conscience which must be obeyed before all else, even if necessary against the requirement of ecclesiastical authority."

In Phoenix, Arizona, in May 2010, Bishop Thomas J. Olmsted excommunicated Mercy Sr. Margaret McBride for allowing a late-2009 abortion at St. Joseph's Hospital in Phoenix to save the life of the mother, who was eleven weeks pregnant and suffering from pulmonary hypertension. McBride, vice president of mission integration, was on call as a member of the hospital ethics committee when the surgeon explained the situation. The hospital stated, "If there had been a way to save the pregnancy and still prevent the death of the mother, we would have done it."

Janelle Lazzo of Roeland Park, Kansas, wrote,

> Certain members of the hierarchy have tunnel vision. There is one standard of right and wrong—two extremes, no gray area. Of course, real life is seldom that way. . . . No one wants to take the life of the unborn child, but it cannot live independent of its mother. Here it would seem that logic would enter. The child will be lost whether the mother lives or dies. But that is not how Phoenix Bishop Thomas Olmsted sees it. To him abortion is abortion is abortion. No gray area.

NCR's response was to have Tom Roberts look at the case through the lens of Catholic ethicists, followed by Jerry Filteau examining it through the lens of Catholic canon lawyers. The black-and-white church-in-Rome does not accept gray areas. The readers, however, understood that while church leaders deny gray areas exist, other Catholics don't have to. Teresita Schaffer of Washington, DC, restated the actuality: "At a gestational age of 11 weeks, a baby cannot survive outside the womb. If the mother died so would the baby. The choice was therefore between letting two people die and giving one of them—the mother—a chance at survival. Why is it moral to insist that two people die when one could be saved?" Reader Anna Lee Brendza of New Philadelphia, Ohio, added, "Abortion is never permitted under any circumstances but it is perfectly fine to kill an adult woman. Thanks, boys, for letting us know."

Later, Olmsted declared the hospital no longer a Catholic institution, but lifted the excommunication order on McBride.

Boston College theology professor M. Shawn Copeland in August 2010 challenged more than 750 women religious at the meeting of the Leadership Conference of Women Religious to live in a state of radical openness. "Even as we may disagree about the nature of our predicament, on nearly all accounts, we admit our tradition is in crisis. The whole church is quite bewildered by what we are (or are not) doing, by what is (or is not) happening to us, by what we are (or are not) doing to ourselves." Copeland concluded women religious today have become a "living protest of perhaps unintentional, but nonetheless real reduction of ourselves as church to the law-abiding, but lukewarm; the unthinking, but self-righteous; the domineering, but fearful. . . . You must not, indeed you cannot allow or submit to this. The very nature of prophetic ministry opposes patronage and true prophets are never on sale."

Bad news took a turn for the even-worse-than-ridiculous as the Vatican swung the hammer and rang the bell at the top of the misogyny index pole. Said Rome in July 2010, the attempted ordination of women is a "grave crime" to be dealt with according to the same procedures as the sexual abuse of minors. Columnist Jamie Manson noted, "The church's statements only reinforce the idea that female bodies are not of equal value in the eyes of God."

Fr. Charles Curran called out,

> We white Catholic moral theologians in the United States have rightly been criticized for our abysmal failure to recognize the evil of racism in our country and our church, and the consequent white privilege that we enjoy. Catholic feminists have reminded us of the patriarchy that continues to exist in our church and society. Libera-

tion theologians have recalled for us God's preferential option for the poor and the need for this to be an important hermeneutic principle in Catholic social ethics. . . . We cannot put our heads in the sand."

Wrote Cynthia Vrooman of Sonoma, California,

Some princes of the church, notably Bishop Thomas Tobin of Providence, R.I., Bishop Lawrence Brandt of Greensburg, Pa., and the former archbishop of Saint Louis, Raymond Burke, are out to get revenge on the religious sisters who deigned to support the recent health care bill or who chose to retain the integrity of their personal and communal lives. Since the bishops appear to be losing their credibility, it is no wonder their egos took a setback.

Which did not mean women undervalued priests. *NCR*'s director of mission and long-range planning, Denise Simeone, wrote a personal account of the support and encouragement she'd received from priests during her education and career, and she responded in kind: "Your ministerial choice has enhanced response to your baptismal call to be among those who lead and shape the life of our parish communities."

17

2010: JOE FEUERHERD

Fox, editor and publisher pro tem once more, used his Editor's Note to periodically introduce newsroom and business staff to the readership. The latter included business manager Wally Reiter when *NCR* was recognized by Kansas City United Way. Reiter, a father of four, volunteers at his Overland Park Christian Church—and has a six-stroke golf handicap. The newsroom staffers included Teresa Malcolm. With "a small editorial staff," Fox wrote, "each of us does more than one task, and none more tasks than Teresa Malcolm" who organizes and compiles the special sections, edits the copy, proofreads pages, searches for photos and "manages the flow of editorial content. To put it bluntly, the content and quality of *NCR* depends on this woman's well-being."

Next, in his Editor's Note, he welcomed Joe Feuerherd as the new publisher and editor in chief. "Actually we welcome him back to *NCR* for a third time. Most recently he was Washington correspondent from 2002 to 2007, a period during which he produced award-winning reporting, especially in the area of church finances and accountability."

There must be something about *NCR* editors and shovels. When Tom Roberts stepped aside as editor to begin a sabbatical, his Editor's Note began, "My mind these past few days has been turning, in its idle moments, to a growing mound of dirt in my backyard."

When Fox returned as editor pro tem, the headline of his Editor's Note was "Back from the compost pile." He began, "I was turning the compost in my backyard . . ."

Had anyone accused soon-to-be-named editor in chief Feuerherd of being a gardener, Feuerherd would have been found not guilty. His idea of the great outdoors was a racetrack. Feuerherd's first connection with finances came from climbing over the fence at Belmont Park racetrack—close to his Garden City, Long Island, home—to find some adult who'd place his bet for him.

Later, in the summers away from studying history at the Catholic University of America in Washington, Feuerherd worked as a counselor at a Pennsylvania summer camp for handicapped children. As did his brother David. As did Rebecca Bartron from small-town Montrose, Pennsylvania. Joe and Becky were soon in love, but Feuerherd was still only a nineteen-year-old student. So he did what he'd done before: play the horses. His trifecta hit gave him a several-hundred-dollar payout. He then brought Bartron to New York for dinner at the Four Seasons, a proposal and an engagement ring.

A teenage wedding that defied the odds, Feuerherd gave up playing the ponies. Their next trifecta was three children: Zachary, Bridget and Benjamin.

Joe's dad, Victor, served in World War II and became an accountant and corporate executive, latterly with SCM, the typewriter company. His mother, Lillian, was a homemaker looking after Victor, Elizabeth, Peter, David, Stephen, Joe, Mary and Matthew. Mary died as an infant and Stephen at age three of leukemia. (Among the storms Joe and Becky Feuerherd weathered was the fear that son Zach's leukemia mirrored Stephen's. It didn't: Zach is a cancer survivor.)

When Vic and Lillian's own children were still at home, a famous Feuerherd family incident involved an infamous situation. Vic and Lillian moved lock, stock and family to South Dakota, where Vic had been named chief financial officer of a local corporation. When the company expected Vic to cook the books, he promptly quit and, jobless, moved the family back East, initially into Grandma Lillian Dolan's Brooklyn brownstone. There were some tough times in Brooklyn, and then in Garden City, New York, until the family got back on its feet.

Joe Feuerherd was precociously political in a dinner-table politically conscious family. He reveled in being a student in political Washington. Though in his element, what Catholic University history major Joe (brother David also was a CUA graduate) needed was entrée. In 1984, "wet behind the ears" (his own words) college junior Feuerherd became an *NCR* Washington intern.

A decade-and-a-half later, in a column, "From intern to publisher," he wrote,

> I'd been raised in a journalistic tradition—my grandfather city editor of the New York Sun, two brothers in the business, and reading NCR (and the New York Times, the New York Post, the New York Daily News and Newsday) since my early teens. Still, it came as a revelation that a future could be made interviewing cardinals and members of Congress, peace activists and conservative supporters of the contras, mandatory celibacy opponents and Latin Mass advocates. In January 1985, I got a bump up to political affairs reporter (at the princely pay of $100 a week) and spent more time writing and reporting for NCR than on my history studies. (Most of my professors, however, were reading my NCR copy, resulting in some generous grading.)
>
> I came and went. First to Capitol Hill as a congressional press secretary and legislative assistant, then to editor of a weekly publication (the *Economic Opportunity Report*) focused on federal anti-poverty initiatives, then back to NCR (1988–1991) as Washington bureau chief. Other stops intervened. I was public affairs officer at the Montgomery County Housing Opportunities Commission (1991–1997), editorial director and associate publisher at United Communications Group (1998–2002), and then back to NCR as Washington correspondent (2002–2007).
>
> Now I return again to NCR, this time as publisher and editor in chief.

There's a tale Feuerherd didn't tell, from his time at the Housing Opportunities Commission (HOC) in Montgomery County, Maryland. There, in 1997, a key moment in Feuerherd family history repeated itself. The commission's executive director, Bernie Tetreault, described how, after twenty-four years, when "I was unceremoniously fired from HOC, Joe was the community relations officer, a senior staff position that reported directly to me. When the board asked him to spread falsehoods about me and my departure he refused, and resigned. For that the staff nicknamed him 'Saint Joe.'" Ineffably decent, Feuerherd promptly searched for another job.

When, for a final time, *NCR* beckoned, Feuerherd was working on housing issues at the national level. He was also enrolled in the American University's graduate history program under Professor Allan Lichtman, a historian and authority on applying quantitative methods to national elections.

Editor in chief Feuerherd's inside knowledge of and fondness for Washington was soon revealed in a major undertaking. Feuerherd was at the helm of "*NCR* Washington Briefing," which brought together "policymakers, legislators and opinion-shapers from the Catholic world to talk over today's key issues." The impressive roster in the 2010 gathering cosponsored by Trinity University included Republicans such as GOP National Committee Chairman Michael Steele, a Catholic; Patricia Weitzel-O'Neill, outgoing Washington archdiocese superintendent of schools; former U.S. ambassador to the Holy See Jim Nicholson; Helen Alvare, former U.S. bishops' pro-life activities director; and House Speaker Nancy Pelosi (D-CA). Feuerherd wrote that the hundreds of participants, who came from various parts of the country, "heard from a wide range of liberals and conservatives, Democrats and Republicans (and even an independent or two). Beliefs and opinions were reinforced and challenged in an atmosphere of both civility and vigor, the Catholic community at its best, providing a model of civic engagement."

Feuerherd's strategy was to provide a venue in the public square "where Catholics of goodwill but differing viewpoints end up talking *to* each other . . . rather than *at* each other." It worked, a major step in Feuerherd's visionary future of a new element in the newspaper's role.

Before the 2010 calendar year was out, Feuerherd wrote poignantly from a rehabilitation center in a nursing home that "serious illness is not something you can do alone." He'd had a large cancerous tumor removed from his right buttock. He wrote of his dependency on his wife, Becky, and children Zachary, Bridget and Ben, and the support of his *NCR* and wider circle of friends. His description of life and conditions in the nursing home, and his journeying with cancer from its discovery, was the product of a stern discipline delivered with a light touch. Personal journalism at its toughest.

Five months later, on May 25, 2011, Joe Feuerherd died. He was forty-eight.

When Feuerherd's death was announced on ncronline.org, of all the tributes flooding in, only one is excerpted here—from Douglas Kmiec, a legal scholar and retired U.S. ambassador to Malta.

> Just a few weeks ago I had the benefit of Joe's writing in an April 8 column entitled "Kmiec takes friendly fire" . . . Joe's analysis of an event that should otherwise not have been newsworthy: namely, a routine Office of Inspector General report that found my then-Embassy in Valletta, Malta, to be accomplishing, even exceeding, its mission goals.
>
> The Ambassador (me), coming from an academic background was said to be a bit "unorthodox in method," but well thought of and on task. Before the report would be made public, my overall favorable review mutated into a rebuke for wandering outside the core mission of the Embassy by showing sensitivity to faith and even seeking to advance interfaith diplomacy.
>
> With brevity and clarity, Joe pinpointed the incomprehensibility of calling the improved relations between Muslim and Catholic and Judaic faiths to be something outside the core mission of a U.S. embassy . . .
>
> Without Joe's discernment, the story of the inspector general's over-reach would have been unlikely to grab the attention of the LA Times ' columnist, Tim Rutten. . . . Joe bolstered *NCR*'s fidelity to the full Gospel, and not just those parts conveniently appealing to natural born conservatives. . . . Joe also knew when a story narrative had more to it than—not atypically—government wanted told . . . for he would follow the trail wherever it led, even if embarrassing to an ideological favorite . . .
>
> [He] could parse [Capitol Hill] bureaucratese, and in the case of our Embassy's OIG report, he knew the glowing original report sat uneasily with the hypercritical later-added challenge to our interfaith diplomatic efforts . . .
>
> Joe possessed the wit to assist others less facile with words to grasp the possibility of improved human understanding across religious traditions. Joe was a progressive, but he called 'em as he saw them. The one constant being: Joe always saw 'them' (the important issues of the day) in a faith-savvy way.

Earlier, Joshua McElwee and Tom Fox reported that the bishops had chosen to not follow their own bishop-theologian dispute guidelines when criticizing St. Joseph Sr. Elizabeth Johnson's *Quest for the Living*

God. Johnson defended her book in a letter to the U.S. bishops' Doctrine Committee. In turn, the Doctrine Committee was sharply criticized in a chapter-by-chapter, thirty-page Catholic Theological Society of America rebuke. The society issued a strong defense of Johnson's book.

Readers were not amused when, on November 2011, NCR editorially suggested "making do with a faulty translation," a bromide for swallowing the third edition of the Roman Missal, a new English-language translation. Nationwide, opposition to the translation has not relented, though the translation is in use.

Fox, appointed publisher once more, then announced the most significant 2012 internal *NCR* story. He appointed Dennis Coday editor effective January 1.

18

2012: DENNIS CODAY

Twenty-two-year-old Dennis Coday spent the summer of 1983 in Kansas City, Missouri. He was completing a bachelor's degree in English and secondary education at Jesuit-run Rockhurst College. Nebraska-born Coday was in seminary formation with the Society of the Precious Blood, and he followed the schedule of a religious: lived in a community house, prayed the Divine Office. "My head was focused on religious life and studies," he said, "but my heart had been kidnapped."

He was required to do a few hours of community service each week. While his classmates volunteered in schools and parishes, Coday looked for something different. Formation director Fr. Mark Miller suggested Holy Family Catholic Worker House at 31st and Troost. "It had just reopened. Why didn't I try something there?"

"I called," said Coday, "and they said they needed help on Saturday afternoons when they had large amounts of vegetables to process—vegetables salvaged from the city's large green markets' dumpsters." He sorted through boxes of tomatoes and then cut up the good tomatoes to be cooked down for pasta sauces and soup base for the next week's meals. ("I recall," he said, "that the staff forgot I was working in the kitchen of their second house, not the main kitchen from which they served the daily supper. They left me there alone about three hours—a memory those same staff members now challenge.")

> The life of these Catholic Workers captured my imagination. I read the Dorothy Day books and was drawn ever closer to that life. It mixed the gritty day-to-day encounter with people at the margins,

with an intellectual and spiritual tradition that was thoroughly Catholic. It exemplified what I was learning in seminary formation as well as at classes in school. The staff members themselves blended this spiritual and intellectual foundation with a personal activism that was very attractive. I found myself spending more and more time at Holy Family House. Soon I was joining them in the dumpster-diving and staying late on Saturday night to share a meal and long talks with the staff. This would be an influence on the next chapter in my life.

Dennis Coday was born in Atkinson, a small town in Central Nebraska on the edge of the Sand Hills, the fifth son in a family of five sons and three daughters. Their parents, Michael and Dorothy, were from large farm families that raised cattle. Coday's mother was of German stock; his father, Irish. Both were devout, practicing Catholics. He father would say that in eighty-three years he missed Sunday Mass only once—when he was standing in line to get his discharge papers from the Army in 1945.

Coday Senior studied business under the GI Bill and then embarked on a career in retailing. At various times he owned an IGA grocery store, a Standard Oil gas station and a Western Auto store. He spent the last twenty-five years of his working life with Gibson's Discount stores, a small Midwestern retail department store chain.

Dorothy Coday's work was in the home and raising the children—until the youngest was in grade school. She became a school secretary and studied library science in the evenings. She retired as the school librarian.

Beyond family influences, "the most influential book I've read," Dennis Coday said, when he was a junior in college,

> is *Bread Broken and Shared: Broadening Our Vision of Eucharist* by Blessed Sacrament Fr. Paul Bernier. The book begins with a description of a potluck supper in a barrio in Juarez, Mexico. To think of that as a eucharistic meal shocked me. Bernier wrote that the Eucharist should be a communal experience and outward-looking. It should be active if not downright activist. The Eucharist should drive us out into the world and to work building the kingdom of God, he wrote. "If we do not [do this work], our liturgies are empty: A true Eucharist is never a passive, comforting moment alone with God, something which allows us to escape the cares and concerns of our everyday life. Eucharist is where all these cares and concerns come

to a focus, and where we are asked to measure them against the standard lived by Jesus when he proclaimed for all to hear that the bread that he would give would provide life for the entire world."

Suddenly that summer there was a second influence on seminarian Coday. Mitch Snyder had arrived. He and the motley Washington, DC–based Community for Creative Non-Violence crew camped out on a hillside park overlooking Kansas City's Union Station. They were in the shadow of the towering Liberty Memorial that honored World War I fallen. The memorial also houses the national World War I Museum.

The Reagan recession had given the country double-digit unemployment; the jobless and the homeless had become part of the evening news broadcasts.

Snyder's crew knew that stashed in the limestone caves underneath Kansas City was the largest cache of food commodities in the world: tons of cheese and powdered milk, bags of rice and beans and flour; tins of beef and pork. The U.S. government bought up this surplus food to support farmers, storing it to keep it off the market and support commodity prices. Some surplus food went to aid foreign lands, but much was stored until it spoiled.

The Community for Creative Non-Violence was in Kansas City to liberate that food. They wanted it to feed the families standing on Reagan's breadlines and staying in homeless shelters. Snyder led a group of about a half a dozen activists, mainly Washington people, in a water-only fast. They would fast until the food was released. It was an unusually hot and dry Missouri summer. During the early weeks, they attracted a further forty or so fellow fasters, homeless men, Vietnam Veterans for Peace, a few college-age students and other young people who hiked in from Iowa, Minnesota and elsewhere.

Cody recalled,

> Hungry, drinking only water with squeezes of lemon or lime in it. Dressed in tank tops and halter tops and cut off jeans. Shorts and light blouses. Unkempt hair. Unshaven. Not dirty, but soiled and sunburnt. They lived in tents—and if they couldn't make the 15-minute car ride to shower in the basement of the Catholic Worker House, they bathed in public restrooms of the park. They looked miserable on that unshaded hillside, growing thinner daily, but attracting more and more attention. Eventually the national news net-

works showed up. Back at the Precious Blood House, I watched Mitch and his people on the nightly news. But I had also been up there, on the hillside for the daily prayer meetings they held. I had listened to the witness of Mitch and his companions.

It was the first people's revolt I had ever witnessed. I remember clearly I associated this group on the sun-drenched hillside of Liberty Memorial Park with the prayers we prayed in community every morning, the Canticle of Zechariah: *Blessed be the Lord . . . He has raised up for us a mighty Savior.*

Summer ended. Snyder and his crew finally persuaded the U.S. government to release those commodities. They declared victory and announced a community potluck supper to celebrate. ("I remember," said Coday, "that Mitch and his crew, all experienced fasters, ate very lightly that night. Fruit and juice mainly. Maybe a little plain bread. The inexperienced who had joined the fast stuffed themselves with fried chicken and hamburgers, salads and mashed potatoes—and they suffered that night and the next day for their overindulgence.")

After six weeks of study and retreat, he and five other Precious Blood seminarians were each given assignments in various Midwest parishes. At his request, Coday would spend September 1983 to May 1984 assigned to St. Mary's Parish in Garden City, Kansas. The region was suffering through the double-digit unemployment of the Reagan Recession crisis as unemployed oil workers and others in their thousands took to the road looking for work.

Said Coday, "The parish had a ministry to these folks, Emmaus House, modeled on the Catholic Worker House, but informed by the Protestant and evangelical churches that also supported the ministry and were more interested in helping the poor raise themselves from poverty than in living with the poor in solidarity. But that is why I wanted to be in Garden City."

Garden City is the crossroads of two routes (U.S. Highway 50 and U.S. Highway 83) that cross the Plains states. Folks were either coming from the west headed to the east or headed west from lost jobs east of the Mississippi. "Poor people avoid traveling the U.S. interstate system," said Coday.

Stretches on interstates are too long and remote. If a car breaks down, you can go hours without help, or have to walk miles to find assistance. U.S. secondary roads and state highways, however, bisect towns large, small and tiny. Small towns mean lots of churches. Each church has a fund to help a traveler on his way. Even a couple of dollars worth of gas could get him to the next little town. Travelers could count on a voucher to buy some bread and sandwich meat to keep hunger away from the kids. If travelers struck really lucky, the church might put them up for a night in a local motel—a good, hot shower and a bed for the wife. Maybe even some TV for the kids before moving on the next day.

Garden City's other draw was that it was the center of a massive cattle industry that raised cattle from newborn, fed them to maturity on ranches, fattened them in feedlots and then slaughtered them "in huge, unimaginably huge slaughterhouses," Coday said.

In Finney County, Kan., cattle outnumbered people by about 10 to 1. Slaughterhouse workers are itinerant folks. The work is too hard to keep people at non-union wages. The slaughterhouses were built in this part of Kansas because they were close to the cattle, but also because wages could be kept low. The workers were poor whites looking to make enough money to keep the family moving down the road to the next place; poor blacks also looking for two or three or four weeks of paychecks to fix the car and move down the road; Mexicans of dubious documentation, mostly men, who would sleep 20 in one house, three taking shifts in one bed. Saving money and sending it home. Wintering in mild Kansas until it was time to go back to summer landscaping jobs in Chicago or fruit-picking in Missouri and Michigan and Campbell Soup tomatoes in Ohio.

Last of all, he said, were the

Vietnamese (plus a few Cambodians), ripped by the American war out of their homelands. The Vietnamese of the first generation were not itinerant. The horrors of the slaughterhouse jobs held no terrors for people who had survived in makeshift boats and refugee camps. They lacked the language skills to become supervisors or trainers, but were able to save and build, reinvesting their wages in family businesses run from their homes. Their children, educated in Kansas public schools, went to college to earn computer science and medical degrees, and to move their parents and grandparents to the coasts. That would happen years after I left Garden City.

The Anglos and Mexican core of Garden City had been there for at least a couple of generations. They were proud of their town and the roots they could trace back to farming and ranching. They had the natural compassion of people who know a disaster is just one lightning storm (one lightning bolt could burn out an entire field of winter wheat), or one drought, or one tornado away. They had the natural faith of people who put a tiny seed in the ground and watched it multiply. They knew hardship and didn't mind—too much—the itinerant meatpacker workers: If you worked to the best of your ability and kept faithful with God, you were OK.

Coday worked Sunday through Thursday as a fourth-grade teacher's aide in the parish school, along with the RCIA (Rite of Christian Initiation of Adults) program and with the music ministry. Thursday night until Saturday morning, he worked at Emmaus House.

The white, wood-sided, two-story house had an L-shaped porch. It was entered into up the south porch steps directly into the dining room. There were three rooms for families on the second floor and in the basement an eight-to-ten-man dormitory.

Coday explained,

> Guests could stay four days and three nights. Day one, get a job at the meat-packing plant. After three days on the job, a worker could get an advance or letter of credit that was enough for a deposit on an apartment or rental house. Once they moved out, they could come back for meals, dinner at noon and supper at 6 p.m. No cafeteria line. Meals were served family-style with plates of meat and bowls of rice, potatoes and vegetables set before them. Cooked by the women of the churches and served by their husbands and children. People sat around two folding tables set end to end donated from a church social hall. A bench ran down one side and the chairs were mixed and matched, castoffs from a half dozen dining sets.
>
> Dipping into the common pot, men and women and children, meatpacker fathers sat with wives and their toddler children in high chairs next to single men who were sleeping downstairs. I don't mean to romanticize it, but the scene looked very much like Fritz Eichenberg's "The Lord's Supper"—especially to an idealistic 22-year-old seminarian.

One of his most vivid memories, he said, could have come out of *The Grapes of Wrath*.

I was on the porch with two or three male guests—a huge tree shaded most of the yard from early afternoon until late evening. It must have been early evening, just before supper. A big car pulled up in front of the house, a late 1970s Oldsmobile 98, two-door, tan or yellow with a vinyl roof. A cargo carrier was strapped down with boxes and bags and furniture. The rear was slung low to the ground. The driver's side door opened first and an average height, lanky man stepped out stood and looked across the roof to us on the porch. The passenger door swung wide open, the man's wife stepped out onto the lawn and two little kids scrambled off the front seat and tumbled onto the lawn.

"We're looking for a place for the night," the man said. "We've come from Arkansas today [a good seven hours drive]. Headed for California. We just need a bed of the night. And a meal if it's not too late," he said. "I've got a voucher from the Brethren church."

"Come on in," I said. "We can get you checked in before supper."

"OK," the man said to people still in the car. "Get out."

I saw the front seat back pushed forward on the passenger side and out stepped a man, shortish, wiry in his early sixties. The father of this family's wife, as I recall. The grandmother stepped out on the driver's side and stood by the lanky man. "Much obliged," she called out to me.

Then from the rear seat stepped another full-grown man, the wife's brother and two young teenagers, a boy and a girl. They untangled themselves and stretched. Pushing and poking, teasing the little kids. The mother shepherded them into the house. The driver and the grandfather led the way up the long sidewalk. They stopped at the foot of the stairs and greeted the men on the porch with nods of the head.

"Can a man pick up some day labor in this town?" he asked the porch sitters. "I'd like to pick up a couple days of work before we head off again," he said. I can't remember if they found work or not. I do remember two days later we gave them sacks of bread and day-old sweet rolls, and they crawled back into that Oldsmobile. Later in my stay at Emmaus House, we would include government surplus food in the bags we distributed: blocks of cheese, bags of rice and flour and beans. The very food Mitch Synder and crew had liberated that hot, dry summer of 1983.

Coday was at his own crossroads: seminary studies versus a stronger pull to be with the people of Emmaus House, the guests and the volunteers. Coday praised the education he received from the Precious Blood priests and brothers. "[They] first wanted to form good Christians and Catholics, concerned for and at service to others. As I have reengaged many classmates in recent years, I'd have to say the Precious Blood did a pretty good job on that score. A few became priests, one of whom is my own brother Timothy, after 26 years still a missionary in Tanzania."

Coday remained at Emmaus House another two years, the sole live-in staff member. "The work still inspired me, but as an early twenty-something, the social life in Garden City, Kansas, was stifling. The evolution of the house, too, was shifting its focus toward more of a professional social-service agency. The house needed someone with those skills."

In the summer of 1986, he took up residence again in Kansas City's Holy Family Catholic Worker House. Each staffer also held part-time or full-time jobs to help out, "a lawyer, a couple of teachers, a parish staff person, a social worker and me." When high school teaching didn't work out, Coday fell back on something he'd dabbled in before: newspapering. "Being a Catholic Worker, I could, of course, draw on Dorothy Day's fine example of blending hospitality and mission with journalism," he said. At high school in Liberty, Missouri, he wrote for its newspaper, and freelanced high school basketball coverage for the *Liberty Tribune* weekly newspaper. During college and again from 1986 to 1989, he worked part time at the *Catholic Key*, the Kansas City–St. Joseph, Missouri, diocesan newspaper.

The inner cities of most if not all metropolitan areas in the United States were engulfed in a violent, bloody war. Crack cocaine had turned cities, including "my city, Kansas City," into war zones. "Crack brought violence on an unprecedented scale," Coday said. Users used violence to finance their habit; gangs used violence to gain and rule their territories; police used violence to protect the citizenry. Holy Family House was on the front lines of that battle, but so were the half dozen or so area Catholic parishes. Coday wrote of parish and neighborhood activists seeking to eradicate crack houses from neighborhoods and combat gang violence with outreach and education. "Those articles weren't great journalism," he said, "but they showed me how journalism, in that half of my life, could be as useful as the Catholic Worker direct service and activism."

By 1989, restless, Coday determined to do journalism that would make a difference. He left Kansas City for Milwaukee and a teaching assistantship at the Journalism School of Marquette University. Through connections there, he met Maryknoll Fr. Robert Astorino, founder and executive director of the Union of Catholic Asian News (UCAN), an Asia-wide Catholic news service with full bureaus in Delhi, Manila and Jakarta and part-time offices in nearly every Asian capital.

In January 1992, he joined UCAN at its Bangkok editorial headquarters. The news was written by Asians, but Astorino needed native English-speakers to work with the copy so UCAN could be marketed to big funders in the West (Europe and America).

Things didn't work out. UCAN needed Coday as a copy editor, not a reporter. Accustomed to journalistic involvement, he chafed at this. On the upside, at UCAN he met the woman he would marry, Jaratsri Piewklieng. Their first son was born in 1995. Coday, with Foreign Correspondents' Club of Thailand membership, freelanced for seven years until 2003, when he joined *NCR*.

Freelancer Coday edited and wrote for magazines that covered Thai manufacturing.

> I was the correspondent for a Kuala Lumpur business and lifestyle magazine; I edited company reports and industry analysis reports for finance companies in Bangkok. I filed stories for *NCR* about Burmese refugees escaping into Thailand; about Asia's 1997 financial crash from a people's perceptive; Cambodia coming out of the shadows of the Khmer Rouge; about Korean "comfort women" [sex slaves to the Japanese Army during World War II] seeking reparation from the Japanese government and earning respect from the Korean nation after four decades of living in shame.
>
> One freelance job had a most significant impact in my life— working on the website of Thailand's Board of Investment. Writing HTML code was still a fairly unique niche skill in 1998. It was on-the-job training for me, but it proved invaluable to my future.
>
> By 2001, we had three sons. My wife and I realized we would not be able to afford a quality education for them in Bangkok on a freelancer's salary. When I began making enquiries in the United States, *NCR* had a spot for me—in 2003 they would relaunch their website and wanted someone with the blend of skills I had.

On February 22, 2003, the five Codays landed in Kansas City. "Two days later we were engulfed in a snowstorm. My wife and boys put on their flip flops and ran outdoors—and quickly ran back inside, flabbergasted that something so beautiful could be so cold."

19

ROME'S WAR ON THE NUNS

The relatively quiescent Congregation for the Doctrine of the Faith now returned to a favorite target: the Leadership Conference of Women Religious (LCWR). In 2009, the congregation had launched its "investigation" into LCWR (not to be confused with Cardinal Franc Rodé's simultaneous 2009 investigation of the "quality of life" of U.S. women religious generally under Mother Mary Clare Millea).

(Given the secretive nature of all Vatican operations, what the Vatican was really up to in harassing U.S. religious provided many rumors. This book has not dealt in rumor. Here is the exception that proves the rule. Some astute Catholics outside and inside the congregations of women religious feared the Vatican likely wanted to take control of the U.S. sisters' remaining assets. This rumor, or speculation, grew mushroom-like in the humus of a similar Vatican attempt some two decades earlier to obtain the Roman real estate of a declining-in-numbers order of German nuns.)

In May 2012, the doctrinal congregation formally condemned LCWR and ordered the group to reform its statutes and submit to the control of an archbishop, Seattle Archbishop J. Peter Sartain. He was given wide-ranging authority over the group and would oversee the changes. (This fitted with the rumor—first pick off the leadership, then go after the orders one-by-one.)

A May 2012 *NCR* headline stated, "Censure stings: The Vatican's move against women religious leadership has been met with widespread support for the sisters." Joshua McElwee wrote, "Support for the sisters appeared in columns in secular newspapers, in demonstrations planned outside city cathedrals, and from priests praising the sisters from the pulpit in Sunday homilies."

- Two *New York Times* columns criticized the order. "In one . . . Nicholas Kristof wrote that Pope Benedict XVI was 'crazy to mess with nuns' who are 'among the bravest, toughest and most admirable people in the world.'"
- A Washington, DC–area congregation "stood up and broke into applause during their pastor's homily . . . (praising) U.S. sisters and the work they have done for the church," with similar reports from Ohio, Montana and Michigan. "A parish in Portland, Ore., erected a remembrance wall, where parishioners can post photos of and notes about women religious who have inspired them."
- "At least four petitions have appeared on the petition aggregation website change.org urging the Vatican to rescind its order. At press time, the largest had gathered about 32,500 signatures," and social media campaigns were created.

Benedict retired Rodé. In 2012, John Allen described Rodé's successor, João Braz de Aviz as "a personable if little-known figure with a reputation as a moderate conservative, who apparently comes to his new job without a strong personal agenda regarding religious life."

At the 2012 St. Louis LCWR meeting, Barbara Marx Hubbard told those present that LCWR is "the best seedbed I know for evolving the church and the world in the twenty-first century . . . one of the best hopes for the continuation of humanity."

In June that year, Mercy Sr. Margaret Farley rhetorically asked the 67th Catholic Theological Society of America meeting, "Is it a contradiction to have power decide matters of truth?" Farley was described as one "trying to balance her commitment as a Catholic, as a Sister of Mercy, as someone who loves the church, with her conviction that, as she said, 'people are suffering.'" Bringing "people are suffering" close to the people and local media coverage, sister-members of NETWORK, the Catholic social-justice lobby, became "Nuns on the Bus." Hundreds of supporters waited for them at each stop of their eight-state tour.

In Kentucky, the Sisters of Loretto celebrated two centuries of touching lives. Later in the year, the Sisters of Charity of Nazareth, Kentucky, also marked their bicentennial.

Catholic women's quest for ordination received moral support when John Allen reported Lisbon's Cardinal José de la Cruz Policarpo said that "there's no fundamental theological obstacle" to the ordination of women as priests in the Catholic church. Benedictine Sr. Joan Chittister had referred to Benedict's papacy as an "in-between time." Now, as this chapter covers the six weeks to February 11, 2013, that time comes to an end. Rapidly because, despite much news, there was one overriding story. As clerical sexual abuse dominated the headlines in the 1980s and 1990s, now the major news theme was the Vatican crackdown on U.S. women religious in particular, and Catholic women's expectations in general.

As the chapter concentrates on the two years immediately prior to Benedict's resignation, there is one major news theme (women), and one minor (in coverage terms) theme (U.S. bishops/Vatican). These are offered to highlight—as Benedict departs and Pope Francis enters—the near-total break between thirty-five years of a monarchic-papal dictatorship and the new moment. (As this book goes to press, the U.S. bishops continue in their role as Rome's senior vice presidents and vice presidents, taking their guidance exclusively from the Vatican with not even a nod to the concerns of American Catholics.)

The bishops-oriented news flow highlights included Milwaukee as the eighth U.S. diocese to file for bankruptcy due to sexual abuse–related settlements and legal costs; the bishops declared New York's June 2011 gay and lesbian marriage recognition legislation a "profoundly unjust law"; editorially, NCR noted "poll after poll indicates waning opposition to gay marriage"; and Santa Fe, New Mexico, Archbishop Michael Sheehan told nonmarried Catholic couples to stop living in sin and to not take Communion.

Twenty-six years after it first became front-page news, the U.S. bishops released "a major study of abuse by clergy"; a poll showed Phoenix Catholics overwhelmingly sided with Mercy Sr. Margaret Mary McBride and against Thomas Olmsted, the local bishop, in her handling of the situation of a seriously ill pregnant woman. The Knights of Columbus bought the John Paul II Center in Washington, DC, for $34 million. NCR declared editorially that Cardinal Adam Maida's committing the ailing Detroit archdiocese to support the Maida-built center's $40 million shortfall was a "colossal and vapid manifestation of episcopal arrogance."

Reader Mike Magee of Carlsbad, California, commented the John Paul II Center sale revealed the episcopal arrogance in common with the sex abuse scandal: "If the Vatican will not permit meaningful reform, including strong lay oversight of major financial commitments, then canon law becomes useless for those seeking justice. At this point, criminal/civil law must step in."

Criminal law stepped forward in Kansas City, Missouri, where Kansas City – St. Joseph Bishop Robert W. Finn was indicted for failing to protect area children; diocesan staff asked Finn whether he'd consider resigning. He was said to have replied, "If the Vatican calls and asks me to leave, I will." He agreed to give the county prosecutor near-total oversight of the diocese's handling of sex abuse cases for the next five years.

NCR editorialized that Finn "repeatedly demonstrated an astounding lack of judgment" in handling an accused priest pornographer. "Yet the unspoken expectation to be inferred by Catholics is that Finn will continue as bishop simply because he is a bishop. The church in Kansas City deserves better." A later editorial added Finn should "resign or be replaced." (In January 2013, Finn criticized NCR and revived Bishop Charles Helmsing's 1966 request that the newspaper drop "Catholic" from its title.)

Reader Robert Brannon of Liberty, Missouri, disagreed with NCR : "Finn has apologized several times. He has also done good things for the church here. A friend calls him a visionary for his purchase of a new Catholic Center. He has also taken a stand against the nuclear weapons plant in our city and been strong against the scourge of pornography." As if countering, Liz Donnelly of Kansas City wrote in the same issue, "God bless the principal who risked her job by reporting [the accused's] unusual behavior, and the two women at the diocesan office who knew how bad the situation was and urged top officials to call the police. . . . I do not think of the bishop as a leader."

An example of a bishop-leader's loss being mourned was that surrounding the death of retired Bishop Samuel Ruiz of Mexico's San Cristóbal de las Casas for twenty-four years until 2000. Proclaiming "the

Gospel has to be incardinated in every culture," Ruiz strove to build a "more just Mexico—egalitarian, dignified and without discrimination."

Some contrast with Chicago's Cardinal Francis George. He appeared to be bidding for the title of the city's chief scold as he likened the gay community to the Ku Klux Klan "demonstrating in the streets against Catholicism." (It may have played well in the Vatican that year. But will he shoot from the lip in the same way under Francis?)

As for Latin America, on the Wojtyla-Ratzinger liberation theology front, in June 2012, John Wilkins interviewed Munich Jesuit rector Fr. Martin Maier. Maier said John Paul at first saw liberation theology "as leftist and, given his experience of the Soviet system, he was very critical and suspicious that Marxism should play an important role in it. . . . There was an evolution. You can see this working out" in the difference between his April 1979 meeting with Archbishop Oscar Romero and the January 1980 Romero meeting, by which time "John Paul had reached a much better understanding." The Jesuit said Ratzinger went from his 1983 "Liberation theology is dangerous" statement to, as pope, "a remarkable speech at the opening of the Latin American bishops' conference at Aparecida in Brazil," and dialogue between Ratzinger and Gustavo Gutiérrez "took place . . . and understanding grew."

The Vatican turned its guns on the Jesuit quarterly *Theological Studies*—columnist Phyllis Zagano wrote, "The Vatican Thought Police" were after it; the U.S. bishops formed an ad hoc committee for religious liberty—as enshrined in the Constitution; and on opposing pages of NCR, Los Angeles Auxiliary Bishop Gabino Zavala resigned because he was the father of two children, and former Bishop Raymond Lahey of Antigonish, Nova Scotia, was freed after serving a child-pornography possession sentence.

The U.S. bishops' lawyer demanded twenty-three years of internal documents from the Survivors of those Abused by Priests (SNAP) group. From Poland, Jonathan Luxmoore filed a two-part series on how Polish bishops covered up clerical sexual abuse, moving abusing priests and blaming the victims. Most abusers remained in office as "clerical power thwarts victims in Poland."

In Milwaukee again: During Archbishop (now Cardinal) Timothy Dolan's tenure, the archdiocese shifted $55.6 million on the church's balance sheet to the cemetery fund to shield it from payouts. Rome approved. The archdiocese had also paid accused priests to leave. John

Allen reported on a four-day summit on sexual abuse in Rome. "There seems to be a new determination in the Vatican and across the Catholic world to use the tools of church law to hold the bishops accountable."

The readers were active. Regarding Bishop Daniel Jenky of Peoria, Illinois, comparing President Barack Obama to "Hitler, Stalin and others," Bill Staudenmaier of Wauwatosa, Wisconsin, wondered "whether calumny is no longer considered sinful in our church." Following Allen's article "New gung-ho archbishops known for aggressive style," and NCR 's editorial "The 'culture-warrior' model" of bishops, reader Michael Petrelli of Haddon Township, New Jersey, asked, "Are they going to turn our magnificent church into a 'small cult in search of heretics'?"

Headlines included "Incoming San Francisco archbishop [Salvatore Cordileone] apologizes for drunken driving"; "On Philadelphia, bishops take a wait-and-see stance" as a grand jury found thirty-seven priests suspect. Dublin Archbishop Diarmuid Martin told a Marquette conference "the truth must be told"; Bishop John Magee of Cloyne, Ireland, was found to have taken "little or no interest in the management of sexual abuse cases until 2008." In the wake of the 2011 Cloyne Report, which said the Vatican had been "entirely unhelpful" to Irish bishops trying to deal with abuse, Irish Prime Minister Enda Kenny was praised for accusing the Vatican of adopting a "calculated, withering position." Kenny said the Cloyne Report "excavates the dysfunction, disconnection, elitism and narcissism that dominate the culture of the Vatican to this day." And fifty-seven U.S. dioceses were found not in compliance with the U.S. bishops' charter on sexual abuse.

Asian Catholic bishops planned a summit on the impact of pedophilia—"Let us not be complacent that pedophilia is a problem for the West . . . it is equally prevalent in many countries of Asia."

Was Benedict XVI's Vatican attempt to revive eucharistic adoration a move to get people's minds off the church-in-Rome's inability to govern?

In Rome, it was the "Butlergate" leak season with the headline "In the Vatican, did the butler really do it?" When promptly arrested, papal butler Paolo Gabriele admitted he leaked papal documents—to protect the pope. Gabriele had provided a topic for some entertaining writing in the Italian and Western media. (The "saddened" pope forgave the butler after he'd been found guilty and released.) The other shoe dropped for the Vatican when the Council of Europe finally released its insider investigation of the Vatican bank and money laundering.

Meanwhile, in the United States, it was the political season. NCR columnist Michael Sean Winters suggested the U.S. bishops were in danger of overplaying their hand in demanding more religious exemptions from Obamacare's contraception coverage than Obama was offering.

As the New Year of 2013 opened, no one remotely anticipated what would happen forty-two days later. In an otherwise routine meeting on proposed canonizations, Benedict XVI calmly announced he was retiring, effective February 28, seventeen days later.

20

NCR: ONLINE AND GLOBAL

In the first six months of 2013, ncronline.org consolidated its position as the "go-to" source not only on what was happening in the Catholic church, but on what it meant. Ncronline.org had now become what NCR had been until, in 2006, it switched from a newsweekly to twice monthly: the major source of current independent Catholic reporting.

In the summer of 2013 as this chapter was being written, two streams of events were playing out in each of these two worlds—ncronline.org and *NCR*—that dramatically affected the newspaper and will have a bearing on its future. These two *NCR* forms are interdependent—and evolving. Ncronline.org represents and feeds off the newspaper, and vice versa. It is *NCR*'s circulation income and advertising income, along with the essential support of "Friends of NCR" that makes ncronline.org possible. To use an increasingly archaic term, ncronline.org has become a Catholic "daily newspaper."

In the summer of 2013, Coday received a phone call from the former circulation manager for the *Sun Herald*, *NCR*'s precursor from the 1950s. "He told me that he was the one to blame for the *Sun Herald*'s demise because he couldn't figure out a way to get the newspaper distributed," Coday said. "Ncronline.org solved the nationwide distribution problem."

Ncronline.org isn't just a website where we post news stories, columns and analysis, said Coday,

> it is a hub of an integrated network. It is the place where readers stay connected to the issues and personalities they believe are important.

While the newspaper-reading habit is fading, people are more connected to news than ever before. In a world where people follow events real time on Twitter and Facebook, where people look for updates and alerts first on their phones, it is the connectedness that ncronline.org provides its readers that keeps the news outlet in the consciousness of news junkies, church professionals (including bishops and their staffs), academics and the devout faithful. That is the future of news content. The trick now is to find a financial model to sustain it.

Editor Coday explains,

NCR has depended on the traditional subscription-advertising business model for its survival for 48 of its 50 years, but this model no longer works for anyone. Truth be told, the subscription-advertising business model never worked perfectly for NCR at any time. The newspaper has always been sustained by other business products—Credence Cassettes and *Celebration* magazine, for example—to make ends meet. These were never the complete answer. Subscriptions-advertising was a very significant and dependable source of revenues. NCR has maintained an 80 percent and better retention rate—every year more than 80 percent of subscribers renew—for as long as I have been with the paper. I suspect this high rate will continue. The question will be how long we can continue to find a new 20 percent of new print subscribers year after year.

To provide further illustration, Coday discussed the national background to the current print-newspapering decline. He said the Tribune media conglomerate, whose flagship company and its namesake was the *Chicago Tribune*, owns other major properties such as the *Los Angeles Times*. Tribune announced it was selling off its newspaper properties to focus on the more profitable local television-station business.

"That signaled for me the real beginning of the end of major U.S. newspapers," said Coday. The biggest papers with national reach may well be able to survive for some time, though the more "regional" *Washington Post* has been sold to Amazon's founder Jeff Bezos. "The message in the *Washington Post* sale is that content is king, but the delivery vehicle—print, tablet, videos or desktop computer—is incidental," Coday says. Local newspapers that cover small communities and have loyal local readers will survive in print form for some time. The vast majority that exist in the middle ground—the *Baltimore Sun* or the *Kansas City Star*, for example—will either evolve into something quite different than they are now or die. The *Detroit Free Press* and the New Orleans *Times-Picayune* are online dailies, but only print three times a week.

> This affects *NCR* because our core audience—an early and late middle-aged general readership, and a church and academic professional readership—is losing the newspaper habit. However, equally apparent are the possibilities for online-only news sources that are either tightly focused on a geographic community, like the *New Haven Independent* (Conn.) or the *Voice of San Diego* (Calif.), or with a particularly topical focus, like *Politico* for government and politics. These experiments are encouraging for *NCR* because many have adopted—and so validated—the funding model that *NCR* has grown for the last 10 years, namely seeking funding from grants, gifts and endowments.

Then, on February 11, a prime illustration of ncronline.org's utility became immediately evident: Pope Benedict resigned. "By luck or fate, we didn't face the same dilemma the newsroom faced at 9/11. The resignation came at the beginning of an off week—a week we don't produce a print paper—so all immediate energy and focus was on the website. Decisions about the print issue could be put off," Coday said. "Our coverage began with a headline, 'Pope Benedict resigns,' a paragraph with a Vatican City dateline, and the pledge: 'More news to follow. Check back with ncronline.org throughout the day.'" And people did come back to ncronline.org again and again. Web analytics showed a new one-day record that day with 110,000 unique visitors. The following days would see similar traffic. John Allen was in Rome filing reports as fast as his fingers could type while stateside reporters and columnists filled in background, reactions and commentary. "All of it went on the website, and we kept readers abreast of our coverage with e-mail alerts, Twitter feeds and Facebook postings," Coday said. The website would record more than 2.4 million visitors in the month from Pope Benedict's resignation to Pope Francis's election.

> As the initial shock wore off and the news buzz eased, we turned our focus on the print issue. The headline on the newspaper couldn't simply read "Benedict resigns" because by the time our readers had

that paper in hand, that wasn't news, but they desperately wanted to know what the resignation meant. We gave that to them in spades, by pulling off the website our best analysis and commentary and publishing that in print. By then, we could see what holes existed in the online coverage and we could commission special pieces for the newspaper.

The result was a twenty-four-page newspaper wrapped in sixteen pages of special coverage devoted to the papal transition. The front-page headline read, "Pope Benedict XVI resigns: The church is in crisis. Benedict's honesty in recognizing that reality should be honored with even bolder initiatives."

The second front page, around the news flow and Arts and Opinion Section, offered Jason Berry's "Anatomy of a cover-up: To protect their interests, Vatican, Legion of Christ kept silent"; "Settlement spurs scrutiny of LA funds"; "Cardinal [Cologne's Joachim Meisner] gives leeway on contraceptives in rape cases." Inside, the St. Louis archdiocese gave up the fight over the Polish breakaway parish. St. Stanislaus Kostka relinquished its Roman Catholic status.

With the print issue put to bed, Coday and Joshua McElwee traveled to Rome (flying out of Kansas City in the calm between two notorious Midwest blizzards) to meet up with Allen in time for Pope Benedict's last Sunday angelus and his last Wednesday general audience. They were joined a few days late by Jesuit Fr. Thomas Reese, former editor of *America* magazine, who had signed on as a senior analyst. Over the next three weeks, Allen would provide the depth and analysis coverage that this historic event warranted—the first papal resignation in six hundred years. McElwee would be filing to the website daily news stories piecing together the events as they happened—truly a first draft of history—and Coday would coordinate coverage between Rome and Kansas City and the rest of the world. Reese added commentary and analysis with Web postings as he could, but more importantly, he became the explainer in chief to the plethora of media outlets covering the proceedings. Reese made innumerable appearances on all the major American cable and broadcast news shows, plus the BBC, Al Jazeera and several European news programs. "Every time he spoke, he was identified as *NCR* senior analyst, and he plugged the website as often as he could," Coday said. "Reese's appearances along with John

Allen's ubiquitous presence on CNN help spread the *NCR* brand worldwide."

The March 13 election of Jesuit Cardinal Jorge Mario Bergoglio of Buenos Aires, Argentina, was good news for the church, but a trying time for news outlets. Bergoglio had not been in anyone's Top 10 picks, though *TIME* magazine online said that when Bergoglio's name was announced, John Allen's online biog of the new pope was all the media knew about Pope Francis.

21

EXIT BENEDICT; ENTER FRANCIS I

The world watched and wondered. The Vatican II Catholics of the world held their hope-filled breaths. American Catholics could scarcely contain their excitement, except for those who wanted no change from the immediate past. The *NCR* newsroom, its editors, reporters and columnists, examined what they had to go on, then dared a cautious optimism as they tapped out their first few words on the keypads. The front-page headline (March 29–April 11, 2013) was "The spirit of Francis: A church of the poor."

Senior correspondent John Allen wrote,

> Two days before the conclave opened March 12 to elect a successor to Pope Benedict XVI, Cardinal Philippe Barbarin of Lyon, France, candidly confessed to reporters outside his titular church in Rome that the voters didn't have their act together.
>
> "There are three, four, maybe a dozen candidates," Barbarin said, leaving observers with the impression of a crowded field lacking a clear front-runner and perhaps a long and difficult election ahead.
>
> As things turned out, Barbarin needn't have worried.
>
> It took the cardinals just five ballots to settle on Jorge Mario Bergoglio of Buenos Aires, Argentina.

Staff writer Joshua McElwee summarized,

> By the end of the sixth day of his pontificate, Pope Francis—formerly Cardinal Jorge Mario Bergoglio of Buenos Aires, Argentina—had made signs big and small that his might be something of a different

papacy . . . the new pope seemed to be trying to define the nature of his power of the world's 1.2 billion Catholics. . . . Francis acknowledged he is the 265th successor of Peter, which he said "involves a certain power" given by Christ to Peter.

"But what sort of power was it?" the new pope asked, looking up from his prepared remarks at the crowd in front of him.

"Let us never forget that authentic power is service," Francis continued after a pause. The pope, he continued, "must be inspired by the lowly, concrete and faithful service which marked St. Joseph."

Other *NCR* headlines provided a variation on the theme of a reforming—if that was the case—Francis. "Serious change may be nigh for the Curia" (Allen); "Election raises alarm for some Latin Mass fans" (staff writer Brian Roewe); "[Bergoglio's] Record on [Argentina's] Dirty War, sex abuse cases under scrutiny" (editor at large Tom Roberts); "One of new pope's allegiances [*Communio e Liberazione*, or Communion and Liberation] might tell us something about the future" (Jamie Manson); "Listen to the hopes of a weary people" (Benedictine Sr. Joan Chittister, columnist); "'Reform' is in the eye of the beholder" (Jesuit Fr. Tom Reese, correspondent); and on it went through fifteen pages of "Meet Pope Francis." In its traditional spot on the last page of the forty-eight-page issue, *NCR* editorialized,

> The symbols from the start were breathtaking. For a community whose narrative is woven deeply with symbols great and small, those advanced by Pope Francis since he stepped onto the balcony . . . in a simple white cassock became more awe-inspiring as the days wore on. . . .
>
> If the journey's primary focus is on the poor, our bet is that he will have an enormous and newly energized following. If his papacy is one founded in humility, dignity and justice, we presume that all the rest, including the list of contentious issues, will make for a rich conversation—and maybe even conversion—along the way.

"By August," said Coday, "Pope Francis had already stamped a unique mark on the papacy that his immediate successor, no matter how soon he comes aboard, will have trouble not adopting." Francis's rejection of the splendor of the papacy, his embrace of simplicity in dress, abode and action, his preference for the title "bishop of Rome" over "pope" has been so widely and enthusiastically received, the next pope will have difficulty if he would try to reverse these measures.

Now back to the news. *NCR*'s welcoming coverage of Francis was inspiring and euphoria-tinged. Reader Sister of Mercy of the Holy Cross Celine Goessl wrote,

> I picked up my *NCR* from my mailbox on Good Friday and what a good day it was for me. I spent a long time on that day reading the entire paper from front to back and was more inspired and overjoyed with the turn of each page. . . . I am one of those weary people that Sr. Joan Chittister speaks about, but on this day I have new hope, a new zest for my spiritual life in the new church, and a new anticipation that we now have someone who will rebuild the church in the style of St. Francis of Assisi. . . . Thank you for the reassurance you have given to us, your readers.

In this period, columnist Jamie Manson remained dubious, in that she reserved judgment on what Francis's attitudes might mean to gays and lesbians.

Then came that second front page covering Francis's emerging pontificate (April 26–May 9) and the chilling "Pope reaffirms last year's assessment of LCWR": "Thirty-three days in, and for some at least, possible cracks in Pope Francis' luster began to show. Hopes that the Argentine pope might dial back potential points of tension in the U.S. church were tamped down April 15 as the Vatican announced Francis had reaffirmed a sharp rebuke of the main leadership group of U.S. sisters" (Joshua McElwee). The editorial stated, "Francis should meet with the sisters." "Amen" was the probable response of all thirty-five thousand subscribers.

Below the fold, "Eight cardinals to form Francis' sounding board." They were geographic as well as strategic appointments: Italy, Chile, India, Congo, Germany, Australia, Honduras and the United States— Boston's Cardinal Sean O'Malley, who "seems poised to become under Francis what Cardinal John O'Connor was under John Paul II, and Cardinal Timothy Dolan under Benedict XVI: the pontiff's go-to guy not just in the United States, but North America and much of the English-speaking world" (John Allen).

In his Editor's Note, Coday quoted *USA Today*'s Cathy Lynn Grossman: "The honeymoon between progressive Catholics in the USA and

Pope Francis . . . may have ended when he 'reaffirmed' last year's stinging rebuke of most U.S. nuns." Coday, under the heading "Reasons to wait and see," perceptively noted, "Perhaps the honeymoon is over, but anyone who has been married a long time knows that the marriage really gets better after the honeymoon."

John Allen had flown to Buenos Aires, not only to talk to the pope's sister, Maria Elena Bergoglio, but to many others. Francis's sister was a treasure house of observation: "Nobody is going to be able to force him to compromise on what he believes in." Asked for an example, she said the best "would be his option for the poor. Many times that made his life difficult here in Argentina, both in terms of his relationship with the government and also with some business people who wanted him to shut up about it. But he always chose the poor people, no matter what, and frankly in this country it can cost you to speak out in favor of the poor."

As ever, clerical sexual abuse and cover-up was back in the news. In Los Angeles, Cardinal Roger Mahony's protect-the-priests redoubt was falling to grand juries and archival research. Tom Roberts's account of letters from the archives of Justice Anne Burke, who served as chairwoman of the U.S. bishops' National Review Board, revealed the extent of Mahony's "obstructionist" attempts to head off the investigation by the John Jay College of Criminal Justice.

Columnist Manson wrote, "I'm getting weary of bishops and cardinals who tell me how much they love my gay and lesbian friends and me, while at the same time willfully misunderstanding us, refusing to talk to us and devaluing our relationships. (I would include my transgender friends here, but no hierarch to my knowledge has even uttered the 'T' word yet.)"

She wrote, "Don't call it love, (New York Cardinal Timothy) Dolan and (San Francisco Archbishop Salvatore) Cordileone." Dolan had told a television interviewer, "Well, the first thing I'd say to (gays and lesbians) is, 'I love you.'" Countered Manson,

> Dolan said this just three months after his infamous interview with "60 Minutes" where he likened same-sex marriage to incest, saying, "I love my mom but I don't have a right to marry her." So, until, Dolan, Cordileone and their fellow prelates are willing to offer gays and lesbians and transgender persons mutual dialogue, deep listening and authentic presence, I respectfully ask that they stop telling us

they love us. Call it politeness, call it tolerance, but please don't call it love.

A couple of issues later, reader Tom Luce of Berkeley, California, echoed the thoughts. He wrote, "The church must stop attempting two contradictory things for us lesbian, gay, bisexual and transgender folks, loving us, then condemning us to hell if we won't abide by total abstinence."

The May-June-July pace seemed to accelerate: "Contradictions cast doubt on Philadelphia [sexual abuse cover-up] verdict" (Ralph Cipriano). By the end of the year, Msgr. William Lynn, the first church official jailed for his part in the cover-up, would be free on bond, pending an appeal. There was a Hans Küng essay, "The paradox of Pope Francis"; "'His heart is with the poor': Pope spotlights social teaching with blunt call for ethical economy" (Michael Sean Winters); "New group [Catholic Whistleblowers] aims to hold bishops accountable" (Ben Feuerherd); and "The landscape of faith-based humanitarian aid reflects a world in flux" (Chris Herlinger).

An editorial, "Philadelphia was a shallow victory," turned to the sexual abuse cover-ups by successive Philadelphia Cardinals John Krol, Anthony Bevilacqua and Justin Rigali. "The Philadelphia archdiocese was one of the worst examples of high clericalism in the United States and of what the clerical/hierarchical culture could breed in its single-minded determination to hide the crimes of sexual abuse and protect itself. In the end, it did neither."

The readers' letters in the three issues that ended on June 20 ranged widely. "I am appalled at Brother Francis' move to continue the 'investigation' of U.S. sisters," wrote Ronald Boccieri of Hadley, New York. Jeanette Blonigen Clancy of Avon, Minnesota, cautioned, "Pope Francis' rejection of papal pomp and his solidarity with the poor, welcome and attractive as they are, do not make up for his apparent acceptance of female subordination." Returning the topic to lay issues, Tim Cronley of Ellenton, Florida, wrote, "Pope Francis recently appointed eight cardinals from around the world to look into ways to reform the church. There should be well-informed laypeople included in the group." Christian Br. James Loxham of Freeport, New York, saw the eight-cardinal appointment as "a source of hope and encouragement" given that "only two of these men are from the Northern Hemisphere." Readers Franciscan Missionaries of Mary Sr. Maureen Conway of New York City, Jean Dooling of East Rockaway, New York, and Helen T. Kock of St. Paul, Minnesota, received columnist Michael Leach's suggestion for a "worldwide forgiveness Mass" with "enthusiasm" (Conway); "What an idea!" (Dooling); and "I pray someone puts this front and center on Pope Francis' desk" (Kock).

In May, someone may have put something on Francis's desk, for in early June, the pope, in a private conversation, told a delegation from the Latin American and Caribbean Conference of Religious Men and Women not to worry if they found themselves under scrutiny or investigation: "This will pass! Perhaps even a letter from the Congregation for the Doctrine [of the Faith] will arrive for you, telling you that you said such or such thing. . . . But do not worry. Explain whatever you have to explain, but move forward."

Fr. Tom Zelinski of Marathon, Wisconsin, had a different take on what Francis had inspired. Wrote Zelinski, "My simple request of the Catholic people is simply: Please participate [in the liturgy]. Actively, consciously, as Vatican II called us to do. . . . I urge, plead with, cajole Catholic people everywhere to stand up, speak up, sing out as though you mean it."

What stood out as the most significant reporting on the laity in these issues was McElwee's revelation that a "spate of firings happen without official policy" in the murky area of some church employees' lives not matching the tenets of church teaching. The reporting rested on the case of Carla Hale, teacher in a Catholic high school, a Methodist whose mother had died. The funeral report mentioned Hale's domestic female partner, Julie, among her mother's survivors. Columbus, Ohio, Bishop Frederick Campbell dismissed Hale, who had taught at Bishop Watterson High School for nineteen years. Accounts of pastors and bishops firing at will in Georgia and Wisconsin revealed there were no adequate guidelines to cover the rights, role or privacy of employees who were gay or in same-sex relationships, including marriage.

Meanwhile, Francis was cementing his appeal through modest crowd-pleasing gestures. In the June 27–July 4 issue, John Allen summarized the pope's first one hundred days: "Quiet on the Vatican front," apart from his eight-cardinal advisory group appointments. Then Francis announced an optimistically aimed bridge-building double canonization afoot: John XXIII and John Paul II. The action was a bold peace plan; the very names indicating the width of the church divide. Francis's first encyclical, *Lumen Fidei* [The Light of Faith] was another bold peace plan and welcome, an appeal to those who generally disdain institutional religion.

The Vatican bank had been a reliable source of scandal and corruption allegations for four decades. Routine headlines. With the latest—Italy's arrest of bank financial officer Msgr. Nunzio Scarano—Francis moved quickly to throw open to transparency the inappropriately named Institute for the Works of Religion, the official name for the Vatican bank. With its intermittent rumors of crooked politicians and archbishops laundering money to one Vatican bank-associated scoundrel being "suicided" in an Italian prison (Michele Sindona) to another found hanging under a London bridge (Roberto Calvi), financial reporters will miss the dirty bank once it is scrubbed clean.

In church news, progressive: Austrian reform movement priest Fr. Helmut Schüller embarked on a U.S. tour; conservative: *NCR*'s Allen pulled off an understated observation coup. At World Youth Day in Brazil, Allen interviewed Philadelphia Archbishop Charles Chaput, who said Francis will "be required to make decisions that won't be pleasing to everybody. This is already true of the right wing of the church. They generally have not been really happy about his election . . . He'll have to care for them, too, so it'll be interesting to see how all this works out."

In August, four months after Francis stepped onto the papal balcony, editor Coday could write,

> I have greeted the election of Pope Francis with great caution. The outward signs have been compelling. . . . He calls for a church of and for the poor. He has said repeatedly that a church that never leaves the sacristy is in danger of becoming a museum piece. . . . For years we've heard some say that the church might need to be smaller and purer, now we hear Francis preaching a church wide open to all: "God doesn't belong to any particular people . . . Jesus doesn't tell the apostles and us to form an exclusive group of elite members." . . . Cracks begin to appear in the wall of my caution.

Perhaps Benedictine Fr. Dan Ward felt the same way as he decided to step down as executive director of the Resource Center for Religious Institutes. Jason Berry reported that for fourteen years the monk-lawyer—much to the Vatican's extreme annoyance—had quietly dispensed advice to religious orders on their canonical and financial rights.

Cry Pax! Patrick O'Neill, in the lead essay of a Peace & Justice special section, asked, "What peace movement?" and answered that given the lack of church leadership, "activists seek [a] more creative approach." *NCR* editorially offered the late Eileen Egan and Gordon Zahn as role models of Catholics who refused to stand by as those in power made decisions that impacted human dignity worldwide. It pointed to twenty-three activists arrested in July at the construction site where miles of a new National Security Campus in Kansas City, Missouri, now loom. "The vision for a Catholic peace movement cannot cease. Perhaps those tending it at the national level could look to Kansas City for guidance." (Among those attending were veteran nuclear protester Fr. Carl Kabat of the Missionary Oblates of Mary Immaculate; the Oblate's new provincial superior, Fr. Bill Antone; and Jesuit Fr. William Bichsel. They did not attend their hearings, but were represented in court by fellow activist and lawyer Henry Stoever.

Responding to an editorial on criteria for bishops—quoting Francis's words, "gentle, patient . . . animated by inner poverty"—Benedictine Sr. Catherine Higley of Ridgely, Maryland, wrote of Wilmington, Delaware's spiritual leader, Bishop W. Francis Malooly, he "goes so gently and with sincere simplicity and graciousness." From Phoenix, Naola T. Conner said that "church power, as exercised by one man, or a few men, totally ignoring the fact that a majority of God's people are hearing God's voice differently, is self-defeating. . . . Give the church a new heart, a humble heart, a heart that understands that God is not chained by the law."

The front-page headline on the August 16–19, 2013, issue was "The stage is set." It referred to the "Francis revolution still to come." It was equally apropos to the other top story that week: "Vatican overseer to attend LCWR annual meeting." It read, "One former LCWR president said the group's members are preparing with 'an ominous feeling.'" McElwee was in Florida for that meeting at which LCWR leaders asked the group's members not to discuss with the press their meeting with Vatican overseer Seattle Archbishop J. Peter Sartain. The most that emerged was a post-meeting soft-shoe diplomatic shuffle: Sartain "had been listening intently and heard the concerns voiced by the members, and their desire for more information. The extraordinarily rich and deeply reverent conversation during the board meeting gave us a greater understanding of Archbishop Sartain, and we believe he now also better understands us," LCWR said in a statement. The closed-door meeting provided Sartain "little opportunity" to answer LCWR members' questions. Meanwhile, *NCR* editorialized on Francis wanting a "messy church." How messy remained the open question, and reasonably begs the question of whether an "extraordinarily rich and deeply reverent conversation" could ever be part of the mess. Reader Deborah Rose-Milavec of Cincinnati wrote she was at the meeting as a representative of FutureChurch.

> The calm self-assurance of LCWR leaders was evident . . . These women seem to be clear about where they stand and where they are going . . . In the end, it was ironic to see two men (Sartain and [Apostolic Nuncio Archbishop Carlo] Viganò) wearing miters, standing alone on the elevated stage preaching and enforcing hierarchical concepts of obedience to a houseful of faithful, talented, wise and, dare I say, holy women.

At the same time, Ursuline Sr. Deana Walker of St. Louis could note, regarding *NCR*'s LCWR meeting reporting, her disappointment

> in the tone, and I sense in *NCR* a very small bit of the disconnect we have experienced with the church and are committed to working through now. There is a historic and delicate process at stake here and most women religious are holding fast to the hope that we can establish a more open and mutual relationship with the hierarchical church. I have to believe that members of the hierarchy and the laity also want that. Those who have been following closely have been awed by the manner in which LCWR leadership have conducted themselves.

In September, John Allen reported, "Francis rebooted the Vatican system with [a] new secretary of state," while ethicists found the proposed U.S. Syria air strike "tough to justify." The most telling Christian story on the front page was an essay by Jeff Dietrich of Ammon Hennacy House of Hospitality in Los Angeles, the oldest Catholic Worker west of the Mississippi. The essay, headlined "Grace, guts and luck," reached deep into the Gospel call, therefore it was timeless. In a church already two thousand years old, it could be part of the lay canon the next time the millennium turns. It delved into the heart of Tertullian's Christians—"See how they love one another." Yet more, for readers saw in Dietrich's essay how the Catholic Workers love all comers, and how hard-stretched that love can become on a 24/7 basis; how severe that love, that mercifulness becomes when it simultaneously incorporates the pacifist message that involves arrests and prison.

There's love like that in Minneapolis' tough Northside neighborhood. There, the six contemplative Visitation Sisters in Zoe Ryan's article could uniquely attest to the fact that for only the third time in fifty years, the U.S. poverty rate had reached 15 percent. "Some days the doorbell rings off the wall." The sisters hand out bus tokens or the grocery gift cards they keep on hand. They refer neighbors to social-service programs, and invite them to visit again or come to pray. Wrote Ryan, the sisters have been a presence there since before the 1990s, "when the city earned the moniker 'Murderapolis.'"

Coday, in his Editor's Note, signaled an additional global concentration announcing a Conrad N. Hilton Foundation $2.3 million grant to the National Catholic Reporter Publishing Company. The grant was given "to expand our coverage of women religious and to amplify the voices of countless Catholic sisters around the globe." The three-year project will rely on "a network of editors and reporters" with dual tasks: to report on the sisters' work, but also "to help them develop their own communication skills by working with them as columnists and bloggers."

The Hilton grant means that the ever-expanding *NCR*/ncronline.org news and commentary network takes *NCR* in its entirety into coverage at the grassroots of the church around the world. All this in a company and newsroom that in the six years since 2007 also had a fair amount of editorial/managerial change to absorb (though with one constant factor, Fox): three editors (Roberts, Fox, Coday), two editors in chief (Larivee, Feuerherd) and three (or four?) publishers (Fox, Larivee, Feuerherd, Fox again). In a follow-up note to Coday's announcement, Fox said the Hilton grant "will require some internal company changes as we work to build our coverage networks. Specifically, by year's end I hope to relinquish my responsibilities as company president/CEO. . . . I will continue as publisher [and fund raiser in chief], collaborating with Coday and the new president." Fox stressed that "as grateful as we are to receive the Conrad N. Hilton Foundation grant, the long-term life of *NCR* depends on endowing the *NCR* mission."

To find bishops prepared to take risks siding with the poor, *NCR* still had to look outside the United States. Roberts in Guatemala wrote, "Much has been made of Pope Francis' job description for diocesan bishops. They must live simply, divested of royal trappings and unafraid to smell like sheep." Meet, Roberts wrote, Bishop Alvaro Ramazzini, a courageous man representing Guatemala's indigenous, whom Roberts proceeded to introduce.

NCR reported on Francis's "forthright" manner in interviews: a fifty-minute unscripted Q-and-A with journalists after World Youth Day; a 2,500-word commentary to leftist, atheist journalist Eugenio Scalfari. Francis sat for what became a rapidly and widely circulated twelve-thousand-word interview with Jesuit Fr. Antonio Spadaro, editor of *La Civiltà Cattolica*. "The church sometimes has locked itself up in small things, in small-minded rules. . . . This church . . . is home of all, not a small chapel."

Not everyone was likely to be comforted. As reader Lucy Fuchs of Brandon, Florida, had earlier written, "Ultimately, Pope Francis is a churchman and it is the church that he will defend. We cannot look to him for change on issues such as ordination of women or reaching out more to gay persons." *NCR* editorially asked what Francis could have in mind. The pope, en route to Rome from Brazil, said on women's ordination, "The church has spoken, and she said no." What then was Francis referring to when he now could tell Spadaro, "The challenge today is this: to think about the specific place of women also in those places where the authority of the church is exercised"? Women cardinals? Women deacons? "Surely," *NCR* editorialized, "Francis *must* be talking about something beyond the very important, but also very limited, roles women now play in the church."

The church-in-Rome's traditional horror at the thought of women's ordination puts into play wonderment about those male priests. There are, particularly, those clerics who become bishops and seemingly doff their moral and ethical values—to say nothing of their common sense—the moment they don their miters.

The latest two *NCR* editorialized on were Minneapolis–St. Paul Archbishop John Nienstedt and Trenton, New Jersey, Bishop David O'Connell. It was the same old hide-the-abuser-priest story. Well,

Nienstedt didn't exactly hide the man; he appointed him pastor. In Trenton, a priest who'd been treated at an inpatient facility and previously had outpatient counseling for aberrant sexual behavior was appointed to a parish where neither pastor nor parishioners were informed. Nothing was said until the diocese was forced to act publicly because of a forthcoming newspaper story.

NCR summed up this latest round of cover-ups and abuse of power this way: "These two cases clearly show why Catholics continue to mistrust bishops. . . . Priests can be removed from ministry with just the suspicion of wrongdoing. Bishops and their staff face no consequences."

In 2015, it will be thirty years since NCR first reported the nationwide cases of clerical sexual abuse and the concomitant cover-ups. Not one bishop has yet gone to prison. So was anyone surprised, as 2013 was rolling into 2014, that seventy-one U.S. dioceses had not updated their codes of conduct to include child pornography as a prohibited behavior under the updated Charter for the Protection of Children and Young People?

The next NCR issue burrowed into another Nienstedt uproar. The front page stated, "Faced with 'disregard' for canon and civil law, archdiocesan official resigns and takes her case to the police and the press." Brian Roewe interviewed that official, the thirty-eight-year-old former Minneapolis–St. Paul chancellor for canonical affairs, Jennifer Haselberger. She drew her courage to act, she said, from a phrase from her days at the College of St. Catherine University, "Be loving critics and critical lovers of the institutional church," and from "the examples of women religious and the selfless ministry of the majority of priests and bishops." NCR would name Haselberger—as one of a handful of Catholic whistleblowers—its Person of the Year for 2013.

Women to one side, which is where the institution in the past frequently preferred them, by November 2013, Francis had signaled "a step toward change on two levels," one affecting many laypeople, the other affecting internal Vatican governance. Allen and McElwee reported from Rome that an October 2014 Synod of Bishops would take up "the vexed question" of Communion for Catholics who have divorced and remarried without an annulment. They also reported Francis might parcel out half of the Vatican secretary of state's duties. Currently, the post demands the secretary be responsible for both foreign relations and internal governance of the church, i.e., overseeing the

Vatican congregations and Curia. A new Vatican position might be created to coordinate the work of the various congregations, most of which operate as if individual fiefdoms.

22

VATICAN: MALE SUPREMACY ENDURES

For the Catholic Church, 2014 did not turn into the Year of Women. It is the topic on which Francis knows he is walking on eggshells as he lightly treads forward, gently pulling many topics and people along with him, people he wants to walk alongside him. The most recalcitrant recipients of Francis's all-together approach may well be the bishops. Their very appointments were based on them having characteristics that do not mesh easily with a popular people's church on pilgrimage. They don't want to smell like sheep. Some of them don't even seem to like the sheep.

Catholic women seeking change may not mind smelling like sheep, but they sniff cautiously when Francis unveils yet another pronouncement. *NCR*'s November 8–21, 2013, headline, "Women resist call for new theology," reinforces the thought. "I want to talk about a theology of men and women together," lawyer and theologian Helen Alvare told *NCR*. She was one of a hundred women from twenty-five countries who attended a Vatican symposium marking the 25th anniversary of John Paul II's *Mulieris Dignitatem* [On the Dignity and Vocation of Women].

The *NCR* board, well aware of the multifaceted leadership talents of women, announced that for the first time a woman journalist, wife and mother would head the NCR Publishing Company. Effective January 1, 2014, Caitlin Hendel, previously managing editor, was to be *NCR* chief executive officer and president. The company manages the newspaper, ncronline.org and the liturgical planning resources *Celebration* magazine and celebrationpublications.org. Board president Annette Lomont said the board appointed Hendel with "the greatest confidence and enthusiasm."

If, under Francis, women still aren't in the top tier of church management, church reform is. The news flow included St. Joseph Sr. Christine Schenk's report from Austria on the first international meeting of reformist priest organizations for six countries. In this pontificate, they can meet with some hope the pope is listening. In Minneapolis–St. Paul, Nienstedt was not listening to, or at least not responding to, clamorous Catholics calling for his ouster.

Catholic bishops were in the spotlight again in *NCR*'s editorial "Questioning our assent to militarism." The topic was the annual collection for the Archdiocese for the Military Services, in the most militarized country on earth. "Long overdue in the American church is a reasoned and deep discussion of U.S. militarism, the proper use of force, the state's responsibilities to protect and defend, and the role of the people of faith in all of this."

Plans for a discussion, but on a far broader scale than U.S. militarism, were soon laid before the world's 1.2 billion Catholics. Pope Francis asked bishops' conferences around the world to survey their Catholics for their opinions on topics such as contraception, same-sex marriage and divorce in advance of the 2014 Synod of Bishops on the family. A measure of how little confidence some Catholics have in the U.S. Conference of Catholic Bishops: To ensure the U.S. bishops not try to limit the survey's range of questions, *NCR* made the entire questionnaire available. The editors wrote that the documents "were sent to *NCR* by someone who feared the questionnaire from the Vatican about [the 2014] Synod of Bishops on the family wouldn't get as wide a distribution as intended. . . . The instructions from the U.S. Conference of Catholic Bishops didn't seem to push for the widest possible distribution."

In the following *NCR* (December 6–19), staff writer Roewe could begin his synod survey article, "If you can't find a synod survey these days, then you're likely not looking. . . . As of Nov. 22, at least 46 dioceses have solicited some type of response related to the October 2014 Synod of Bishops." Francis, meanwhile, was pulling the rungs out of one ecclesiastical career ladder. Normally, reported John Allen, secretaries of the Italian bishops' conference were "named to major archdioceses that put them in line to become princes of the church and heavy-hitters of the first order." Francis also made it clear he'd like a change in the Italian bishops' conference statutes so the bishops choose their own president and secretary—currently appointed by the pope.

Meeting in the Philippines just before the terrible cyclone, N. J. Viehland reported sixty-five women religious from Asia and Oceania committed themselves to deepening their spiritual bonds and strengthening cross-cultural and international cooperation to better serve the needy.

Benedict Sr. Joan Chittister, who before Benedict's retirement and Francis's election had spoken of the "in-between time," now had a new moment in time: "We are at a tipping point." She had reflected on the 50th anniversary of the assassination of President John F. Kennedy, the 50th anniversary of the death of Pope John XXIII, fifty years after the rise of Martin Luther King: "We have lived in an era of spiritual giants. . . . They warned us, all of them—JFK, Martin and John—to examine our policies and change our hearts." As Chittister surveyed the greed-riven, even punitive U.S. political, economic and social scene, she concluded,

> The struggle has been too long; the confusion too deep; and the politics of every institution, too unholy to abide much longer.
>
> We are choosing now between discussion and dispute, between winning and growing, between the old and the newly imperative.
>
> From where I stand, with an African-American in the White House, a South America from the Peronista era in the Vatican and 10 million undocumented immigrants among us, it looks as if we are at another moment of possible conversion. We are choosing between past and present, between life and death.
>
> But with JFK, Martin and good Pope John gone, the only question now is: Which way are you yourself tilting? Who would know it? And why not?

Editorials sometimes come from one pen, sometimes from several. The next one was a twosome. Editor at large Tom Roberts introduced the editorial topic, "Things are different under Francis," with these thoughts:

You've probably seen or heard quotes like these:

"The religious and secular left grossly misinterpret the statements made by Pope Francis."

"It's disgraceful that some would manipulate the words of Pope Francis to get us in line with their agenda."

"What the pope meant to say was . . ."

Such statements have become—particularly for those who wish to contain change in the way of challenging any notion that a pope could be different, other than cosmetically, from a predecessor or from the church of centuries earlier. We saw very similar arguments about the hermeneutics of discontinuity and continuity, often from the same parties, over the meaning of the Second Vatican Council.

With Francis it has served as a dismissive meme, a way of brushing off what is patently obvious: In Francis, we see a great deal of discontinuity with Popes Benedict XVI and John Paul II. And it is about time. How can Francis' Nov. 24 apostolic exhortation, "The Joy of the Gospel," be seen as anything but a clarion call for discontinuity?

During the interregnum of 2005, it was virtually impossible to make a critical case against the papacy of John Paul II, and the reasons were understandable. He was a giant of an age and had taken the church along dramatically new paths on the world stage. For those accomplishments alone, he should be called blessed and will soon achieve sainthood.

But as *NCR*'s John Allen expressed it in the obituary he wrote, John Paul left a world more united by his actions, but a church more divided. Outside the church, Allen wrote, he built bridges; inside, he was "a bruiser."

Dennis Coday picked up the theme:

It is only natural that some would be distressed at the change in direction. We've discovered in very embarrassing ways that the church is not a perfect society, as popes once declared, and that change is sometimes imperative. Things *are* different under Francis, who seems far more comfortable applying pastoral theology first and consulting the moral texts and canon law later. If that's a mistake, the church has survived far worse.

No pope is perfect; no community of Christians ever, anywhere, is a complete expression of the fullness of God. . . . Whatever magnificence of thought and action John Paul and Benedict brought to the modern papacy, it was also obvious that serious flaws and deep corruption had taken over significant areas of the church and its governing apparatus. The assembled cardinals recognized the need for deep change. They voted for it.

"I dream of a '"missionary option,'" Francis writes in "The Joy of the Gospel," "that is, a missionary impulse capable of transforming everything, so that church customs, ways of doing things, times and schedules, language and structure can be suitably channeled for the evangelization of today's world rather than for her self-preservation."

And then it was 2014.

The first issue of *NCR* to carry the date 2014 was also the Christmas issue. The entire company, but the editorial staff past and present in particular, understood that the months directly ahead were aimed at preparing for the October 2014 50th anniversary of the newspaper's founding. At the same time, the Christmas theme and coverage took the newspaper and the company back to Christianity's origins. The Christmas issue (December 20, 2103–January 2, 2014) focused again on the reason the word "Catholic" appears in the masthead of this brave little newspaper in a small city in the American Midwest that has an outsize influence on the shape of the discussion in that global church.

Dennis Coday announced the appointment of Stephanie Yeagle as *NCR*'s newest managing editor. Yeagle replaced Caitlin Hendel who had been appointed CEO/president of National Catholic Reporting Company. Hendel, previously an editor in Washington, DC, at *Congressional Quarterly-Roll Call* where she had covered Congress, graduated in journalism from the University of Kansas. Baptized in New York, journalist Caitlin wed journalist John in St. Peter's Church, Kansas City, Missouri. Hendel, granddaughter of a western Kansas newspaper publisher, welcomed her return to her Kansas City family. "I'm a mom and wife and sister and an aunt. Family is so important to us." January 1, 2014, Hendel would take charge of *NCR*'s business operations, freeing up Tom Fox, who remains publisher, to focus on development and management of the Hilton Foundation Global Sisters reporting project.

As *NCR* makes its way through 2014 to October and its anniversary, it notes that it began covering the third session of the Second Vatican Council. In October 2014, it will be covering on its anniversary the Synod of Bishops considering family and evangelization. As a half century ago, *NCR* will be holding the church-in-Rome accountable as its reporters get to the stories behind the stories behind the activity.

From a council to a synod. Synchronicity of a sort.

At fifty, *NCR* is getting a little gray in its hair. It is proud, therefore, to honor—as this book closes—its offspring, ncronline.org: journalism with a reach that the newspaper, even in its prime, never quite achieved.

What the *National Catholic Reporter* editors *have* achieved, however, is quite remarkable. Yes, they have maintained the highest standards of their journalistic cause and calling. Yet they are also Catholic journalists. They have, equally, served another cause—the social Gospel mandates as espoused and encouraged by the Second Vatican Council.

That is the story behind the story.

THE CORPORATE REPORT

THE NATIONAL CATHOLIC REPORTER PUBLISHING COMPANY, 1964–2014

As you know, in 2014, the *National Catholic Reporter* and the National Catholic Reporter Publishing Company celebrate their 50th anniversary.

NCR, the newspaper, looks and feels similar to what debuted fifty years ago. It is a lay-led, independent Catholic newspaper with well-designed, important front-page stories, good graphics, and features vital to the broader church throughout. It takes progressive to aggressive editorial stances—and is an uncensored advocate for those who have a story to tell.

After fifty years, the newspaper might seem to be an icon of stability. To close observers, however—to the more than seventy-five persons who have served on the corporate board of directors, to the nine publishers (and especially Tom Fox, who has held that position at three different times), to the multiple business managers, to the editors and staff of the dozen subsidiary newsletter publications, to the directors of Credence Cassettes, Leaven Press and Sheed & Ward publishing subsidiaries and to those who have been the readers and subscribers to *NCR* publications—this half-century is known to have been a tumultuous roller-coaster ride.

This brief company history serves as context for *NCR's* exciting story. Like ancient Gaul, this recap is divided into three: 1964 to 1979, 1980 to 1996 and 1997 to the present.

While the initial period, **1964 to 1979**, was externally a spectacular playing out of the Second Vatican Council (1962–1965) and subsequent tensions within the church, internally, at *NCR*, it was a struggle for survival and sustainability, a hectic search for the right pricing niche and a time of tensions between the publisher and editor.

NCR began in 1964 as a national version of the local Kansas City–St. Joseph diocesan *Catholic Reporter*; the two shared staff and facilities until 1966. *NCR* was launched with a readership of 11,000. The circulation doubled the first three years and rocketed to a high of more than 88,500 by the end of 1968. At the same time, the subscription price did not cover the costs of production and distribution. Consequently, the *NCR* corporate board dealt with increasing deficits from the start until they changed the way of doing business in 1971–1972.

During 1969–1971, *NCR's* circulation tumbled to 58,000. Its financial deficit rose to more than $90,000 ($500,000-plus in today's dollars). Robert Hoyt, *NCR's* enterprising and heralded initial editor, was dismissed at a time of subscription losses, excessive financial debt, internal conflict with publisher Don Thorman and Hoyt's impending divorce. Publisher Thorman became CEO-publisher-editor in 1971. He saw *NCR* as a "communications" company, not limited to the newspaper. In January 1972, he launched *Celebration*, a monthly "creative worship service" magazine still flourishing today. Thorman debuted Credence Cassettes in 1972, inaugurating a very successful business recording conferences and headliner speakers around the country then selling the cassettes to an appreciative audience of Catholic religious and lay educators.

New board member Msgr. John Egan of Chicago had an eighteen-month experiment with a newsletter, *Link*, "connecting ideas and services for people in pastoral and community ministry." The new communications business, coupled to internal adjustments and increased advertising and fundraising, moved the *NCR* corporation over to the positive side of the financial ledger, a position that continued into the 1980s.

Dan Herr, leader of the Thomas More Association and *The Critic* magazine, chaired the board from 1968 to 1970, followed by Frank Brennan, a Kansas City insurance and marketing executive, 1970–1979.

Of the first 17 board members in this phase, 14 were male, 3 female; 14 were laypersons and 2 were priests. In 1972, Franciscan Sr. Francis Borgia Rothluebber was the first religious on the board.

Thorman was only fifty-two when he died in November 1977.

Editor Arthur Jones was named publisher-editor of *NCR* and CEO of the National Catholic Reporter Publishing Company.

In 1978, a new era began in Rome with the election of Pope John Paul II.

NCR's circulation, from a low of 37,000 in 1973, by the late 1970s had increased to about 44,000. In 1979, *NCR* corporate gross revenues rose to $1.9 million, its net worth for the year to $100,000, about the same amount that came in from advertising and fundraising. Its cumulative net worth at that point was more than a quarter-million dollars. (These financial figures come from the nonprofit corporation's annual report to the IRS, and circulation information comes from the annual report to the U.S. postal service, both of which are public information.)

The National Catholic Reporter Publishing Company, as a total operation, had firmly established itself: *NCR* chronicled the church's momentous changes and growing tensions, and *Celebration* and Credence Cassettes reflected and nourished the liturgical, intellectual and spiritual life of what has been estimated as a majority of parishes in the United States.

The years from **1980 to 1996**, the second phase, might be seen simply as the "Tom Fox years." There was a flood of activity internally. The board, publisher and staff of the National Catholic Reporter Publishing Company were deeply involved with bringing a host of new pastoral, liturgical and spiritual resources to Catholic parishes, along with the weekly *NCR*. Jason Petosa was the new publisher, a former priest who had carved out a second career in marketing and had been assisting Arthur Jones. *Celebration* magazine, under Bill Freburger, and the Credence Cassettes recording and distribution venture, led by Clarence 'Clink" Thompson, were doing well. *Celebration* had more than 9,600 subscribers, mostly parishes—almost half of the nineteen thousand parishes in the United States at the time.

Art Winter, an *NCR* writer since 1966 and a mainstay of *Celebration*, sensed there was a growing need for a publication specifically about spirituality. He designed and lobbied internally to create *Praying*, a bimonthly that started as an *NCR* supplement in October 1983 and became a separate publication with its own subscribers in mid-1986.

Resource Guide, an attempted regular listing of Catholic conferences and resources, in partnership with another major Catholic organization, did not survive a test run in the early 1980s. Then came a series of parish-oriented aids that were more successful.

- *Eucharistic Minister*, a four-page monthly newsletter, was an extra price add-on to *Celebration*, aimed as assisting liturgical celebrants. It started in April 1984 under Freburger's editorship.
- *Catechist's Connection* followed in October 1984, published ten times a year, aimed at the adult instructors and leaders of the now widespread RCIA (Rite of Christian Initiation of Adults) program in Catholic parishes. Adult educator Jean Marie Hiesberger was editor. (She would later be the general editor of the breakthrough *Catholic Bible: Personal Study Edition*, 1995, the most accessible, high-quality commentary of its time, using the New American Bible.)
- *The Caring Community: For the Homebound and Hospitalized to Share in the Life of the Church*, a monthly four-page handout of the Sunday readings with commentary, brought the Word of the liturgy along with Communion to those not able to attend Mass. The aid was prepared and circulated as part of an optional *Celebration* packet, starting in October 1985.

Publishing books would be next. The National Catholic Reporter Publishing Company had produced some of its newspaper content as paperback books in the late 1960s, e.g., *Special to NCR: The First Five Years of the National Catholic Reporter* (1969); *The Best of Cry Pax* (1969), a collection of the Sister Forum; the significant *The Birth Control Debate: Interim History from the Pages of the* National Catholic Reporter, edited with extensive commentary by Robert Hoyt and the *NCR* editorial team (1968); and *Reassessing* (1980) by Arthur Jones.

In 1984, Petosa launched a new brand, Leaven Press: books, booklets, video cassettes and newsletters. Petosa moved quickly to hire for Leaven editor Robert Heyer, formerly of Paulist Press. In Petosa's quickness, not all the board knew of the move before it was made. In March 1985, the National Catholic Reporter Publishing Company acquired the common stock of book publishers Sheed & Ward from Universal Press Syndicate, an arm of Andrews McMeel.

For the National Catholic Reporter Publishing Company, Sheed & Ward was good news and bad news. The good news was that it had a significant history and brand, although it had lost impetus. Soon Sheed & Ward had a thirty-two-page catalog. One element of the bad news was that the publishing business was changing. Desktop publishing was the new wave. The lifespan of a book was shortening, generally to less than five years. Sheed & Ward was building a large inventory, but book reading tastes were changing, competition was stiff and there was uneasiness over funds allocated for the newspaper being used to shore up the book division.

The board chose as its new publisher William L. McSweeney Jr., who had an extensive business background with Hallmark Cards. He started in January 1986 and was instructed to make sure *NCR* the newspaper survived. Under Fox, circulation had continued its slow but steady climb from 45,000 in 1980 to more than 50,000 in 1985—and continued to a high of 53,000 in 1986.

The paper was never completely self-sustaining; advertising and fund development were not strong. With the startups, investments in needed new computer equipment and multiple rising costs, the overall cumulative debt of the corporation reached more than $400,000 in 1986.

Then, during four straight positive financial years, 1990–1994, and with the debt nearly halved, but with *NCR* circulation declining (to 48,000 in 1995), publisher McSweeney and Heyer, director of subsidiary communications, opted to drop one newsletter and add four in a new round of publication startups.

- *Eucharistic Minister* ceased as a separate publication in November 1992, its content absorbed into *Celebration*.
- *Christian Initiation* was introduced in August–September 1993 as an eight-page bimonthly newsletter "for those involved with the initiation of adults and children," adding children to the parish mix. Freburger picked up the editing for the first three years.
- *Lector* followed in September 1994 as an eight-page monthly to provide background and assist those doing the first and second Sunday readings. Beatrice Flo was the editor.

- *Cantor* was the next add-on, for a price, to the *Celebration* package for parishes, eight pages, monthly, started in September 1996, also edited by Flo.
- *Parish Sacrificial Giving* was tested out by the communications division and initially thought promising but dropped within two years.

McSweeney announced his intended early retirement a year in advance, effective December 1996. The board succession plan prepared editor Fox as the next publisher.

In the years 1980–1996, the board was better balanced than before: 9 women to 12 men; 15 laypersons, with 3 priests and 3 religious. John Caron led the board for over a decade (1977–1989), succeeded by John McMeel, who was chair from 1989 to 1995. There were no term limits in the earliest phases and long terms were not unusual. Outstanding examples: Frank Brennan (15 years, to 1979), Joseph Cunneen (14, to 1980), Jesuit Fr. Joseph Fichter (20, to 1986), Rose Lucey (20, to 1996), William D'Antonio (18, to 1998), McMeel (14, to 1996), Benedictine Sr. Joan Chittister (17, to 2000), Blessed Sacrament Sr. Mary Roger Thibodeaux (13, to 1998), Marist Br. Cyprian Rowe (11, to 1999) and Jesuit Fr. Howard Gray (14, to 2003).

As McSweeney resigned, the corporate balance sheet, for the first time in over a decade, was out of the red, although a very modest $10,000. One of Fox's prescient moves, as he ended his long stay as editor at the end of 1996, was to set up the corporation's first website, www.nathcath.org and to write *Catholicism on the Web*, a survey of what five hundred Catholic institutions were doing with the new technology.

The rapid growth of the Internet signaled the beginning of a new world for any publishing company.

The third phase in this overview, **1997 to present**, was even more tumultuous. The issues: the aging, waning population of "Vatican II Catholics," the impact of so many priests and sisters leaving institutional roles and changing technology. Credence Cassettes, started in 1972, had passed its peak and was losing customers and money. *Celebration* survived, guided by its talented new editor since 1997, Patrick Marrin, and an extensive team of parish leaders from throughout the country. Sheed & Ward was inventory rather than income.

Fox named Michael Farrell, *NCR*'s features editor, *NCR* editor. Farrell's mark in three years at the helm was a redesign of the paper, sprightly features, and the millennium project, a special "Jesus 2000" supplement, published December 24, 1999: 60 portraits and images of "Jesus for the new millennium" culled from 1,678 presentations from 1,004 artists in 19 countries.

Under Fox, Rita Larivee, a Sister of St. Anne, joined the corporation as director of operations. Her overall analysis of *NCR*'s situation pictured *NCR* functioning like two side-by-side companies: the newspaper and all the other communications, a relationship judged unhealthy by mission standards, with two operations competing for major capital investment resources.

In November 1997, the board voted to divest the corporation of Credence Cassettes and Sheed & Ward. The National Catholic Reporter Publishing Company would then focus on the newspaper, while keeping *Celebration* and *Praying* magazines. A month later, Sr. Rita Larivee was named associate publisher.

In 1999, all the supplementary newsletters and magazines except *Celebration* were discontinued. The *NCR* library and archives document the National Catholic Reporter Publishing Company contribution to the pastoral leadership of the Catholic church over a quarter century: *Praying* (1983–1999, 93 issues), *Catechist's Connection* (1984–1999, 154 issues), *Caring Community* (1985–1999, 171 issues), *Lector* (1994–1999, 59 issues), *Cantor* (1994–1999, 34 issues) and *Christian Initiation* (1996–1999, 36 issues). In the same year, ncronline.org was redesigned and a major part of the week's paper became available to subscribers through the Internet. At the time, *NCR*'s circulation was above 49,000 and *Celebration* was holding at around 8,500.

Other major changes: a shifting readership, the growth of online communications, sustaining the leadership of the *NCR* venture, and building a community of supportive "Friends of NCR."

In 2000, Fox named Tom Roberts editor. Dennis Coday, brought on earlier as a writer, in 2003 became coordinator of ncronline.org. At the end of 2004, a tired Fox resigned after seven years as publisher and seventeen as editor. The board chose Larivee as the new publisher.

A major makeover of ncronline.org meant subscribers could access the entire paper, but the process was overly complex and too small a number subscribed to sustain that experiment. An "e-series" of newsletters was tested to parishes as subscribers but discontinued within a year due to inadequate subscriptions. NCRCafe, featuring two-way communications, was introduced alongside ncronline.org in 2006. "Cafe" offered multiple "forums," but interaction was weak unless someone introduced some extensive, specific starter content. Still connected to the *NCR* team, Fox led a series of "podcasts" on wisdom leaders. NCRCafe was dropped as a duplicate online offering in 2008 and ncronline.org was rebuilt.

To save on costs and beef up content, the newspaper dropped back from forty-four issues a year to twenty-six. Newspaper subscriptions tumbled. Total circulation dropped from near 45,000 in 2005 to 38,000 in 2008 and to 35,500 by 2010.

At one point, *NCR* as a print newspaper nearly became extinct. Larivee and her marketing manager were planning ways to appeal to younger Catholic adults. The board at their May 2007 meeting approved a motion to change the newspaper to a monthly magazine, designed to appeal to younger readers, subject to available financing.

Over the next year, there were staff cutbacks. Roberts stepped down as editor, taking on the title of editor at large. Larivee became editor in chief, Pamela Schaeffer became executive editor. Capital investment to support a magazine did not develop. In 2008, with Larivee's three-year contract at an end, and with the Sisters of St. Anne electing Larivee to lead the religious order, the *NCR* board opted to stick with the newspaper and set up a search committee for a new publisher.

The exciting promise of Joseph Feuerherd as publisher (2008–2011) and the dismay at his startling early demise have been described. Feuerherd had persuaded pro tem editor Fox to resume full-time editorship. Now the board had to lean on Fox to assume Feuerherd's publisher role after Feuerherd's death. Coday moved from managing editor to editor in January 2012.

In the final third lap of its first half-century run, the *NCR* corporate board changed significantly. Term limits were enacted during this phase, so members had shorter stays. Women made up a stronger percentage of membership than men: 55 percent to 45 percent (16 to 13). And they exerted critical board leadership: Ann Weick was chair 1994–2001, Joan Neal chair 2001–2003, Patrick Wade 2003–2009 and Annette Lamont 2009–2013.

The reassuring news amid these shifting sands of sustainability has been the solid support of the "Friends of NCR." The *NCR* team has been fortunate to have Wally Reiter as business manager from 1996 on and Connie Stucki as development director from 2005 on. With the new focus, the *NCR* publisher also has become "fundraiser in chief." A capital campaign in 1997 brought in well over half a million dollars. That was duplicated in 2002 and buoyed to more than a million in 2009. In the other years, those who loved and cared about *NCR* shored up their lifeline to a reform Catholicism with sufficient annual contributions to keep the National Catholic Reporter Publishing Company as a whole in the black.

The other bright news has been the rapid growth of ncronline.org. In 2013, Coday could announce that ncronline.org was the "most visited Catholic news site" in the United States "the premiere online source for independent Catholic news"—and "about to get better." There were 6 million visits to the website in 2012; halfway through 2013, the number of site users had already equaled the previous year. From the announced resignation of Pope Benedict XVI to the election of Pope Francis, more than 2 million people turned to ncronline.org.

The redesigned website was launched in October 2013. Some twenty bloggers now post regular stories and essays.

Celebration has its own website, www.celebrationpublications.org. Readers can subscribe to print or online and have access to an archive of issues from 2010 on. In 2013, the corporation began publishing special collections of *NCR* print material as e-books, starting with *Best Catholic Spirituality Writing 2012* and following with *Pope Francis at 100 Days: The World's Parish Priest.* And, course, one could now access both www.ncronline.org and www.celebrationpublications.org through links in Facebook and Twitter, as part of the social media era.

Effective January 1, 2014, Caitlin Hendel became the first female journalist, wife and mother to head the National Catholic Reporter Publishing Company. The board unanimously elected Hendel, briefly managing editor, as CEO and president at the November 2013 board meeting. Fox continues as publisher, fundraiser in chief, and coordinator of the newspaper's new online outreach to women religious around the world.

Fox was instrumental in securing a $2.3 million Hilton Foundation grant to create an online website on which sisters globally will write, report and blog as they find new ways to coalesce as a sisterhood.

Fox had already traveled to Asia to assist nuns there in contributing to the new site. So yes, *NCR* may look and feel a lot like when it began. But what a story it has taken to keep it alive, to have been awarded first place for excellence as a general newspaper by the Catholic Press Association many times in the past and recently thirteen years in a row (1999–2012) and to have changed the way the Catholic church is reported on in North America and around a large part of the world.

As Hendel assumed control, *NCR*'s circulation was at 35,000, and Editor Coday could report ncronline.org was now achieving 1.2 million hits a month.

Larry Guillot

NATIONAL CATHOLIC REPORTER PUBLISHING COMPANY

As *NCR* started into 2014, its 50th anniversary year, here are the people, board and staff who make *NCR* happen.

BOARD OF DIRECTORS

Annette E. Lomont, chair; Tom Bertelsen, vice chair; Zeni Fox, secretary; John Weiser, treasurer; Maryjeanne Burke; Mary Dacey, SSJ; Thomas C. Fox; Jim Frey; Tom Gallager; Helen Garvey, BVM; Jill Marie Gerschutz—Bell; Jeanne Marie Lee; Rachel Lustig; Joan McGrath; Steve Miller; Peter Phan; Kathleen Pichon; Jeanette Rodriguez; Landon H. Rowland (emeritus); Patrick J. Waide (emeritus); Patrick Whelan, M.D., Ph.D.

STAFF

President/CEO—Caitlin Hendel
Publisher—Thomas C. Fox
Editor—Dennis Coday
Editor at Large—Thomas W. Roberts
Editor, *Celebration*—Pat Marrin

Administrative Assistant to President, Publisher, Editorial and Development—Tracy Abeln

EDITORIAL STAFF

Copy Editor/Special Sections Editor/Photo Coordinator—Teresa Malcolm
Layout Editor/Art Director—Toni-Ann Ortiz
Web Editor—Pam Cohen
Web Developer—Robyn Haas
Books Editor—Jamie L. Mason

WRITERS AND CORRESPONDENTS

Vatican Correspondent—Joshua J. McElwee
Correspondent, Washington, DC—Michael Sean Winters
Correspondent, Oakland—Monica Clark
Correspondent, Seattle—Dan Morris-Young
Staff Writer—Brian Roewe
Bertelsen Interns—Coleen Dunne, Megan Fincher
Business Manager—Wally Reiter
Accounting—Dorothy Flemington
Advertising/Accounting—Kamin Rea
Advertising/Purchasing—Vicki Bershears
Advertising Sales—Terri Lynn
Web/Accounting—Michel Tisdale
Maintenance—Alex Merch
Reception/Classified Ads—Velva Dewberry

DEVELOPMENT AND MARKETING

Director of Mission and Program Development—Denise Simeone
Development Director—Connie Stucki
Marketing Manager—Sara Wiercinski
Circulation Manager—Jo Ann Schierhoff

Circulation/Customer Service—Orlena Bolder
Circulation/Customer Service—Tina Padilla

ACKNOWLEDGMENTS

Saying "Thank you'" is always a pleasure. (It means the book is finished.) It is, too, a timely reminder that the solitary writer doesn't do it all by himself (or herself). I certainly didn't.

This look at *NCR*'s first fifty years would not have been possible without the generous support of Annette Lomont, Charles Raaberg and Landon Rowland, all of whom who have been central figures in the *NCR* family.

Foremost among those who were key to the early insider material for this book was Larry Guillot. Many of the details essential to the telling of *NCR*'s first six years are due to Larry's personal history (he appears in the pages), industriousness, organizational skills and instincts as a researcher. There's more, however: Throughout the process he has been my adviser, researcher and aide-de-camp—as well as the person who wrote the corporate report for the appendix. Thanks so much, old chum.

Quietly pulling necessary strings here and pushing levers there was Denise Simeone. You gem!

Tracy Abeln's deliveries darkened the skies. Like a squad of condors, black-bound volumes flew in from Kansas City with monthly regularity as I went through page after page and decade after decade of the *National Catholic Reporter*. Thank you Tracy, for ensuring that these volumes and much else arrived on schedule. Thanks also to the Cristo Rey High School volunteers you dragooned into copying some pages for me.

Only Teresa Malcolm and I know how much she has contributed to the smoother flow and accuracy of this book. Thank you, Teresa, and copyeditors Brian Roewe and Pam Cohen. Thanks also to *NCR*'s Vickie Breashears for a cameo of Bob Hoyt. We go back a long time together, Vickie.

Before I'd typed a word, Jesuit Fr. Raymond Schroth had generously sent me a copy of his slim but important file containing details I could not have located elsewhere. The Hoyt-Fox correspondence is an example. At one point, this book might have been a solid *history* rather than a journalist's *story*—with Ray as author. Alas, for several reasons to do with *NCR* rather than Ray, time ran out. Thank you, Ray, for your generosity and encouragement. Try not to groan too loudly when you read the result.

Mike Hoyt, Bob's son, was a willing cooperator in the dig into his father's background. I'm grateful for both the information and your enthusiasm, Mike.

The family of Donald J. Thorman, editor and publisher, kindly provided additional background on Don. Particular thanks to Betsy, Peggy and their aunt.

Reaching back in time meant being in touch with Tom Blackburn and Art Winter, Patty Edmonds and Rick Casey—thanks for your help. And when did I ever write a book in which Jean Blake didn't play a part? Thank you, Jean.

I'm grateful to Pat Marrin for a thumbnail sketch of *Celebration* magazine's formation. It got me off to a good start, Pat, thank you. Others to thank at *NCR* who provided key information at just the right time included Connie Stucki, Sara Wiercinski, Jo Ann Schierhoff, Toni-Ann Ortiz, Michel Tisdale and Robin Haas. Robin unveiled the mysteries of the *NCR* website, as did Dennis Coday. They had a difficult student.

This fifty-year story would not be told without the keen interest displayed by the *NCR* board, and the particular support of two board members. I am deeply grateful.

The archivists at Marquette University provided an almost complete set of the *Sun Herald* daily newspaper, a vital precursor to the *NCR* story. Diane Wagner at St. Norbert College, De Pere, Wisconsin, was instrumental in unearthing documents regarding Bob Hoyt's college and seminary years. Thanks, Diane—and all because of a chance meeting in California.

The researchers at the Detroit Historical Society were particular helpful in providing material relevant to the Hoyts' background, as were other public libraries in Michigan. With the passage of time, I fear I may have forgotten several people who provided a key bit of information. If so, the likelihood is I looked up from the keyboard, called them, typed in the information, then forgot the source. If so, my apologies to any I have overlooked.

The person who did the final proofing checks, Alden Perkins, has my particular thanks. She caught the errors that almost got away.

The person to whom I owe the largest debt is my wife, Margie. I was abstractedly AWOL for twelve months. My apologies, thanks and love, My Love, for putting up with me.

ABOUT THE AUTHOR

Liverpool, England–born **Arthur Jones** was educated at the sixteenth-century Boteler School in Warrington, and Ruskin College, Oxford (Dip.Econ.,Oxon). He did further work in Catholic history at the Catholic University of America, auditing Msgr. John Tracy Ellis's lectures.

In 1963, as a young British journalist, Arthur Jones, was the only Western reporter in Fidel's Cuba. He filed articles about the suppression of the church there for the *Catholic Star-Herald* of Camden, New Jersey, and the Associated Press. "I'm typical of many journalists in my generation of Brit newsmen," says Jones—"simultaneous journalistic careers." He writes on both Catholic and financial-economic-political topics.

Following a mandatory stint in the Royal Air Force, Jones spent a year, 1958–1959, in the United States. In the early 1960s he worked on London's Fleet Street for the British *Catholic Herald*. Since his return to America in the 1960s, Jones, long a U.S citizen, has spent two-thirds of his career in the United States.

He was a New York associate editor and European bureau chief of *Forbes*, editor (1975–1980) of the Kansas City–based *National Catholic Reporter* and subsequently its editor at large. In 1985, for *NCR*, he wrote the first exposé of the nationwide nature of the Catholic clerical sexual abuse crisis. He has also served as a *Financial Times* correspondent, and an international correspondent for *Financial World* and *World Trade* magazines.

He has reported back from more than two-dozen countries world-wide. His wide-ranging economic overviews and his interviews with figures such Iranian Prime Minister Amir Abbas Hoveyda, Swedish Prime Minister Olof Palme and Fiji's Ratu Sir Kamasese Mara remain typical of his political-economic writings.

His dozen books reflect the same spread of interest and concerns as his journalism; see http://arthurjonesbooks.com.

Married for fifty-two years to Margie O'Brien, Jones has three chil-dren and two grandchildren. He lives in rural Maryland.